CULTURE SHOCK!

A Survival Guide to Customs and Etiquette

SAN FRANCISCO

Frances Gendlin

T0294096

Marshall Cavendish
Editions

This edition published in 2019 by Marshall Cavendish Editions
An imprint of Marshall Cavendish International

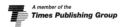
A member of the
Times Publishing Group

Other Marshall Cavendish Offices:
Marshall Cavendish Corporation. 99 White Plains Road, Tarrytown NY 10591–9001, USA
• Marshall Cavendish International (Thailand) Co Ltd. 253 Asoke, 12th Flr, Sukhumvit 21
Road, Klongtoey Nua, Wattana, Bangkok 10110, Thailand • Marshall Cavendish (Malaysia)
Sdn Bhd, Times Subang, Lot 46, Subang Hi-Tech Industrial Park, Batu Tiga, 40000 Shah
Alam, Selangor Darul Ehsan, Malaysia.

Marshall Cavendish is a registered trademark of Times Publishing Limited

National Library Board, Singapore Cataloguing in Publication Data

Name(s): Gendlin, Frances.
Title: CultureShock! San Francisco : a survival guide to customs and etiquette /
Frances Gendlin.
Other title(s): CultureShock!
Description: Singapore : Marshall Cavendish Editions, 2018. | Includes index.
Identifier(s): OCN 1046624055 | ISBN 978-981-48-4103-0 (paperback) |
ISBN 978-981-47-7978-4 (ebook)
Subject(s): LCSH: San Francisco (Calif.)--Social life and customs. | San Francisco (Calif.)--
Description and travel. | Etiquette--California--San Francisco.
Classification: DDC 979.461--dc23

Printed in Singapore

Photo Credits:
All photos by San Francisco Convention & Visitors Bureau, except page 68 (Age Fotostock/
Adam Jones); page 74 (Age Fotostock/Renaud Visage); pages 7, 37, 133, 234, 258
(Photolibrary). Cover photo by Ivana Cajina (unsplash.com).

All illustrations by TRIGG. Map on page xviii by John Zaugg.

ABOUT THE SERIES

Culture shock is a state of disorientation that can come over anyone who has been thrust into unknown surroundings, away from one's comfort zone. *CultureShock!* is a series of trusted and reputed guides which has, for decades, been helping expatriates and long-term visitors to cushion the impact of culture shock whenever they move to a new country.

Written by people who have lived in the country and experienced culture shock themselves, these books provide all the information necessary for anyone to cope with these feelings of disorientation more effectively. The guides are written in a style that is easy to read and cover a range of topics that will give readers enough advice, hints and tips to make their lives as normal as possible again.

Each book is structured in the same manner. It begins with the first impressions that visitors will have of that city or country. To understand a culture, one must first understand the people—where they came from, who they are, the values and traditions they live by, as well as their customs and etiquette. This is covered in the first half of the book.

Then on with the practical aspects—how to settle in with the greatest of ease. Authors walk readers through topics such as how to find accommodation, get the utilities and telecommunications up and running, enrol the children in school and keep in the pink of health. But that's not all. Once the essentials are out of the way, venture out and try the food, enjoy more of the culture and travel to other areas. Then be immersed in the language of the country before discovering more about the business side of things.

To round off, snippets of basic information are offered before readers are 'tested' on customs and etiquette of the country. Useful words and phrases, a comprehensive resource guide and list of books for further research are also included for easy reference.

CONTENTS

DEDICATION

To Judith and Gerry

ACKNOWLEDGEMENTS

San Franciscans, you will come to understand, are an opinionated lot. My friends and colleagues in the City by the Bay cheerfully gave me helpful suggestions for information to be included in the original edition of this book almost two decades ago, and they were no doubt either gratified or disappointed upon reading it. (None said they were disappointed. I didn't ask.) Nonetheless, I truly did appreciate their comments, and mentioned them happily in the several later editions. Now with this new effort after another decade, I am grateful especially to Claudia Schuster, who gallantly tried new restaurants with me and who helpfully told me her opinions of this city she also knows so well. I'm grateful too, to David Handy for having driven me to the far reaches of the city; his understanding of the emerging neighborhoods South of Market helped enormously. And thanks to Laurie Armstrong at the San Francisco Travel Association and its retail outlet the San Francisco Convention and Visitors Center, whose materials were timely and helpful.

NOTE

With so much varied and detailed information, all guide books, no matter how current, suffer from some suddenly outdated information or an error or two—especially in San Francisco where "new" has always been at the forefront. So, regardless of all our efforts, there may be an error here and there concerning a business that has suddenly disappeared or a neighborhood that has changed seemingly almost overnight. If there are any such anomalies, they are, of course, mine alone, despite all the research and checking—and perhaps, the fickleness of the San Franciscans. Some things are sure, however. There is an old joke among chauvinistic San Franciscans, that "one of these days there will be a big earthquake here, and the rest of the country will fall into the sea." But as of the book's publication, at least, the city was intact: the "big one" had not hit and San Francisco and the rest of the continent were still firmly attached. So, if other things have changed, as of course they must, try to take it in your stride. Just enjoy San Francisco for what it is, on that particular day. The next day it might be something different, after all. One of the Tourist Office's quotes actually is "Never the same. Always San Francisco."

But note that guidelines about regulations, addresses, and Internet sites were current as of Summer 2018, to the best of our research and knowledge. Neither Marshall Cavendish nor I can bear responsibility for any changes in immigration laws (which are being tightened considerably and continue to change seemingly with little notice or explanation), prices that have risen since this writing, quality of products or accommodations, the disappearance of a shop, the occasional unsatisfactory meal (yes—rare but true even in San Francisco) or any other such inconvenience. San Franciscans may be faithful, but as you will see, they are always looking ahead, causing the city to appear to be changing day by day.

Examples Described

Readers may be surprised to find some spelling inconsistencies and should understand that this has more to do with the American psyche than a malfunction of the word processor. Although our American ancestors rebelled against the British and forged their own spelling of certain words—"theater" and "center," for example—some current Americans seem to find British spelling more elegant. Thus there might appear here a "shopping centre" or two and a "theatre" or two amid the centers and theaters, but it doesn't matter, for they are American in every important regard. The same holds true for the word "cafe," which is American, but which may variously be spelled "caffè" or "café," depending on the nationality or whim of the owner of the establishment. And all prices are in US dollars.

Throughout the categories we describe hundreds of services and restaurants that are, in fact, representative examples, for there are surely already more in any category, and while some leave, others will no doubt appear. Of course, recommendations are subjective. Each guidebook has its favorites, or at least indicates something the writers have found of interest. That they differ in their listings only means that there's more exploring to do in this town that offers it all. In Chapters Six and Seven—about restaurants and entertainment—along with various suggestions, we mark a few interesting items with a ✦, just to say, "this one is worth paying more attention to."

Internet addresses have been included for information that readers might reasonably want to access online—such as housing options, visa formalities, business advice—but not for every Internet address in this totally cyber-friendly city.

Sometimes it's best just to put "10 best" of something into your browser and see what currently pops up. San Francisco may have everything, but it has to be found, for locals and tourists alike. Of course, the "10 best," in San Francisco change, as do websites, but those listed here were active when the book was published. And we only hope they stay that way—at least for some time.

Also, whether for tourism or living in this information-heavy city, you can download apps to your phone. Check your app store.

It's not surprising that here in a city where people want everything everywhere, categories overlap. What might be listed as a pub might well have upscale, elegant food. A sushi bar might also have a sauna, a restaurant might have a movie schedule, too. This is what makes San Francisco fun, but it also sometimes makes it hard for guidebooks to list attractions in only one category. When possible, just check the websites for the most current information—on just about anything.

In Chapter Six, all restaurants are introduced by location, making it easy to understand where they are. And throughout the book, where location is important for particular services or shops, they too are listed by the neighborhood closest to them; where the services might be needed no matter where they happen to be (e.g. churches), they are listed alphabetically or by category.

INTRODUCTION

"You wouldn't think such a place as
San Francisco could exist."

— Dylan Thomas

Welcome to San Francisco, certainly the most open and probably the most tolerant city in the United States. This is a city where not only can you openly be who you are, you can also try being whatever it is you want to be. Just about anything goes, whether you have come to make a fortune or to squander one, whether you are part of the traditional culture, the ever-emerging digital scene, or any one of the counter-cultures that has at one time or another called San Francisco home. Just think of the city's changing nicknames. In the 1850s the city was called "The Barbary Coast," when rowdy gold miners recalled the old-time Barbary pirates. For a time it was even called "Baghdad by the Bay," when that city was still exotic and untouched. Current appellations, however, demonstrate the city's pride in what it has accomplished: "The City That Knows How," or even the proud "City by the Bay." But most San Franciscans just call it "The City," as though it were the only one—as for many residents it is. One nickname it does not ever have—at least for locals—is Frisco. Do not call the city Frisco.

A San Francisco Tourist Year
- 25 million visitors
- 9 billion spent by visitors
- 562 million in tax and fee revenues for the city
- 74,000 jobs supporting the visitor industry
- 35,000 hotel rooms

- 14 per cent hotel tax
- 6400 daily cable car rides
- 39 million vehicles cross the Golden Gate Bridge annually

About 25 million visitors a year come to "everyone's favorite city." You might think the reasons obvious: San Francisco is the most beautiful—ravishing—cosmopolitan city in the United States, with clean air, sparkling water on three sides, steep hills rising in the middle of the city, and breathtaking views. Quaint cable cars clang up and down the hills, and exotic aromas waft through the streets. People are outgoing and friendly. And when the sun shines and the sky is bright blue, it feels as though there is no other city in the world where you would want to be. But although beauty and charm stretch far, they do not tell the entire story. The deeper story unfolds as you come to understand the city and its residents, as time goes on.

Some of San Francisco's substance is clearly in plain view. Perched on the Pacific Rim, the city is home to some of the most important banks and trade institutions in the country. It is the northern focus of Silicon Valley—an area that may not appear on any map, but which nonetheless commands much of the world's technological innovation, and using that technology, it has become home to world-famous, cutting-edge medical and bioscience research. It is a port for some passenger cruises. It has an outstanding opera company, symphony orchestra, and ballet, plus impressive art museums and galleries. It has excellent universities, hospitals, and research institutions of all sorts. It has a glorious climate and beautiful parks and promenades from which to enjoy it all. And, deliciously, it has some of the best restaurants in the country. Knowing all this, many of the world's largest and most influential corporations have brought their headquarters and many thousands of employees here.

You can find all this in a standard tourist guide, of course. Such guides describe the city and its unique attractions in detail, review restaurants, and suggest hotels of all categories. Each has its own approach to capturing the spirit of this enchanting city by the sea—and in the most eye-catching manner possible. All, however, have one thing in common: they are designed only for people visiting for a short while—visitors who think that what they see in a week is what the city is all about.

It is true that you can get a general idea of the magnetism of this city in a short time, and that is a good start. Certainly, many of the things you have heard about the City by the Bay do ring somewhat true. Definitely it is charming at its core, always vibrant, ever pushing toward the future. And its beauty does stretch far. That Tony Bennett has sung to the world "I left my heart in San Francisco" is no mistake. But it is also odd, offbeat, perhaps even amazing in some ways, and its outright iconoclasm contributes a great deal to its delicious mystique. When you begin to appreciate the city's wholehearted acceptance of the unusual and its constant search for any next frontier, you will be on your way to understanding what the city is really all about.

And, if you are here for a while, you will need that extra look, those extra clues as to how the city works. This book, thus, although offering information for the first-time visitor, also focuses on where tourism ends and where daily life begins. Whether your stay is for a month or two or a year or two, the type of information you need for a successful stay is different—deeper and more detailed than that found in the standard tourist guides. How to choose a neighborhood that suits you, where to find the most interesting markets and shops, how best to get up and down the hills or commute in for work, how to cope with the difficulties of finding housing or the right school for your children, and how to find out what is going on at any day of the year—these are just a few examples of basic information that should help you manoeuvre comfortably within the San Francisco scene.

So, what will you find here? A city to take seriously, no matter what you have heard about the eclectic lifestyles and iconoclasm of its residents. As in any city in the world, daily life rules: if San Franciscans are known for playing hard, they work hard, too. In the soaring skyscrapers of the Financial District and SoMa, in the medical complex of Mission Bay, or in the funky warehouses of the Inner Mission (sometimes called Multimedia Gulch), workers earn salaries that, on average, are among the highest in the country; more than half of the city's residents hold college or professional degrees and 85% have training beyond high school. Locals spend their dollars in some 13,000 retail businesses and eat out in more than 4,000 restaurants, all of which must appeal to a population that demands creativity and excellence—and something ever new to tickle its fancy for novelty.

Even the municipality itself is constantly doing its best to make its urban life meet changing times and needs. Where other cities have seen their downtowns collapse as people fled to the suburbs, San Francisco conscientiously keeps upgrading its own. Half a century of neglect south of Market is now hardly thought of. Think of the Moscone Convention Center and Yerba Buena Gardens, the expanded Museum of Modern Art, the enormous baseball stadium, the improvements to the public transportation system, opening up of the exquisite bayfront, and the intentional reclaiming and development of the former wastelands at Rincon Hill, China Basin, Mission Bay, Bayview, and Dogpatch. Welcoming also the vertical skyscrapers and thousands of new residential possibilities in SoMa, these "new" neighborhoods are now among the trendiest. While retaining its spirit—prosperous and adventurous—the city is moving into the future as it must.

Businesses that manage to capture the changing, eclectic tastes of San Franciscans tend to succeed. Yet those that do not, often see failure as an opportunity to start again, to reinvent themselves with a different –even more novel— approach. The city has always been known for its creative energy, and, since Gold Rush times, for taking risks. If the area is on the cutting edge of technology and finance now, think back to 1853 when Levi Strauss came to San Francisco to work with his brother-in-law. By 1871, they had received a patent for securing the seams of their duck twill work pants with copper saddlebag rivets. Today, the headquarters of the multi-million dollar Levi Strauss & Company sits in its own lovely green park along the Embarcadero, as important now as it was then.

On the other hand, there is a lot not to take too seriously in the City by the Bay. What contributes to the very energy and essence of San Francisco is the attitude that makes living here downright fun. This book also describes the area's myriad sporting opportunities, the friskiness of the population, the varying Asian cuisines—both upscale and definitely not—and some cultural—and decidedly non-cultural—events. What it cannot impart in detail—but you will soon find out for your-self—is how the light-hearted and quirky sides of the city's populace contributes to what makes San Francisco the way it is, a place like nowhere else. When "normal" city festivals aren't enough, how about a "macaroni and cheese cookoff", or a competition to see which dog has the best costume? Or the How Weird Street Faire, or the annual Bay to Breakers race, which brings out the scanty costumes as people run across the city—just for fun.

The city, of course, has its problems. Although it is often rated near the top of "quality of life" surveys, and its work-ers earn well above the national average, the cost of living in the Bay Area also ranks at the highest in the country. This is partly owing to a lack of affordable housing, brought about by a shortage of housing in general yet also the influx of thousands of well-paid tech-professionals willing to pay high rents and purchase prices. So, housing in the Bay Area—for both purchases and rentals—costs significantly more than in most areas of the country. As the demographics change and income inequality has become more prominent—with lower income non-professionals being forced out as more educated professionals move in—people are concerned that San Francisco may soon become a city dominated by the interests of the rich. And it is true that some families with children are finding life in other regions of the Bay Area more affordable and just about as pleasant. Fortunately, community-minded corporation executives are also beginning to notice this and are considering how to find a solution.

Unfortunately, as in other major urban areas, there are too many homeless people on the streets. Some tent communities have established themselves under the freeways, and the city has long been trying to figure out what to do. Now, facing this head on, the Department of Homelessness and Supportive Housing is taking steps to construct and provide subsidized housing and support systems and to end homelessness in the city. This will take some time, but it is a high priority, so change will come.

Other problems facing the city's residents are the impossibility of driving downtown, with few parking spaces and too much traffic. Again, fortunately, the public transportation system is being expanded and upgraded. The convenience of Uber and Lyft helps decrease the number of private cars circulating, but there are so many each day that the streets are just as congested, if not more. The multi-national headquarters in SoMa and the housing and services adjacent are creating new full-service downtown neighborhoods where cars are not necessary, and this eventually should help.

So, as one can see, when supported by the populace, what actually makes the city work is that this is a city of action: when there's a problem, the city government works to solve it: new affordable housing and support for the homeless, more efficient public transportation, more green space, a major and obligatory recycling program. Responding to those San Franciscans who work hard and play hard and who love their city and want to keep it the way they—and the rest of the world—like it, the city moves on.

All in all, as you will shortly discover, San Francisco is—and it also is not—just like any other city. This book should help you find that out as you begin to make your way. Scout out the neighborhoods it describes, stroll the outdoor markets, experiment with unfamiliar dishes in offbeat Asian eateries. Get to know your neighbors and your colleagues at work, for San Franciscans are welcoming folk. Volunteer in your community. Spend Sundays in one of the city's beautiful parks, go whale watching not far offshore, and find the view that best makes your own heart soar. San Francisco's Convention & Visitors Bureau once said that the three commandments when visiting San Francisco were to "explore, experience, and enjoy." When you join long-time San Franciscans in following these "commandments", you too will soon understand what led the city's beloved writer Alice Adams to term San Francisco "the last lovely city." Welcome home.

MAP OF SAN FRANCISCO

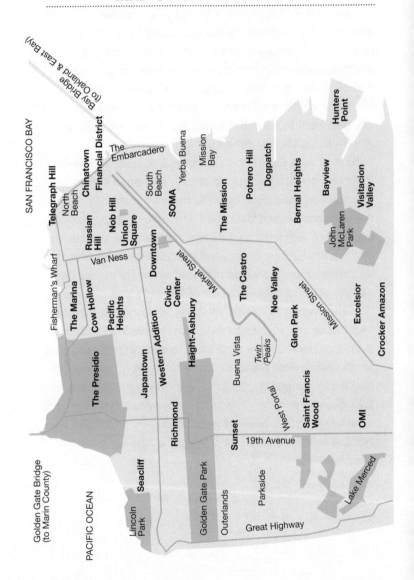

CHAPTER 1

FIRST IMPRESSIONS

> ❛No city invites the heart to come to life as
> San Francisco does.❜

— William Saroyan

On the summer morning your plane arrives in San Francisco, you've already been wondering if everything you've heard about the city is true. Is it really the most beautiful city in the United States? The most cosmopolitan, like a European city? Well, you're here for a meeting and have come two days early, just to find out. So, after your cab has deposited you at a downtown hotel on what looks to be a cool, cloudy day and you've checked in, you set out to see for yourself, city map showing on your cell phone. You'll start with the famous Union Square area, then see if you can find that green Chinatown gate people talk about, grab a bite to eat, and perhaps go to North Beach on one those cable cars that also seem to be symbolic of the city. You've heard that the Italian cafés in North Beach not only have good coffee, they're excellent for "people watching," too. You carry a jacket—just in case.

And then as you start your walk, the wind hits you full force. Unrelenting, damp. It's whipping along the canyons of tall office buildings as you forge your way through the Financial District up to Union Square. You can't see the tops of the buildings for the fog. So, you've got your jacket on, zipped up, and are glad that you read somewhere that only uninformed tourists wear shorts and sandals in "summery" San Francisco. People talk about the lovely climate here. Surely, they can't mean this.

You cut through the Crocker Galleria, three levels of open balconies with shops and cafés that look interesting, and you make a mental note to come back. And soon ahead you see Union Square, up some steps. A group of colorfully-dressed Latin American musicians are playing their pipes, creating a lively air. One of the musicians nods at you as you pass by on

A cable car climbs up the steep hill on California Street. The Sing Chong Building (circa 1908) with its Chinese styled roof makes it clear that the attractions of Chinatown await.

your way up. And suddenly you are charmed. The old plaza—no matter how modernly restored—is captivating, overlooking its bustling surroundings. There's a human scale, the buildings are low, and there aren't any fogbound skyscrapers here. You can imagine what it must have looked like a century ago. Down the steps again, you circle the square to browse the windows of Saks, Tiffany, Nieman Marcus, and Macy's, and you even wander in to look at the lobby of the famous century-old but totally up-to-date Westin St. Francis hotel. The cable car is clanging by as you come out, and people even seem to be hanging off the sides. Watching as it works its way up a steep hill, you decide that yes, this isn't to be missed.

Chinatown is showing on the map, so you walk past the huge Apple Store and turn on Grant Avenue, glancing right and left, and then you look up, straight ahead. And there it is: the Dragon Gate! Spanning Grant Avenue where it narrows, it's a tall welcoming entrance with a tiled roof like a pagoda, painted red and green, the Chinese colors of prosperity. So here you are, possibly being beckoned into another world. You quicken your steps, not minding the upward incline. At first there are gift shops to the right and left: the windows show jade and gold, silks, artworks, and Chinese tourist kitsch, of course. But buying souvenirs for the family is for another day, so you walk on. It's not so cold now, and a bright blue sky is showing through in patches as the fog is beginning to lift. In fact, you're almost ready to take your jacket off.

And then the restaurants appear, their wafting aromas trying to lure you in. "Eat where the Chinese do," your boss advised, so you look in. But there are Asians in all of them, so you keep on. You turn up steep Washington Street and see that the signs are all in Chinese! Now on Stockton it doesn't seem like America any longer. Ancient-looking women with their shopping bags are shouting in Chinese to the fruit vendors, gesturing at piles of vegetables, the likes of which you've never seen before. The descriptions are in Chinese but the prices are not, and they are incredibly cheap. The fish markets, open to the sidewalk, also have their lines, if this pell-mell assortment of people can be called a line. Buckets of fish line the floor below those above that are in cases or on ice. Some of the women in mismatched clothes and black cloth sandals—they could even be great-grandmothers—have fabric slings tied firmly across their chests, with a baby snuggled, almost swaddled, behind.

Now you notice there are so many little eateries you don't think you could make a choice. So, you just go into the next. There are cooked, crispy ducks hanging in the window, and a huge vat of what must be soup is bubbling on a burner, as well. And it's clear that no one is speaking English, not one word.

The waiter zipping by points to a large round table where five businessmen in suits are talking in Chinese while eating their lunch, chopsticks in one hand, rice bowl in the other. They don't look up as you take the remaining seat. There's a pitcher of water on the table, and at your place a handwritten menu that, thank heavens, has English translations under the listings in Chinese. There are also a yellow plastic glass, chopsticks, and a paper napkin, but no fork. You look to see what the men are eating. Are those chicken feet? And what is that meat in brownish sauce? The guy next to you is shoveling it in, so it must be good. You've heard about authentic Chinese food in San Francisco. It looks like you've come to the right place.

So when the waiter halts just briefly in front of you, although you had been thinking of that delicious-looking duck, you point to what your neighbor is having. And instead of tea, which all the others are drinking, you take a chance and order a Diet Coke. It may be China, but it's America, too, is it not? And in almost the blink of an eye, an enormous meal is thrust in front of you: first soup, and then the main course with rice, along with the Coke. The man next to you gives you a quick nod of approval, but then looks down to his rice bowl once again. You don't know exactly how to describe your meal—"beef and vegetables" doesn't do it justice—but you'd come back for it again, any day. Being here reminds you that there's a celebrated Asian Art Museum, a must for tomorrow, the last free day before your meeting begins. Finally, when the bill is set before you, you can't read it, for it's scrawled in Chinese, but since it's under $10.00 including the Coke, you couldn't care less. On the way out you give your own nod of approval at two other tourists who have come in and are now looking around, wondering what to order.

And when you're back on the sidewalk, contentedly replete, something is different. You realize that the entire sky is clear and the air is warm. In fact, the sky is of a blue so startling it almost takes your breath away. The street seems to sparkle as you walk up to Mason Street to wait for the cable car. You realize as you climb, that you've walked just about across the whole downtown, and that San Francisco is a "walking city", despite the hills you've climbed and see just ahead. You don't wait long, but when the cable car arrives, it's full, or so you think. Yet people adjust themselves to make a space for you, so you jump on, finding a pole to hold on to steady yourself.

You flash the City Pass you bought near Union Square, the gripman rings his bell, and off you go.

North Beach is too close, so you ride until the end of the line, only a few streets from the famous Fisherman's Wharf. The meeting organizers have planned for a group dinner out here one night, so instead of stopping here, you stroll along the promenade, noticing a brightly colored antique-looking trolley car discharging passengers for their own afternoon at the Wharf. But you're going to Pier 39, where you've heard that there are actually sea lions living right in the city, and darned if it isn't true! Dozens, or maybe hundreds of them. An official sign cautions people against bothering them in any way. Along with everyone else, you take a picture or two. Then, before doing anything else, you get a cup of coffee and walk around to the end of Pier 39. Musing, you wonder if you should have lunched here in one of the inviting restaurants with their views, but you put it out of your mind. Your own experience in Chinatown was one you'll long remember.

And there at the end is the most incredible panorama a city could ever have! Unbelievable! The glistening bay, the Golden Gate itself, mountains across the water, and the glorious unending sky, still that piercing blue, the air now quite warm. You lean against the rail, sip your coffee, never wanting to move. But you do. Finally, you whisk past the tourist shops, you glide along the moving walkway of the Aquarium, and then you are out once again onto the street. You're thinking tiredly of the long walk back to your hotel, and perhaps of a nap.

But San Francisco accommodates, and there approaching the corner is one of those colourful, vintage trolley cars, and you—along with several others—flag it down, somewhat relieved to catch the ride. The tracks run along the Embarcadero, the broad boulevard that parallels the bay, and with stately palms guiding the way, you're soon back downtown, and tight asleep on a comfortable bed only a few minutes

The sea lions of Pier 39, doing what they do best: basking, barking and lounging on their piers.

after that. A fresh sea breeze, a healthy walk, and a delicious lunch are all it took.

Later, in the hotel lobby you run into a colleague also arriving for the meeting, so you agree to spend the evening together. Outside, it's still quite balmy, and the breeze has died down. What will it be? North Beach and an Italian evening, or a walk down Market Street to the Ferry Building? No, you agree to meet there early in the morning to take in the Farmers Market and then the ferry, perhaps to visit Sausalito. And later, the Asian Art Museum for you and the Museum of Modern Art for your friend. There's clearly too much to do, and too little time. You've both got your jackets at the ready, and you decide to take the cable car from its starting point just at the corner and get to North Beach.

For the first few streets, it's flat, but as the car reaches Kearny Street it gets steep, and then steeper and steeper yet. And the car is climbing and both you and your friend are grinning like the tourists you are. You pass Grant Avenue where you had walked earlier in the day, and finally you get off at Powell, where your friend hails another bell-clanging cable car that is coming up the hill. This one is heading north, and as the other chugged up, this one—after a few minutes—glides down, and then down some more. The cable cars are a National Landmark, and you can see why.

When you are once again on foot, you see Washington Square, so you stroll around—amid the people relaxing on the grass—and you look at the works at an art fair there. You chat with a photographer, thinking to buy his photo of the sea lions, but you don't, for you want to see how your own come out. And then you walk south on Columbus, past the famous coffee houses and several Italian restaurants that all look good. But, your friend has heard of Sotto Mare that specializes in cioppino, a seafood casserole. That suits you both just fine, and the place turns out to be as good as advertised. It's crowded, so you sit at the counter and watch the chefs do their stuff. An hour or so later, when you come out (with several business cards in your pocket to give to friends back home), it's cooling off and you put your jacket back on. Suddenly you remember something else you once heard about San Francisco, that it does have four seasons, but they all just happen in one day! You tell your friend, and you both nod in agreement and laugh.

Strolling back to the hotel, you look at the streets, into the restaurant windows, wishing there was more time. And then you hear a low blast of noise. It's a real foghorn, clearly announcing the fog starting to come back in. But now you understand and can't wait for tomorrow afternoon's warm blue sky. And, just before you end this first day, you decide to have a drink at the top of your hotel, where the lounge boasts of a spectacular view of San Francisco and the bay. The lights of the city are twinkling below the fog that is now drifting in, and you and your friend sit rather quietly with your glasses in front of you—a Zinfandel from the Wine Country that the waiter has recommended. You look out at the lights, and you mull over what you've seen on this first day, and whether San Francisco lives up to its reputation for charm.

And if this first day at the city had been yours, what would you conclude?

CHAPTER 2

THE CITY THEN— AND NOW

> *San Francisco is 49 square miles
> surrounded by reality.*

— Paul Kantner (Jefferson Airplane)

Then ...

When the founding fathers of the United States were signing the Declaration of Independence in 1776, what is now San Francisco had only recently been discovered and was still wild lands and sand dunes as far as the eye could see. That people date this "discovery" to 1769 by Spanish soldiers looking for Monterey Bay of course doesn't take into account the thousand years the area had already been inhabited by the native Miwok, Ohlones, and Wintuns, hunters and gatherers who were quickly subjugated by the intruders and then overcome by their domination and diseases. The soldiers and missionaries coming to control and convert these native peoples very shortly did them in.

One wonders whether those Spanish soldiers were as awed by the beauty of their find as we are today. The sandy shoreline they took over was backed by soaring cliffs. Rocky hills were covered with live oaks and sweet-smelling grasses, and the ever-shifting sand dunes reached toward little inland marshes and streams, borne by the constant ocean breeze. But, as with the native peoples, even the bay we currently see, spectacular as it is, is not as the Spaniards found it, for some 40 per cent has been filled in. Bay waters originally came as far as what is now Montgomery Street, lapping at Kearny Street, and the Marina was dredged only for the 1915 Panama-Pacific Exposition. By Francisco and Taylor Streets, there was once a protected sandy cove called North Beach, but now all that remains is the name.

The Spanish named the area Yerba Buena, after those herbal grasses on the hills. By 1776, Juan Bautista de Anza and his contingent of 200 Spanish soldiers had established the Presidio, a fort that commanded a strategic overlook of both ocean and bay, and it remained a military base until just a few decades ago. By 1776, too, the priest Junipero Serra had founded the sixth of the Franciscan missions that stretched up the 600-mile Alta California coast, and just a few years later a church—now known as Mission Dolores—was built, an adobe building which still stands.

Although the areas that are now the Mission District and the Presidio were the first to be settled, the original village of Yerba Buena was founded along the city's eastern-most waterfront. Yerba Buena Plaza, now Portsmouth Square in Chinatown, was the heart of the village, which was first Spanish, then Mexican, and finally, in 1846, American. The town also rolled down the hill to the waterfront and today, the old brick buildings of the Barbary Coast—on streets with names such as Balance Street and Gold Street—still attest to their role during the Gold Rush, more than century and a half ago. It may be that only a few of the buildings from the 1850s remain, but now they anchor an arts and dining district, combining modernity with a spirit that is only San Francisco.

While thousands of adventurers seeking quick fortunes came to the Sierra foothills, clever merchants of all sorts readied their wares to take some of that fortune for themselves. Restaurants, bordellos, hotels and rooming houses, groceries, baths, and laundries almost exploded overnight around the Barbary Coast. Banks and financial services set themselves up toward Montgomery Street. Levi Strauss started producing his trousers. And a sleepy town that a short while before had counted only 500 residents with one newspaper became a city of 35,000 with twelve dailies on the country's western edge. The discovery of silver—the 1859 Comstock Lode—brought more speculation and wealth, immigrants, and workers and services to keep them all. By the end of the century, the city held ten times that 35,000, and today, with the population hovering about 875,000, a different frontier spirit holds—in the soaring steel and glass office buildings, with this century's financial and technological adventurers looking out, this time over the Pacific Rim and beyond. Iconoclastic attitudes toward life are still strong, focusing on opportunities seen and grasped, whether at work or at play.

For the most comprehensive information on San Francisco, get the extensive San Francisco Visitors Planning Guide at the Visitor Information Center, 900 Market Street, downstairs at Hallidie Plaza. Or download it at www.sftravel.com/article/visitors-guide.

And Now ...

Today, the City of San Francisco makes up the entire San Francisco County, the most important of the nine counties comprising the Bay Area. Yet it is the smallest of the nine, and almost half of it is water, most of it San Francisco Bay. In fact, it is the smallest county in the state. Situated on about the same latitude as Tokyo and Washington D.C., the beautiful, hilly, wind-swept city sits at the top of a peninsula, and its land area encompasses 46.7 square miles (121 sq km), just 7 miles (11.3 km) across. Only since 1937 has the city been connected to the north and east by its two famous bridges, and ferries that have long brought people to the city still traverse the sparkling bay. The city itself swells like the ocean tides: each day it accommodates 200,000 workers who commute in from around the Bay Area, plus, over the course of a year, 25 million visitors—tourists and conventioneers—who filter through.

CLIMATE

To simplify what is truly complex, the city's climate is determined by the ocean, by the 40 or so hills that break or conduct the ever-present wind, and by the long Central Valley that cuts down the middle of the state. When the valley swelters in the summer and the foothills are golden and dry, the hot air rises, as it must. This forces cold ocean air to whip through

the natural opening of the Golden Gate to temper the heat, but bringing to the city foggy mornings and brisk winds that move bitingly through the streets. Sometimes the fog burns off by late morning and early afternoons can be clear and warm. Other times, however, the fog hovers and does not move for days, leaving visitors surprised that they need a jacket in mid-summer and residents amused by the tourists in their shorts and tee shirts, hunched against the wind. Conversely, when the Central Valley cools off in September and October, San Francisco can have its sunniest summer days, with its temperatures even reaching about 80°F (32.2°C) for a day or two. This is when diehard San Franciscans complain the most, bemoaning the absence of their beloved fog.

Winter itself is cool and damp, but not really cold. Although climate is uncertain in San Francisco, as it is everywhere these days, until recently there was traditionally a winter "rainy season" and a summer "dry season". But California recently suffered a four-year drought, and although it seems now to have ended, its effects may last for some time. In general, though, in San Francisco, rains can be gentle or hard, but there are rarely thunderstorms, and usually part of each day is clear. With the city rarely seeing temperatures below freezing, flowers bloom outdoors in the winter, athletes play tennis in shorts and sweatshirts, office workers with sweaters eat their box lunches at outdoor tables, and people walk to work wearing light wool jackets, perhaps carrying an umbrella, just in case. On those rare occasions when a flake or two of snow does appear, so do the amazed telephone calls: "Did you see the snow?"

Within San Francisco are about a half-dozen microclimates, depending on which side of which hill or valley you are and the patterns of the winds. No matter where, however, the climate is bracing and the average annual temperature is about 55°F (12.8°C). The areas near the ocean are the foggiest and most cool, as are the summits of the highest hills. Areas away from the ocean and on the lee sides of hills—SoMa and Mission Bay, Bayview, the Mission, Noe Valley, and the Castro, for instance—are often sunny when other parts of the city are socked in or enshrouded by fog, and in fact, these are the warmest parts of town.

EARTHQUAKES

It is a fact one has to admit: San Francisco sits above the intersection of several of the earth's tectonic plates. Earthquakes regularly assault the entire Bay Area, owing to adjustments in the rifts of those nearby plates: the famous San Andreas and Hayward faults, as well as the San Gregorio, Greenville, and Calaveras faults. Two major tremblors, two "big ones," are still remembered with awe: the 1906 quake, registering 8.0 on the Richter scale, whose fiery aftermath all but destroyed the city; and the lesser one in 1989, registering 6.9, which caused great damage and a restructuring of the downtown waterfront.

No matter how long people have lived here, everyone talks about the occasional minor quakes and tremors, and few people get used to the even more rare large seismic jolts. Despite nervous jokes about "waiting for the big one," the dangers earthquakes present do not seem to drive people away. All recently-constructed apartment and office buildings in the city must be "earthquake-proof," which means they might sway during a quake, but should not collapse. Nonetheless, earthquakes remain dangerous, and if they worry you, you might consider living away from the faults in one of the other counties of the Bay Area, where the risk is perhaps somewhat less. Scientists are now saying there is a 70 per cent chance of a major quake within the next 30 years, and although no one knows exactly when the next "big one" will come, everyone knows that it will.

THINKING ABOUT PLACE

San Francisco is, by and large, a residential city. Its major financial businesses cluster in the eastern portion that became the city's financial hub during the Gold Rush, but development is now ceding to the nearby SoMa, Mission Bay and Bayview areas. The rest—extremely diverse residential areas—maintain the local services and shops that residents of each area would expect. The city calls its widespread areas "districts," and their names often reflect their history, such as the Mission or Cow

Hollow. Yet the hills and their microclimates, and the lifestyle each area has molded, have created myriad little neighborhoods with names of their own, and it should not be surprising that in such an individualistic city, each area has its own character, often fiercely defended.

Some of these neighborhoods may take more understanding than others and some may display distinctly different attitudes, even from block to block, such as just along one street: Market, mid-Market, or Outer Market. Many districts are charming and welcoming. Some are warm, sunny, and relaxed, some foggy, wind-swept, and brisk. Some are known for their social activism, a few defined by their ethnicity. Nothing is cheap in San Francisco, but the city has now legislated that all new residential construction offer a percentage of units for affordable housing, under current market rates.

San Franciscans have long regarded the eastern part of the city as urbanized and progressive and the western parts as more suburban and conservative. It is true that although neighborhoods overlap and populations change as prices rise and older districts become gentrified, people still tend somewhat to be characterized by the districts they call home. Yet that is changing, as people live anywhere they can. Now, the ethnic and social population is diffused, and the city's balanced cultural diversity constitutes a great part of its cosmopolitan charm. While Pacific Heights has been known to be predominately wealthy Caucasian, the Castro gay, Chinatown Chinese, the Mission Latino, and the Western Addition African-American, in general there is a pleasing—and sometimes surprising—ethnic distribution throughout the city. Asians are now predominant in the area around Clement Street, and a diverse mix of San Franciscans has moved into the once-Latino Mission. Bernal Heights, Glen Park, Potrero Hill and the hippy-known Haight are all among the areas where savvy investors took advantage of the few remaining reasonably priced homes, and of course now having remodeled them, have driven the

A row of "Painted Ladies" or Victorian style houses. These shown here are in the Italianate design, popular between 1850–1875, and are characterised by bay windows with side windows slanting inward, pipe-stem columns flanking the front door and flat crowns.

prices up. In fact, young professionals—unmarried and often childless—with an abundance of discretionary dollars to spend on housing keep moving into all the different neighborhoods, buying their "fixer-uppers," and bringing life and color to those areas that were once uninspired, or, conversely, that were once considered only private enclaves of the rich. That residents with lower income levels are being forced out is a matter of some concern.

As in any city, some districts are more open, beautiful, or well-kept than others. No matter where you live, however, you will have access to open space, whether it is the sandy strips of the ocean beaches or the wide concrete promenade that runs alongside the bay. If the eastern half of the city, destroyed in the 1906 earthquake, does not see many leafy streets, green squares and large landscaped plazas nonetheless charmingly dot the area, allowing spectacular views of the nearby mountains and the often bright blue, almost iridescent, sky. The five-acre landscaped park above the new Salfesforce Transit

Center will certainly be a welcome addition for a populace that heads out-of-doors whenever it can.

Away from downtown, parks, both sculpted and wild—Buena Vista, Glen Canyon, the large McLaren, and Harding—offer as many attractions, in their own ways, as the city's two most famous, the Presidio and Golden Gate Park. The beloved 13-acre Dolores Park has been completely upgraded (to an estimated cost of $20 million), following a Leave no Trace philosophy, and is a destination for hundreds of park-goers every day—whether to play a sport, have a picnic, or just sun themselves on the grassy hill. And across from the famous Painted Ladies (Victorian houses), Alamo Square Park has also beautifully benefited from a multi-million dollar upgrade.

Each district, naturally, abuts at least one other. Sometimes there is a dividing boulevard or street or a hill, but sometimes just a subtle sense of change. In some areas, just one small street will mean the difference between an area you would consider for housing and one that might not appeal. Although all the districts are given a broad look on the next pages, some mini-neighborhoods may not be mentioned, only partly for lack of space. Some are too small to describe and, given the overwhelming need for housing, some are in the process of change or rebirth. In any case, change is what San Francisco is all about.

Safety

San Francisco—like any major city—has its occasional robberies and muggings. Yet women need take only the usual precautions of staying on well-travelled streets and jogging in the parks with friends on designated paths and in daylight hours. And although the Tenderloin is slowly changing, especially with the many popular Vietnamese eateries, there are still parts of the area where it's better not to enter alone at night.

In this tech-savvy city, thefts are often of cell phones—especially iPhones—so be careful. Don't just leave them on a table while you're drinking your coffee, or carry them in your back pocket while you're walking. It only makes sense.

No matter where you look, remember that San Francisco is is often rated as having the highest average rents for a one-bedroom apartment. Check one of the many websites such as www.numbeo.com to determine the current average prices and cost of living statistics. And then factor in your own personal needs. San Francisco is clearly worth the effort.

DISTRICT BY DISTRICT: FINDING YOUR OWN

The Downtown—moving south

For almost a century, San Franciscans characterized their city as "North of Market" or "South of Market," for these areas that bordered the long bisecting Market Street were like night and day. The North—with Union Square, the Financial District, Nob Hill, Jackson Square, and North Beach—was the focus of the city's life, while the South—a large, sunny, residential area devastated in the 1906 earthquake—tumbled into disrepair, the site of shipyards and their workers (many African Americans and immigrants) in seedy rooming houses, of drab industries and marginalized San Franciscans who could, in effect, live nowhere else.

How this has changed! Union Square north of Market Street may certainly still command the shopping and theatre points of the city, and the Financial District bustles with the business of the Pacific Rim. Hotels and trendy restaurants thrive, and there are many of the city's attractions along the north waterfront— Pier 39, the Ferry Building, the Exploratorium, and Fisherman's Wharf, to name just a few. Residential life remains agreeable and even exciting especially around Chestnut Street or Fillmore. But actually, the daily vibrancy of the city is moving south to a district now proudly called SoMa (South of Market), urban renewal having made its various old districts flourish anew. Thousands of new residences have cropped up in dozens of revitalized streets and more are underway. Major museums and

The Museum of Modern Art in the trendy SoMa—South of Market—district, opened in 1995. Its collections offer works by both modern masters and younger, less-established artists.

a convention center bring tourists and locals alike, an imposing skyscraper is joining others with a brand-new transit complex, two connected vertical shopping centers face out on Market Street, and lovely urban and wild waterfront parks bring green as does the rooftop park of the Transbay Terminal. Two huge sports arenas bring loyal fans, and the University of California a state-of-the-art 50+ acre medical complex at Mission Bay attracted bioscience start-up businesses and international corporation headquarters, apartment complexes and local services. The expanding public rail system and subway will link all this all as far as Chinatown. All this, in fact, is SoMa.

Of course, the districts in SoMa were here all along, just waiting to be reborn. China Basin, Dogpatch, India Basin, Mission Bay, Baview, and Hunter's Point once conjured up thoughts only of dismal and crime-ridden areas to be avoided. Market around South Van Ness was colorless and uninviting. All told, there was little, anyway, to draw San Franciscans south.

By mid-century, the city knew it had to do something, and plans for renewal were made—especially for the areas around what are now the spectacular Yerba Buena Gardens, the Moscone Center and the stunning Museum of Modern Art. For years, condominiums and offices had been starting to appear along the southern waterfront, and in the year 2000, a new 40,000-seat baseball stadium at China Basin cemented the area into the modern San Francisco world—along with the huge 55-acre University of California medical complex in the next area south, Mission Bay. Biotech industries followed and thousands of people came who had never come before to work and to live.

So what are these various districts of SoMa like today? Dilapidated, unused piers are being refurbished with residences and commercial use, bayfront parks are being made more welcome, old public housing is being upgraded, a vast new housing community is already partially completed, restaurants are moving in as are the people to enjoy them. Hundreds of new housing units are creating new residential communities heading south and all the way up Potrero Hill. About to finish construction, across the Mission Creek bridge and almost adjacent to the AT&T Park in Mission Bay, on 300 acres, will be the 18,000-seat Chase Center, an arena area for the Golden

State Warriors (basketball), and in the interest of easier transit, a new central subway line to link it as far as Chinatown. New hotels are opening, more restaurants and bars are appearing seemingly every week, drawing the crowds, and in all, the San Francisco spirit carries on.

Closest to Market Street is where we see that "downtown" will never be the same. In areas near the South Embarcadero—sometimes called Rincon Hill or the "East Cut" (if the name takes hold), a little city is on its way. The spectacular reconstruction of the earthquake-damaged Transbay Terminal around First and Mission, is combining with the tallest building in San Francisco, the 61-story Salesforce Tower. Salesforce has poured many millions into this combined project, that is called The Salesforce Transit Center. Think of it as a force unto itself. The new multi-use and beautiful transit hub connects all eight Bay Area counties by bus and train, and restaurants and retail space, and pedestrian bridges are linked to the surrounds and to the Salesforce Tower. On the rooftop, and in the heart of downtown, a beautifully designed 5-acre Salesforce Park on top of the Transit Center will offer green gardens and trails, a water feature, a children's space, and a restaurant.

In the 61-floor tower, Salesforce itself has occupied some 30 floors, and other corporations are taking the rest. Nearby Facebook is leasing the entire Park Tower, bringing its office space in the city to more than a million square feet, in addition to expanding its major campus in Menlo Park. But seven million square feet of commercial space and 4,400 residential units here are clearly not enough. Other towers are either under construction or in the works, both commercial and residential. This is all bringing many thousands of jobs—and people—to the area, which in turn will bring more restaurants and services. This total city-within-a-city will be ever more in demand.

Of course, all this expansion comes at a price. In some areas in fact—even not just close to Market Street—average residential rents already are currently hovering around $4,000 per month. Yet, as mentioned, all new housing development must provide a certain percentage of "affordable" units; this is true throughout the city.

So, where will all these people live? For decades, people have been moving into SoMa, in highrises along the Embarcadero, in old warehouses converted into lofts, and finally now, taking over the areas south of the Third Street Bridge. The medical and biotech area of Mission Bay sees attractive apartment complexes and, adjacent to the south, along the Central Waterfront the formerly industrial and unnoticed Dogpatch, has also now visibly reinvented itself. Dogpatch? Starting at Mariposa, it may be listed as a Historic District, but modern life here is warm, in the refurbished Victorians, in the artists' studios, and in the burgeoning restaurants and cafés.

Farther south are two large districts, Bayview and Hunters Point. Formerly drab and problematical working class communities seeing disrepute and crime, they are rapidly developing with upgraded public housing, new homes, a public library, open spaces, and new enterprises moving in. Newcomers appreciating these warm and sunny areas along the bayfront are buying the older houses for prices that would have been impossible a decade ago. Keep watching as they continue their redevelopment. At the once-dilapidated Hunters Point—the former site of a Navy shipyard on prime waterfront property—reclamation is owing to community activists along with the city's support. Keeping "the Point"—its longtime artists' community—and with upgraded public housing, new townhomes, the revitalized waterfront parks and the Candlestick Recreation Area, it's only the beginning. The abandoned piers are now planned for housing and neighbourhood commercial services. All these areas—once the poorest in the city, able only to house those who could live nowhere else—are quickly meeting the rest of the city. And the Caltrain, especially at its 22nd Street and Bayshore stations, makes these areas convenient for people to commute to work. Look also at the quasi-suburban Silver Terrace, close both to the thriving Bernal Heights and Portola Districts (across the 101 Freeway).

Actually, Potrero Hill has long been appreciated. Traditionally also a working class district settled by ship builders and removed from the city more in spirit than in distance, in recent decades this Historic District has had a reputation as being funky and fun. Now part of this southern expansion, artists and professionals, straight and gay couples, and young families who have refurbished their properties, are mixing congenially in sidewalk cafés with neighbourhood old-timers; the major commerce of cafés and small shops is along 18th Street. Many now realize that Potrero Hill is an easy commute to the Financial District or SoMa. Clean residential streets that follow the hill's contours seem quiet, and lining the leafy streets are small clapboard houses, large spaces converted into lofts, multi-story Victorians, attached single-family homes, and apartment buildings—a vigorous mix that looks sunnily out over other parts of the city that may already be enveloped in fog. Potrero Hill is the kind of neighborhood its residents swear never to leave. This rather iconoclastic ambience still persists, but with the development activity here on the hill and all around it—for how long? Already on the Potreo Flats below, that once belonged to warehouses and small industries, upgrading is finding a new spot to consider. Galleries have moved in, restaurants are joining the long-time Anchor Brewing Company (now reenergized by its sale to Sapporo), and Dogpatch is just steps away.

The Mission

Still South of Market, the Mission is another of the sections of town that is totally on the move, yet in some ways is the same. It's a large district with distinct attitudes, and basically, you can choose whatever lifestyle you want, for everything is here. Here's another area that let you know what's what: there's the Inner Mission, Mission Dolores and the Latino area, the coveted Valencia Corridor, and the far distant Outer Mission, just to name a few. Some are wildly popular day and night and some are workaday, but all are worth attention. The Mission is totally up-to-date San Francisco.

But first, remember that this is where it all started. Since those Spanish priests established their mission here, the area has maintained a Latin tone, despite waves of other nationalities that have left their mark. Some 50,000 people currently live in the Mission, in a melting pot of races and nationalities; yet despite the changing demographics and some of the Latino population forced out by rising prices, it is still just under 50 per cent Hispanic, which gives the area its colorful, uninhibited flavor.

Mission Street, which centuries ago linked Mission Dolores to the port at Yerba Buena, is the city's longest; as it cuts to the southwest, it takes on the character of each surrounding neighborhood. In the Inner Mission since the end of World War II it has been a Latino main street, with businesses displaying their wares on the sidewalk, taquerias offering inexpensive meals, and neighborhood folk volubly carrying on an outdoor life. Many of the side streets around 24th Street see three-story, bay-windowed flats and other low-rise apartments perched over the neighborhood stores. The original Victorians that have been gloriously renovated bring gentrification, happily to many, disappointing to others who worry about the character of their neighbourhood changing.

Toward the end of the 19th century, the Mission was solidly middle-class. Yet this was one area that did not benefit from the advent of the cable car, for when the hills became accessible, many people moved up. As industry developed near the waterfront, Irish, German, and Italian workers flocked to this sunny area from which they could walk to work. Although the area had been international for decades, what defined it as Latino was the establishment of international fruit and coffee companies that dealt with Latin America.

Now, the Mission has been noticed by more San Franciscans, especially by young entrepreneurs with their families, who saw an area ripe for investment and for a refurbishment of the old, decaying houses. The Mission is a booming town. Drive around the district and you will be convinced. Hundreds of restored large Victorians and small bungalows line side streets between Valencia and Guerrero. Ride along Dolores with its Canary Palms, on Fair Oaks with its Chinese elms, and down streets such as Capp or Hill streets with Italianate Victorians on one side and Stick Victorians on the other. Most are already brightly restored. Chula Lane to Abbey Street is a cul-de-sac of Victorians as well. Crossing over Cesar Chavez, the Precita Park area is a community of small homes on short streets that is suburban in feel. These are all areas home buyers are snapping up, and when you look around you will see beautifully restored homes perching majestically over some that still look as though they would fall over in the next breeze, as well as modern apartment complexes rising in any inch of space.

Unfortunately, some Latinos and older traditional businesses have been forced out by the rising prices; little here would be categorized as "affordable." There's just so much going on. Excellent Latin and non-Latin restaurants, hip bars, galleries, and charming boutiques are following the affluence, causing real estate prices to rise, especially around the now trendy Valencia Corridor—with its independent shops, theaters and restaurants of any level you want. In addition, the average rent

Victorian Houses

Victorian houses are San Francisco's pride. Although thousands disappeared in 1906, some 14,000 throughout the city survived the fire and have been preserved, many in the Mission, Cow Hollow, Pacific Heights, Alamo Square, and the Haight. Victorians may be garish or gracious, they may appear in a number of styles such as Queen Anne, Italianate, or Stick, they may be single-family homes or two-flats, or—as along Union Street—they may have been converted into stores and offices. Regardless of their appearance, Victorians are always sought after and do not come cheap. For an inside look at a Victorian, take a tour of the Haas-Lilienthal House: 2007 Franklin Street, tel: (415) 441-3000; www.haas-lilienthalhouse.org.

for an apartment is more than $3,000. Despite all this, the flavour of the Mission still persists.

Pay attention to the southeast section called Outer Mission, which is really quite a distance away and separated from the Mission scene. Bordering Mission Terrace, Crocker Amazon and Excelsior, it's a small area closer to Daly City, more tranquil and residential, with single-family homes. Prices are fairly reasonable here, and the Balboa Park station makes public transportation easily accessible. Look also at the surrounding districts, such as Noe Valley, Bernal Heights, and around Mission Dolores.

The Castro, Noe Valley and Bernal Heights

Certainly no discussion of San Francisco would be complete without some understanding of the Castro. In San Francisco nomenclature it is actually Eureka Valley, although no one calls it that any more. Originally part of a large ranch owned by José de Jesùs Noe, whose name remains on the next valley over, this multi-colored rainbow district that begins around Market and 16th Street, and climbs up the steep hill to its south, is known simply as the Castro, although little of the Castro is simple at all.

Until the end of the 19th century, this was one of those hilly areas that was seen as remote by San Francisco's elite, and so it remained rural and agricultural longer than its neighbors closer in. But when the cable car made the hill with its 18.4 per cent grade habitable, real estate speculators laid out a grid of streets, built Victorian houses and peak-roofed cottages and sold them to the working-class Irish, Scandinavians, and Germans, who created a traditional Catholic neighborhood—or so they thought.

Look at the Castro today. To outsiders it may look like the city's "gay ghetto," but to most San Franciscans it is much more than that. It truly is a small town with its own set of urban pleasures and problems, its local services and shops, its particular sense of what a community should be. Look at the stylish shops, the crowded cafés, the bright, rainbow-striped flags waving from windows, and you will understand this community's pride and solidarity. Both light-hearted and serious, this is a community that will no longer be anything but bold. The city has the largest LGBT percentage of any city in the United States (15.4%), and also highest percentage of same-sex households.

Most of the old Irish population has disappeared by now. The white-collar workers and professionals continue to step in, refurbishing the houses, setting up shops. This is what gregarious Harvey Milk did in the Seventies, and his subsequent rise in city politics and tragic assassination drew together what had been a rather disparate community, one that has stood its ground ever since. Do not underestimate its political clout; politicians now understand that, like everyone else, gays need public transportation, affordable housing, and reasonable zoning laws. Unlike everyone else, however, they often get out to vote as a bloc. Now, although gays—like all San Franciscans—live anywhere they can afford, the Castro is the community's spiritual and political home. Castro Street is bustling with men doing their daily shopping and errands, cruising, frequenting the late-night clubs, or going to the Castro Theater, along with other San Franciscans who come for the film festivals and for the trendy restaurants nearby.

As a residential area, the center of the Castro is a sunny valley. Steep hills shelter the small houses, and flowers bloom in front or backyard gardens or in pots on the sunny decks. As the streets rise steeply toward Twin Peaks, the homes become larger—Victorians and Queen Anne cottages—and these, when they are put up for sale, are snapped up in the blink of an eye. Rentals are also climbing: at the time of this writing, the average price for a rental apartment in the Castro is above $ 3,600.

Across Market, up towards Corona Heights and Buena Vista Parks, the Castro's suburbs have large, well-landscaped homes on winding, hilly streets. These are more traditional, less remarked-upon areas, agreeable and calm, and prices are rising considerably here. And farther in—below the Buena Vista Park—is the Duboce Triangle, with its own ambience—its small parks, tree-lined streets and its own restored Victorians, which are always in demand.

Just to the south, Noe Valley takes and gives to both the Castro and the Mission, but is another village unto itself. Some old German and Irish might still live here, as in the Castro, but it is now one of the most sought-after areas of town by young couples, by lesbians and gays spilling over from the Castro, and by artists and others with a bohemian outlook. Protected from the fog by three steep hills, this sunny valley is one of the city's most popular areas for young families; mothers pushing their children in strollers do their shopping on 24th Street or sit with their friends at outdoor tables in front of any of the area's charming little cafes. Twenty-fourth and Church is the main shopping intersection, but the shopping district really stretches from Diamond to Dolores. Since the J-Church streetcar line comes here, Noe Valley is a convenient commute for those who work downtown.

The entire area is relaxed in feel, less frenetic than the Castro, more solidly comfortable. Streets are fairly wide, and the small houses that line them are painted in light colors. The streets leading up to Diamond Heights are steep and the large Victorians have exceptional views, although the higher the climb, of course, the denser the fog. The residents of Noe Valley value their village and are trying to keep out the big businesses and chains. They have been doing so somewhat successfully so far.

Only a few years ago, you would not have paid much attention to Noe Valley's neighbor at the southern edge of the Mission valley, a rather placid, uninspired—sometimes rundown—area of small private homes nestled on low-rising hills. Now, however, sunny Bernal Heights is much in demand—some say with the old-time spirit of North Beach, updated. The area's location—with borders also on Glen Park and the Mission—meant that it was a logical expansion for those neighborhoods, as well as for men and women who might also have thought of the lively Castro as their home. Gently winding streets heading up low-rising hills, several welcoming green parks, gentle breezes, and panoramic views from Bernal Hill drew a new generation of San Franciscans, ready to remake the Victorian bungalows and Queen Anne cottages. Bernal Heights is now an area with its own cachet.

Fortunately the area has not lost its traditional multiracial, multi-ethnic character, but it took the work of community activists opposed to excessive gentrification to keep it that way. So far, the neighborhood ambience persists, even on Cortland Avenue, the district's main commercial street, which offers residents all the conveniences and services that a small town would want, plus the presence of the Alemany Flea Market. Private homes still have gardens, the renewed Holly Park is a treasure for families, and neighbors chat together in Bernal Park while letting their dogs romp and play.

Bernal Heights thus remains an area of satisfying proportions. Of course, prices have increased, as they have in the rest of the city. But, clearly, Bernal Heights is a neighborhood to value, and fortunate is the person who can seize an opportunity here.

DOWNTOWN NORTH OF MARKET

Back north of Market, the streets around Union Square—melding with the eastern Financial District neighbour—are undergoing changes, as well. Named after the pro-Union rallies held here during the Civil War, Union Square remains San Francisco's major shopping and theater district. A century ago this area that nestles around the 2.6-acre (1.1-ha) square was wealthy residential, but when the cable car made the steep Nob Hill more accessible, the wealthy moved up or out towards the new elegant district along Van Ness. Yet the high-quality shops and artisans stayed on, and after the 1906 fire, they moved back as soon as they could. Today, the landscaped square is ringed by luxury hotels and stores; most of the original shops are long gone, but one or two—such as Shreve's Jewelers—still exist. The hotels and theaters cluster near Geary and Market Street, and a few of the city's chic restaurants bring locals to the area.

In terms of residences, however, although there are many agreeable low-rise rental apartments north of Geary and on the southern foothill of Nob Hill, some may be too close to the 31 blocks of the seedy Tenderloin, which stretches out toward Polk Street. It's still problematic in many areas, and owing to several city services here, the homeless are more evident around the streets. But a Vietnamese community has established itself well around Larkin Street, with about 250 businesses, including restaurants that serve up delicious and affordable traditional food; this area is sometimes called Little Saigon. Some students are drawn to the lower rents here and easy access to public transportation. But here, especially, it just depends on where.

MID-MARKET TO HAYES VALLEY

Decades ago, the area now called Mid-Market (or Central Market) consisted mostly of the Civic Center—the city's nexus for government and culture. Market Street—starting around 6th Street and heading out past Van Ness—was drab, and just to the west, an elevated freeway blocked the sun of a neighbourhood called Hayes Valley that had little to say for itself. Now, however, with the freeway demolished, Hayes Valley sparkles in the sun and with a pulsating life. Mid-Market sees the soaring Federal Building, the Twitter building with its massive Market, Spotify, Dolby, and Uber headquarters, new classy hotels, and theaters and international restaurants. The traditional and stately Beaux Arts buildings of the Civic Center,

City Hall and the Public Library ground the area, along with the famous Asian Art Museum (see page 190). Concerts, ballet, and opera draw night time culture-hounds. And open plazas are welcoming to workers at lunchtime, so the area hums day and night.

Van Ness Boulevard itself is helping the Mid-Market process along, for it too is in the process of upgrading. It is interesting that a century after the 1906 fire destroyed it, the Van Ness corridor is once again an upscale residential area, with its condominiums, supermarket, and chic restaurants in all directions. Now the large intersection of Market and Van Ness is on the road to modernization with ongoing building and plans for even more office spaces and residences. Luxury hotels are already opening, and these will bring more restaurants and services—probably soon with a new neighbourhood name of its own.

To the west of the Boulevard is that Hayes Valley that now in the open has blossomed and is showing its true character to the world. Residents are proud of their community: concert-goers come here to dine in any level of restaurant—or later to hang out in one of the hip nightspots—bureaucrats lunch in the restaurants, neighbors visit in the afternoon over a cup of tea, and shoppers check out unique shops selling handcrafted products or antiques. Hayes Valley is in the perfect position to accommodate them all. Streets that had been hidden under the freeway have cleaned themselves up, Patricia's Green is a pleasing sculptured community park with a playground and art exhibits, and housing here is always in demand.

Financial District to Jackson Square

Stretching east to the Bay from Union Square is the historic Financial District, sometimes called the "Wall Street of the West," but long ago was the "Barbary Coast." As people hurry down the windy corridors of Montgomery and Sansome Streets, they probably do not think about the early days, when everything east of Kearny was mud flats, and the waters of the bay lapped up to what is now Montgomery Street. With just a few steel-shell buildings remaining from before the 1906 earthquake, the FiDi is still home to many of the city's high-rise office buildings, including the Bank of America, Transamerica Pyramid and the four-building Embarcadero Center.

Here, towards the southern end, streets seem deserted when the corporate types go home after work or to the happy hour in locales nearby. But because so many people work in this area, it really is filled with little treasures of restaurants and shops and take-out eateries. The Ferry Building and its Marketplace and other waterfront venues draw people day and night, as does the upscale Embarcadero Center, almost every evening of the year. Yet, if this part is not truly a residential district, another nearby revival is taking care of that.

Stretching inland from the long north Embarcadero promenade, just south of Broadway, you'll find an agreeable mixed-office/residential area. Long in decline, the area took on a new life in the 1960s, when an old produce market was demolished and warehouses were restored to hold offices, television studios, and art galleries. At Jackson Street, the Golden Gateway Center added more than one thousand living quarters in apartments and townhouses, creating an instant neighborhood. The Gateway—with its supermarket and fitness club—is linked to the services and shops of the Embarcadero Center—creating another little city in itself.

Adding to the revival mix here is Jackson Square, on the flat land-filled area that was once the Barbary Coast, its dance halls, boarding houses, and bawdy night life catering to gold miners down from the hills. Now the surviving red brick buildings dating from the 1860s are housing antique shops and art galleries, designers, and the well-known outfitter, The North Face. Retail stores, restaurants—including the exquisite Quince and Kokkari Estiatorio—are nearby, tech companies have moved in, and more. There are several open plazas in this sunny area, in addition to the splendid promenade that runs along the Bay. Sidney Walton Park, with its sculptures and fountain, brings office workers to its grassy knolls at lunchtime. Overlooking the park are the Golden Gateway Commons, spacious red brick condominiums built around private landscaped walkways. These town homes are sometimes rented out by their owners; when put up for sale, their prices, as one would expect, match the vitality of the area.

Nob Hill

Above the Financial District, just to the north of Union Square, and abutting Chinatown as well, Nob Hill is central to everything downtown. And it always has been. Perhaps the best known of the city's hills, Nob Hill still houses some of San Francisco's wealth, but not in any of the palaces ostentatiously constructed at the end of the 19th century by San Francisco's "Mother Lode" and railroad tycoons. The opulent lifestyle that allowed for their 50-room homes came to an end in 1906, today replaced by luxury hotels, elegant apartment buildings populated by professionals working nearby, the Grace Cathedral and Masonic Center, and the lovely Huntington Park holding it all together. One old mansion still exists, just to remind us, perhaps, of what once was. The grand hotels here offer fine dining and exceptional views, so both locals and tourists find their way up the steep hill, one way or another.

Until the end of the 19th century, Nob Hill was too steep for horse-drawn carriages, and it was workers who built little cottages along the lower slopes. But although cable cars allowed the tycoons to claim the summit, after the 1906 earthquake most rebuilt on safer terrain. Small frame apartment buildings began to appear, and many of these buildings—refurbished and modernized—remain convenient today for people working down the hill—in any direction. High-rises appeared at the summit in the Fifties, but here, as in other areas, height limits were instituted, limiting the amount of skyline that could be blocked.

The summit of Nob Hill, dominated by Grace Cathedral.

Today's public transportation has also made this steep hill convenient for Asians, as Chinatown expands up Clay and Sacramento. On the west, low-rise apartment buildings line the narrow streets heading down to the Polk Gulch corridor, and, in fact, stores on California down to Polk are the most convenient. You probably won't find housing available on the top of Nob Hill itself, although on its slopes apartments do become available from time to time.

Chinatown
You may not want to live in Chinatown, but no discussion of San Francisco would be complete without a bow to this colorful, historic area that—the Mission and military Presidio aside—formed the original settlement of Yerba Buena and that in its own way contributes to much of the spirit of the modern city.

Chinatown, that used to extend from Bush to Broadway and from Kearny to Powell, now crosses over Broadway into North

On Grant Avenue at Bush Street, just a few blocks north of Union Square, is the Dragon Gate that marks the entry to Chinatown.

Beach and up Russian and Nob hills. The Chinese community has also expanded out to Clement Street and into the Sunset, but Chinatown remains home base; no matter where people live, many come back on a Sunday for shopping and a family lunch. Although residents complain that their traditional area is becoming too homogeneous in its commercial effort to lure tourists, Chinatown is still a crowded warren of streets and alleys, of small exotic-looking shops and apartments above, perhaps with an open window and laundry waving in the breeze. In fact, behind some of the shabby, unmarked doors in the little alleyways is where the most interesting—and quietly private— business of this sometimes-secretive community takes place. The tantalizing aromas from the restaurants, conversations and audible bargaining in Mandarin and other Chinese dialects, and the inexpensive markets crowded with elderly women carrying their grandchildren on their backs in cloth sacks also conspire to give Chinatown an air of other-worldliness.

Although only about half of the city's Chinese population lives here, this 24-block area is the city's most populated district. Its constant bustle is perhaps at least slightly reminiscent of the original Chinese quarter founded in the 1850s, when Cantonese immigrants flocked to these shores. During the Gold Rush they were cooks, launderers, and shopkeepers, even brothel keepers, and then workers on the railroad. By 1881, some 25,000 Chinese were resident in the city, and so many were coming to the United States that the Chinese Exclusion Act of 1882 was passed to stop the influx, meaning that until its repeal in 1943, the Chinese population became older—and poorer. Only in the post-World War II period did immigration begin once again and did the Chinese come again to Chinatown.

The main local shopping streets are to the west, on Stockton and Powell, which leaves Grant to the tourists looking for gifts. But the spiritual heart of the community is Portsmouth Square, which as Yerba Buena Plaza was originally only one street away from the shoreline. Until commerce moved east to Montgomery Street, this was the center of town, and it was at Yerba Buena Plaza that the discovery of gold was announced.

Rents in Chinatown are fairly reasonable, but conditions may not be particularly agreeable. This is not the cleanest part of the city by any means, nor is there much that is leafy green— except St Mary's Square on a nearby rooftop. So, now the city government is allocating funds to upgrade the area, but surely its iconoclastic spirit will remain. This is certainly the most exotic and fascinating part of the city, yet consider carefully if Chinatown appeals. Chinatown is another planet, deep in the heart of San Francisco.

The North Embarcadero

Nestled below the granite outcropping of eastern Telegraph Hill, several condominium complexes bring quiet residentiality to an area that was enhanced by the construction of Levi

Strauss Plaza, with its fountains, streams, and grassy lawns. Some of these condominiums along Lombard or Montgomery are rented out by their owners, and some come up for sale. The prices are what one would expect. Up Telegraph Hill from North Beach—but on the sheer eastern side that no car can traverse—are the Filbert Street Steps, a landscaped walkway with enchanting clapboard cottages along lanes and terraces that might seem precarious, but that (at least so far)

The eastern side of Telegraph Hill is too steep for roads and cars. On the top of the hill is the famous Coit Tower, a landmark of San Francisco.

have survived earthquakes, rains, and whatever else the San Francisco climate (or politicians) might inflict.

Here, the ancient trolley cars bring tourist families to the famous attractions of Pier 39, with its stunning views, its shops and entertainment, its resident sea lions on K dock, plus a spectacular aquarium. Not far along is the rightly-famous Fisherman's Wharf—generally reached by cable car from downtown—and its restaurants with their fishing atmosphere. Again, not far, on the way to the Marina is the eastern edge of the Van Ness Corridor, and there are high rise buildings and also low-rise apartments dotting the area. These are close to Ghirardelli Square, famous for its chocolate—also with shops and attractions that appeal mostly to tourists, and to discerning locals, as well.

A Valley between Two Hills

North Beach is a sunny valley nestled between the western slope of Telegraph Hill and the eastern edges of Russian Hill. One hundred and fifty years ago, there were a few docks and a little beach along the northern waterfront. Fishermen lived close by, some Basque and Portuguese, but primarily it was the Italians in what came to be called Little Italy who gave the area its flavor, one that is still remembered. Italian restaurants, coffee houses, bakeries, and deliciously aromatic delis draw the crowds, as does the spirit of the "Beat" poets in the Fifties who brought a rather bohemian feel to the area. Nightlife—whether in cafés, restaurants, or clubs—abounds. But the atmosphere in spots has also changed: Chinese restaurants and groceries have crossed their erstwhile boundary at Broadway, and now along Stockton they compete noisily for attention, while in the early morning Washington Square is taken up with devotees of tai chi. The result is an agreeable mix, one that tourists and San Franciscans appreciate to the fullest. North Beach is one of the most treasured areas of the city.

For daily life, the Financial District is only a 15-minute walk away. Low-rise apartments hover above interesting shops and restaurants. On the east, the quiet residential neighborhood of Telegraph Hill rises slowly, and as it does, many of the three- and four-story apartment buildings command excellent views. Long-term residents live in cottages or in old buildings that new arrivals would love to get their hands on. Some properties do become available from time to time, and their prices vary, from the actually reasonable to the usually expensive. Not all of these buildings have garages, and even with a residential parking permit, finding a space on North Beach streets is always a challenge.

Heading up the winding road to Coit Tower, private homes of all sizes and apartment buildings command prices that are as steep as the hill's gradient; the hill is on bedrock, and the views can be spectacular. The old beach itself may be gone, but a beach town it remains: keep your windows open at night and you will hear the foghorn piercing through, and perhaps even the barks of sea lions down at Pier 39.

Practising tai chi in Washington Square.

This holds true, too, for parts of steep Russian Hill, which climbs up from North Beach to the west. Its location could not be better. With trendy Polk Street down the hill on the west, North Beach to the east, Cow Hollow down past the western slope, and Chinatown to the southeast, Russian Hill is ringed by every convenience one could want. If the area took its name from the Russian seal hunters who 150 years ago were said to have buried their dead up here, the area is now very much alive.

People do not talk much about Russian Hill, and few tour buses labor up the hill, which suits the residents well. The small businesses and restaurants on Hyde or Green Streets cater to locals, and in general this is a rather peaceful district with many enchanting lanes of almost-hidden charm. Restaurants and local shops go down the hill to this end of Polk.

On Russian Hill, finding a home would take patience. What everybody does find is a well-kept residential community with an active community association to keep it so. People may live in small apartments above neighborhood shops, in large buildings that push up against the fog, in luxurious condominiums on little landscaped lanes, or even in single-family homes that persist despite the desire of development to encroach. Some streets have Mediterranean villas or simple redwood homes, and some cul de sacs even have houses with gardens in front. Russian Hill seems to have it all. Tourists may thrill to drive down Lombard, the "crookedest street," but locals know that up at the top of the steep hill is Ida Coolbrith Park, more like a garden, a little park with a really big view. Russian Hill is definitely charming.

West of Van Ness—the Marina

Past North Beach and the commercial Fisherman's Wharf area, the exquisite, residential Marina sits on marshland dredged for the 1915 Panama Pacific Exposition, which celebrated the opening of the Panama Canal. If the Exposition was designed to show the world that the city was once again on its feet after the 1906 earthquake, the quake of 1989 that damaged so much of this landfill district showed how fragile that footing actually was. Nonetheless, defying nature's whims, most Marina residents stayed, rebuilt their homes, and are today enjoying their views of the Bay, the Golden Gate Bridge, and the hills—at least until the next "big one" hits.

Looking majestically out over the broad, grassy strip of the Marina Green, a line of elegant Mediterranean-style private homes stands as entry to the peaceful, often fog-shrouded neighborhood. Grand stucco houses, smaller homes, and gracious Art Deco apartment buildings that impose on broad or winding wind-buffeted streets are home to a smart set of young professionals—many singles but also some with families—who enjoy the proximity to the activities at Fort Mason, the greensward of the Marina Green, the eucalyptus-fragrant Presidio, and also to Chestnut Street, the area's effervescent commercial and nightlife scene. The San Francisco Yacht Harbor is here, as well. The area here may be flat, but the prices are quite steep.

Across Chestnut and the broad, commercial Lombard Street, Cow Hollow bridges the Marina below to aristocratic Pacific Heights above. An area of tranquil dairy farms more than 150 years ago, the restaurants and nightspots of Union Street—from Franklin to Divisadero—are today a playground for the upscale singles crowd. Interesting apartments and homes line just about every street, and climbing the steep hill up to Pacific Heights, the houses along Green and Vallejo are generally Victorian. On Union Street itself, the old Victorians have been converted into offices and trendy shops.

Combined, the Marina and Cow Hollow are great areas for living and hanging out. It is hard to park here, so if you are interested in living here, it will be good to have a garage.

The Presidio

How many cities have a National Park right in their heart? San Francisco does: the Presidio, a 1490-acre (599-ha) multi-use expanse which, as already mentioned, was among the original settled parts of the city, a military base for more than 200 years. Decommissioned in 1994 and turned into a multi-use park, it includes a residential program, and lucky indeed are the people who get to live here. The Presidio is part of the wide-ranging Golden Gate National Recreation Area (see page 211).

Jointly managed by the National Park Service and the Presidio Trust, a U.S. federal agency, the 2.3 square mile Presidio is without doubt one of the most beautiful pieces of real estate in the country. Undeveloped areas abound and are officially preserved, including the nearby and gorgeous Crissy Field—wetlands, open space, and miles of beaches that everyone enjoys. And if you play golf, you do not have to go far, with a par 72 course in your own backyard. Tennis courts, too.

The Presidio has some 800 buildings, refurbished and in use. Almost three thousand people currently live here, in apartment duplexes and single family homes formerly used by military personnel. There's so much to do—from art and education, restaurants, those various beaches and hiking trails, children's playground, special wellness events—and more. Film director George Lucas has created a 23-acre headquarters in the former Letterman Hospital—called the Letterman Digital and New Media Arts Center, whose lovely grounds are open to the public. Several hundred non-profit associations operate from here. The Walt Disney Family Museum is here as well.

This may well be the best of all worlds: living in a lovely park with the resources of a modern city, and with San Francisco Bay to one side and the Pacific Ocean on the other.

Pacific Heights

Just up the hill from the Marina, Pacific Heights is one of the most costly and elegant residential districts in the city. In Pacific Heights, luxurious apartment buildings near Broadway and Fillmore quickly give way to beautiful single-family homes, and even these soon give way—as the broad streets head west toward Divisadero and Presidio—to the exquisite mansions of the truly rich. The tranquil, empty streets climb hills and dip into valleys, making the outer part of Pacific Heights a rather removed enclave, with little to disturb its serenity. Properties occasionally come on the market here, and the prices soar above the unbelievable. (In recent years, several mansions sold for upwards of $30 million.)

Yet in Lower Pacific Heights, on streets to the sides of Fillmore, rental apartments nestle among the private homes. This area is less removed, more in touch, as residents are seen with their children at Alta Plaza or Lafayette Park, or walking their dogs. Upper Fillmore Street itself, from Washington to Pine, is busy by day and lively by night, with restaurants, an international cinema in nearby Japantown, a popular super-market that sells high-quality products, and crowds of people strolling and browsing the shops.

Presidio Heights

An extension to the west, Presidio Heights is perhaps slightly less aristocratic in demeanor than Pacific Heights, but the stately houses lining Clay, Washington, and Jackson none-theless offer extremely gracious living in the heart of the city, with tree-lined streets, few passers-by, and the security that a rather suburban lifestyle might provide. Proximity to shopping in Laurel Village and to the commercial Sacramento/Presidio intersection makes the area feel connected to city life, while the leafy Presidio and its edge of Mountain Lake Park make it feel less so. A few apartment buildings ring the edges, but vacancies are rare. Primarily, it is the domain of one beautiful home after another; houses do come up for sale from time to time, and they sell quickly and well.

Starting at California and reaching to Geary are the almost hidden, overlapping communities of Laurel Heights and Jordan Park, whose broad, clean streets are often swept by fog and wind. Quiet neighborhoods of apartments and private homes, they seem underrated, except by those fortunate enough to live there.

Moving West

From Geary, though, there is the Western Addition, stretching to the Panhandle of Golden Gate Park. Although parts of it—in the New Fillmore around O'Farrell and Fillmore and NoPa near the Panhandle or Alamo Square—offer nice apartments and welcoming communities, the entire area is in transition and has always seemed to have been so. Originally a farming community, the advent of public transportation brought it into the workings of the city; surviving the earthquake were its Victorian houses, including those now called the Painted Ladies on Alamo Square.

Japantown—about six square blocks—was once considered a part of this district, but now it has a character of its own. By the end of the 19th century, while the Chinese population was diminishing, the Japanese population increased. Many Japanese immigrants lived south of Market, but others moved out to the Western Addition, buying small houses and settling in the area they called Nihonjimachi, or "Japanese people's town." After the Chinese Exclusion Act, the Japanese bore the brunt of racism, setting the atmosphere for the infamous Order 9066, during World War II, when Japanese Americans were sent to "relocation centers," forcing them to abandon their homes. By 1942, ship workers—many African Americans—found the now-empty buildings, heard of the low rents, and settled in. Ultimately, the Western Addition became known as a "Black neighborhood."

When the Japanese came back, most settled in the Richmond and the Sunset. Only a small percentage of the city's Japanese residents lives in Japantown, now separated from the rest of the Western Addition by Geary's concrete. Nonetheless, the area—anchored by the stunning Peace Pagoda—is once again the central focus of the community. The 5-acre (2.02-ha) Japan Center shopping, cinema, and restaurant complex at Post and Fillmore draws people from all over, but Nihonjimachi remains firmly and locally Japanese. Here there are one-story town homes and apartments, well-kept and quiet. Near the Japan Center and the commerce on Fillmore Street as well as the shopping complex across Geary, this is a desirable area, although homes rarely come on the market.

Across Geary, the Western Addition was long an area poised to go downhill. Fillmore Street near McAllister, the commercial center of town after the 1906 devastation, was more or less abandoned by 1912, when commerce moved back downtown. The lovely 1890s Victorians on Alamo Square—and just about all the others—went to seed. Eventually the area became known only for its shabby housing projects lining the once-tranquil streets, and for crime and drugs.

But not now! Finally, urban renewal stepped in, as did people looking for affordable homes. The Victorians on the once again chic Alamo Square were restored to their brightly-colored glory. The development of a shopping center and several large modern apartment complexes abutting Geary to the southeast, brought stability and vivacity to the area, and people throughout began sprucing up apartments and single-family homes.

NoPa, that sits between Alamo Square and the University of San Francisco, means North of the Panhandle. Abutting the lovely greensward that stretches to Golden Gate Park, NoPa has also enlivened the Western Addition, with its Victorian homes and sought-after restaurants. It's a small, comfortable area with some restaurants and bars popular with students at the University of San Francisco, and being adjacent to the Western Addition and the Haight, everything is within reach.

The Haight

Across the Panhandle from the Western Addition, starts the Lower Haight that then, a few streets west at Masonic Boulevard, turns into The Haight, famous for decades as the Haight-Ashbury and for an attitude that in one way or another is still trying to hold on. The Haight remains identified by its most celebrated moment—the "flower children" of 1967's Summer of Love, when psychedelic hippies found the place they felt they could best exist. Music has dominated, and people come for the exotic boutiques, the offbeat eateries, or to look at the old homes of the Grateful Dead or Jefferson Airplane. But if young seekers still flock to the Haight—which they do—it is the Lower Haight, today at its funkiest best, that draws the locals, with great bars and barbeque joints, ethnic eateries, and almost-reasonable rents for the apartments that hover above.

These young people easily mix with—or more likely ignore—the new homeowners who are refurbishing those original, surviving Victorians that line the side streets and the Panhandle. So, the Sixties have moved on, and unusual shops and eateries are coexisting with upmarket boutiques and restaurants that are gentrifying an area that had become extremely seedy. One can only hope the area will not lose its unique character as gentrification pervades.

This area along the Panhandle was once quite fashionable, as the Victorians attest. During the economic depression of the 1930s, however, it became hard to maintain the large homes, and during World War II, some were split into apartments with cheap rents. When North Beach became too popular and

The Conservatory of Flowers in Golden Gate Park is known as the "oldest public growing house in California". The building was shipped from London to San Francisco in 1875.

expensive, some Beat Generation poets and "beatniks" (their followers) moved here, and by 1962, the entire area was rather bohemian; by 1967, very hippie, but years of decline took their toll. Finally, the City stepped in to subsidize the refurbishing of buildings and to limit the building of new units, which encouraged people to buy and restore the lovely old homes.

In fact, the district around Haight and Ashbury has a rather surprising appeal. The neighborhoods that abut—Upper

Haight, and to the south the dynamic Cole Valley enclave, Parnassus Heights, Buena Vista and just past the upscale Corona Heights which is also a suburb of the Castro—offer an extremely agreeable mix of large and small private homes on tree-lined, sometimes winding, streets. Some of these areas are still inhabited by long-term residents, by young couples who value the backyards for their children, and by faculty members and researchers at the University of California Medical Center, for whom this area is prime.

The Avenues

To the west of Arguello Boulevard (Richmond District) and Stanyan Street (Sunset District) are "the avenues," grid-like streets that start at 2nd Avenue and go west until they can go no more. They stretch on both sides of Golden Gate Park, and it is the Panhandle—the greensward that divides the two adjacent districts. The Richmond and Sunset have much in common: in terms of climate, these are the foggiest districts in the city, and on some days when downtown areas are still basking in the sun, they can both be shrouded in mist, buffeted by wind.

Both these large residential areas were developed only in the 1920s and 1930s; pleasantly culturally diverse, they are solidly middle class, known for their two-story, stucco, pastel-colored homes, sitting side by side, street after street. In each district, however, there are gems of luxury, of magnificent views, of exquisite homes—to be had at a price. These roomy communities—safe, comfortable, and well-kept—are seen by some as far from the city life, and some residents rarely feel the need to go downtown.

But there are differences, too. The Richmond's eastern edges, from Presidio Terrace (really still in Presidio Heights) all the way out to exclusive Seacliff remind one of Pacific Heights, with their mansions standing stately in the fog and backing on the lovely, wooded Presidio. Down in the Inner Richmond, however, the area is increasingly Asian: some 35 per cent of the Chinese community has settled here, making Clement Street the focus of a "new Chinatown." Geary, its neighbor to the south and one of the city's longest commercial thorough-fares, has long been the stronghold of the Russian community, marked by a few delis and stores, and the impressive golden-domed Cathedral of the Holy Virgin. So, this particular set of avenues is multi-cultural at its core.

South of Geary begins the alphabetically consecutive streets, starting at Anza. Residentially, there are low-rise homes and apartments on wide, straight, rather bland streets. As the area heads out towards the Presidio and the ocean, however, it begins to feel like the beach town it is. Lincoln Park at one edge is wild and wonderful, with spectacular views. And right on the ocean, at the very edge of the continent, past the restaurants at Cliff House, the condominiums of Ocean Beach sit along the Great Highway, behind the sandy dunes.

South of Golden Gate Park, in the sunset with its own ambience, the avenues begin their alphabet once again, taking up again at Lincoln and ending far to the south at Wawona.

Years ago, the sleepy intersection at 9th and Irving (in the Inner Sunset) held a few shops, restaurants, and local ser-vices, but not much else. Now, despite the fog that whips in early, it is one of the city's liveliest scenes. Residents of this area—students, faculty, artists, and young Asian families who live in low-rise apartments or two-story stucco homes—have fought against commercialization, forcing businesses to keep the scale and size of stores appropriate to their sites. Several large chains were rejected, and at present the area remains an extremely popular commercial nexus.

Yet in a few streets west, the atmosphere of 9th and Irving begins to fade, and the straight broad streets carry on as far as they can to the west into the chilling fog. The supermarket Safeway on Irving serves both the Inner and Outer Sunset.

Despite seemingly endless rows of small, undistinguished single-family bungalows and semidetached homes, and two-flats, the Outer Sunset has some attractions, including Asian commercial districts on Irving and Noriega, especially around 19th Avenue and then farther out in a sub-district newly-called Outerlands. Several restaurants draw crowds that line up outside to eat here despite the wind.

With access to beaches and several large parks, adjacent to the lively West Portal—with its BART station, and close to the major Stonestown Galleria and San Francisco State University, the residents of the southern part of the Sunset especially seem content. And all along the westernmost stretches, past 19th Avenue and surrounding the long Sunset Avenue greensward, a few of the discreet, pleasantly residential com-munities—Forest Hill, Parkside, Pine Lake Park—seem part of a more tranquil world. Prices here—even for the more elegant and substantial properties—are reasonable in relation to the rest of the city.

The Southwest

Just south of the "avenues" and still in proximity to the uni-versity and Stonestown sits the Oceanview, Merced Ingleside (OMI) set of southwestern neighbourhoods. These green, fra-grant areas are often totally socked in by fog, but their residents enjoy the coastal winds and the smell of the sea. Revolving around Ocean Avenue and 19th Avenue, these are really three middle class neighborhoods working to form a cohesive whole. In general, they are known for pleasant, single-family homes with neatly kept yards—the area is about 75 per cent residen-tial. Some apartment areas exist around Stonestown and Lake Merced, inhabited primarily by both long-term local residents, but also by students at San Francisco State, who come and go. And, Parkmerced is a massive residential complex of low-to high-rise buildlings near San Francisco State University and the Daly City border, east of Lake Merced. With some 9,000 residents, this is actually a neighborhood in itself. An extensive modernizing redevelopment may have changed the look, but not its appeal.

To the west, near the university in its wooded and garden-like setting, near large Harding Park and near Lake Merced, and close to the ocean with its crashing waves, the area begins to take on the aspect of the coastal town it is. Lining the western side of the lake, along John Muir Drive, a large complex of rental units can be seen in a community known as Lakeshore, which is also home to Lowell High School, one of the best in the city.

Ocean Avenue, the northern border of the district, is gently residential to the west of 19th Avenue, but commercial to the east. This is one of the commercial areas that services Ingleside Terrace, known for the looping residential Urbano Drive that follows the course of the long-gone Ingleside Race Track. The comfortable, well-kept houses here exude the atmosphere of suburban living, and, fortunately, one may occasionally become available.

Ingleside and Oceanview themselves continue in a transition that started some time ago. Years ago, when the decaying Fillmore districts were being redeveloped, African American families were evicted with a promise they could return to new housing. Instead, many families migrated outward to the OMI and affordable homes, as the formerly entrenched White communities bought automobiles and moved to suburban living. Decades later, centralized shopping centers and large cinema

McLaren Park

The 312-acre McLaren Park—the city's second largest—is a hilly natural treasure enlivening the central far south. While you are strolling on the trails or picnicking with your family, keep your eye out for the wildflowers on the grasslands, the Coastal Redwoods and Monterey Cypress trees, the California quail, and especially the Great Horned Owl. With seven miles of walking trails, the playgrounds, picnic areas, lake and golf course—and now Its own Bike Park—McLaren is an urban wonder.

complexes forced small local businesses to close, and the area declined. In recent decades, however, an active citizens' effort has brought the area back to its residents, with rebuilt and expanded public facilities and an overall sense of renewal.

The Far Southeast
Also far to the south but on the city's eastern side, are several districts that seem not to fit into the vibrant San Francisco mold. Nonetheless, they have their reasons to exist. Separated from Bernal Heights by Interstate 280, Portola, formerly a generally lower-middle class melting pot, has sprung into its own light. Originally an Italian neighborhood, then Jewish, it is now truly multi-cultural, as evidenced along San Bruno Avenue, with its many Latino and Filipino establishments, Italian butchers, and Asian eateries. People buying their first homes often settled here, but now prices are rising as they are everywhere else, and especially so in this area near Glen Park and Bernal Heights.

Surrounding the large John McLaren Park are several neighborhoods—Bayshore, Excelsior, Outer Mission, Visitacion Valley, and Crocker Amazon—that are generally characterized by middle-income and working class families living in stolid single-family homes. Yet, the foggy, slightly uninspired streets with their rows of little houses are convenient to Daly City, to San Francisco State, and to the city by BART. With older housing ready for refurbishment, neighborhoods are poised to come back. Crocker Amazon has some homes on more interesting streets such as Chicago Way.

The Mountainous Center
To the south and west of Noe Valley the highest hills in the city impose themselves over a dozen interesting communities. Wind-swept and foggy for the most part, Twin Peaks, Mount Davidson, and Mount Sutro command the city's geographical center; many of their neighborhoods are blessed with exquisite

views and park-like settings, some a bit sheltered from the cold ocean wind. Despite the winding and dead-end streets, each area is convenient to—or overlaps—another of interest, and all are in proximity to the city's major universities, making them attractive to faculty and students. There are mansions and private homes, small cottages, and well-maintained apartments, but what you will find depends on where you look, for each area has its own character.

Diamond Heights, which is the major district on the eastern slopes of Twin Peaks, was developed in the 1960s, and its modernity shows in its large apartment complexes and well-designed, single-family homes. Its proximity to its eastern neighbors makes it ever more desirable, as prices in Noe Valley and the Castro soar. "Discovered" also is the attractive, hilly Glen Park district to the southeast, adjacent to the Glen Canyon Park, with its many rental apartments, and Victorians. It had long been a sedate, well-kept neighbourhood, but now some streets are seeing tech-rich people buying and renovating large homes, around Laidley Street, for example. And the Glen Park BART Station makes the Financial District even more quickly accessible than some areas closer in. Nearby, the steep Glen Canyon Park offers a wilderness park, although playgrounds, tennis courts, and a baseball field have tamed it somewhat.

Mount Davidson's summit is foggy and wild, but on its western downslopes are some incredibly beautiful neighborhoods, almost a surprise in this outer part of the city. That they are near the university and the Stonestown shopping area makes them very much in demand. Drive around Sherwood Forest and Saint Francis Wood, for example, to see the lovely homes on impeccably landscaped grounds. Houses occasionally come up for sale here, but as in Pacific Heights, the prices are astronomical. The pleasant homes of West Portal bridge towards the more ordinary Miraloma Park, Westwood Highlands, and Westwood Park, where some areas and streets are more appealing than others.

Just above the UC Medical Center, Mount Sutro and its fragrant eucalyptus forest may be the city's best-kept secret. On the hill's eastern edge, within walking distance of the hospital, the charming enclave of Sutro Heights backs on the forest, and here are several of the most beautiful and flowery streets in the city, especially Edgewood Avenue, which is paved in red brick.

Circling the hill, wild, foggy Sutro Forest sees private homes and apartments in addition to institutional housing for medical students. And around the hill to the west is Forest Knolls, a grouping of more than one hundred small, uniform homes on winding streets, each facing the forest itself.

YET QUESTIONS PERSIST

This overview of the city should help you get a feel for it as you explore it on your own. As you do, you will discover that San Francisco retains its little mysteries, and it always will. Old ones will be resolved and new ones will show up. That's just the way it is. In any case, the architect Frank Lloyd Wright summed up his own thoughts about the city: "What I like best about San Francisco is … San Francisco," he said. For all in all, as San Franciscans believe, the city is unique.

AND AROUND THE BAY

A Different Style of Living

The eight outlying counties of the Bay Area stretch about 50 miles (80.5 km) south toward the major metropolis of San Jose, east past the industrial port of Oakland, and north to Sonoma, up toward what is known as the Delta—that stretches from Sacramento and southward to Stockton. Bay Area counties are generally referred to by their position in relation to the Bay: the North Bay (Marin, Sonoma, Napa, and Solano counties), the South Bay whose farther reaches are called the Peninsula (San Mateo and Santa Clara counties), and the East Bay (Alameda and Contra Costa counties). Thousands of people commute to the city from the nearer portions of these counties, and now even some of the farther reaches are beginning to be regarded as within commuting distance. (For short excursions out of town, see Chapter 8.)

People choose to live in the greater Bay Area rather than in San Francisco for a variety of reasons: the preference for a tranquil suburban or even rural lifestyle, affordable housing, access and proximity to good public and private schools, low crime rates, fewer earthquakes, or perhaps even a more "normal" climate.

Unlike San Francisco, much of the Bay Area sees four distinct seasons. While San Francisco is enjoying its natural summer air conditioning, it is warmest inland, away from the bay. Temperatures in the rest of the Bay Area can soar in the summer, but even in these areas, winter climes are mild, with perhaps a touch of snow in Sonoma, on the peaks of Mount Diablo, or on Mount Tamalpais.

For a city with excellent transportation, and cultural diversity, consider the always up-and-coming Oakland in the East Bay or its intellectual neighbour Berkeley. Both are just across the Bay Bridge in Alameda County, which has the highest population of the Bay Area. Others farther out could be Walnut Creek, Fremont, or Concord. Formerly seen as less desirable than Marin to the north or San Mateo County to the south, the East Bay now holds its own. In the North Bay, Sausalito exudes charm, but Mill Valley and San Rafael have it all: conveniences of every sort and a gentle way of life.

And to the south, as you head to San Jose, known as the focal point of "Silicon Valley" and its Internet entrepreneurs, do not miss San Mateo or lovely Palo Alto, home to Stanford University and just about anything you could want. Silicon Valley is a special place, even if it doesn't have official borders or municipalities. Here in the various towns are the enormous campuses of Apple, Google, You Tube, Facebook & Instagram, PayPal, Cisco Systems, Hewlett Packard, and dozens more. Some employees prefer to live in The City, and they are shuttled to and from work each day. Many thousands of people, however, live in these peninsula communities, and while the lifestyle is quite different than that of San Francisco, it has its charms.

All the adjacent counties are dotted with delicious little towns, gentle and leafy green, linked by country roads and, for the most part, touched by major highways. Living here, thus, requires keeping a car, perhaps more if two people in a house-hold are working, or if a child needs to be taken to school. If living outside the city appeals to you, think about living along the BART line, which goes from San Francisco under the bay to the east, and somewhat toward the south. (See page 135.) Commuting by car during rush hours is slow and tedious, but BART is reliable and fast. From the North Bay, commuting is most often by car, crowding the lanes of the Golden Gate Bridge; there too, however, the public commuter buses and even ferries are reliable and practical; and from the south also come the buses, train, and BART (from Colma), and, unfortu-nately, long lines of cars, and shuttles taking the tech workers to Silicon Valley and back.

Rents and purchase prices vary from the merely expensive to the outrageous, depending on the size of the home and its views of the bay, as well as the town's amenities. But some older areas have more affordable homes, and some of the com-munities have new subdivisions with planned developments of single-family and multi-family homes. Whereas just the towns close to San Francisco were considered an easy commute to the City, now communities as far north as Petaluma or Novato, or as far east as Concord, are being developed and consid-ered within traveling distance. Whatever the price range, the beauty and lifestyles of these more relaxed areas are consid-ered by many—especially young families—to be essential for a well-balanced life. Towns around the Bay Area are never called suburbs, but life there is truly suburban. Check them out.

Taking a Tour

Tours are especially good for an in-depth understanding of a particular site or culture. Many of the tours are to be made on foot, so wear comfortable shoes, and do not forget to bring a jacket.

For reliable and current information, it's always good to access the San Francisco Travel Association—the city's tourist office: www.sftravel.com. And, check your App Store to download information to your cell phone.

- All About Chinatown Walking Tours; tel: (415) 982-8839; www.allaboutchinatown.com. Lively tour, ending with a dim-sum lunch. Call to reserve and for the meeting place.

- Audiosteps; 2590 Greenwich, Suite #1, San Francisco, California 94123; tel: (415) 346-2604; www.audiosteps.com. Purchase and download an audio tour of the city to your device and explore at your own pace.

- Big Bus Tours; 99 Jefferson Street; tel: (855) 854-8687; www.bigbustours.com. Hop on and off these open-top double-decker buses, offering a comprehensive first-look at San Francisco. (See also Gray Line below.)

- Bay City Bike; Extensive bike tours around the city, from five different locations. Bike rentals also available (www.baycitybike.com).

- Blazing Saddles Bike Tours: 2715 Hyde Street at Fisherman's Wharf and other locations; tel: (415) 465-5458; www.blazingsaddles.com. Daily guided bike tours from this well-established company. You may also take a guided audio tour on your own downloaded your device.

- Blue & Gold Fleet Sightseeing Tours; Ticket office at Pier 39. Boats leave from Pier 39 and 41, tel: (415) 705-8200; www.blueandgoldfleet.com. Hour-long cruise on the Bay, seeing Alcatraz, the Golden Gate Bridge, and Sausalito.

- Chinese Culture Center of San Francisco; 750 Kearny Street, 3rd Floor; tel: (415) 986-1822; www.c-c-c.org. Docent-led tours of Chinatown and an introduction to the city's Chinese culture.

- Cruisin' the Castro Tours; 584 Castro Street; tel: (415) 255-1821; www.cruisinthecastro.com. If you want to know everything about the Castro, this tour gives you the history and attractions of the country's largest "gay mecca."

- Dylan's Tours: 782 Columbus Avenue; tel: (415) 932-6993; www.dylanstours.com. Small group tours in a minibus, on electric bikes, or even an e-Tuk, kind of an electric rickshaw. Friendly tours led by locals, through the city or over the bridge to Marin and Muir Woods.

- Edible Excursions: 71 Cuvier Street; tel (415) 806-5970; https://edibleecursionsnet. Walking food tours for San Francisco, Berkeley and Oakland. Taste and feast on some of the best these food-loving cities have to offer. Talk with chefs and learn why the Bay Area is so noted for its culinary creations.
- Gray Line; Pier 41 Marine Terminal and other addresses, tel: (415) 353-5310; www.graylineofsanfrancisco.com. Hop on buses, city tours, and more around Northern California.
- San Francisco Electric Tours; 757 Beach Street, at Hyde Street; tel: (415) 474-3130; www.electrictourcompany.com. Take a tour of the city on a Segway.
- San Francisco Fire Engine Tours & Adventures; The Cannery; tel: (415) 333-7077; www.fireenginetours.com. Tour over the Golden Gate Bridge and then back in a restored, classic, open-air, bright red fire engine.
- Sidewalk Food Tours of San Francisco: 3310 Market Street, tel: (877) 568-6877; https://foodtoursofsanfrancisco.com. Walking culinary tours in three food-lovers' districts—with tastes from Chinese dumplings to pizza and chocolate truffles—and more. Learn some history and culture while you walk and munch.
- Urban Hiker SF; tel: (415) 669-4453; www.urbanhikersf.com/. Guided walking tours—up the hills and stairways and along urban trails. Learn the history of the neighborhoods and even see a eucalyptus grove—and enjoy the spectacular views. The tours have different starting points.
- Victorian Home Walk; 2226 15th Street; tel: (415) 252-9485; www.victorianwalk.com. Tour Pacific Heights, and see colorful Victorians, beautiful gardens, historical houses, and the inside of a period home. Check the website for time and meeting place.

THE PEOPLE BY THE BAY

Certainly when you come to San Francisco you will be wondering just what San Franciscans "are like." In some places, the answer would be easy: in France most people are French and in Beijing they are Chinese, and their families there might go back hundreds of years. But in multicultural San Francisco, it's not so simple. Look around, and you'll soon see diversity everywhere you go—different nationalities, races and languages, plus obviously-different cultural or sexual orientations—people just going about their business, day by day. Among all these distinctions a huge and increasing percentage are well-paid professionals working in the towers of international technological or financial corporations, yet in leisure time they might mingle with long-time less-affluent residents who work in shops or offices behind the scenes. You'll see enormous spending on luxury and wealth and fun alongside mom-and-pop stores, and working parents raising their children as best they can. And, surprisingly, there's a disturbing homeless population that the city is struggling to deal with, some of whom do have jobs, but just can't make ends meet.

This lack of uniformity should not be surprising. In San Francisco, small and dense as it is, Asians make up some 35% of the populace and Latino 15%, in total some 50% of the population. But now even the demographics of these populations have changed from the small shopkeepers and workers of older days. Modern Asians, for example, are also professionals and some 13,000 are entrepreneurs on their own; for those on salary, depending on their skills, they may make about the same average as their Caucasian colleagues, different indeed from just a few decades ago. New arrivals compare San Francisco to their own city and others they have seen, saying, "San Francisco is so Asian," or even "so European," or "it's not like home at all." And they are right, or partly so: San Francisco shows so much of other cultures on every street that it is indeed hard to categorize, but it is like home, because it is home to about 875,000 San Franciscans—those people of all ethnic backgrounds, religions, political persuasions, and sexual preferences—who have created and continue to create—this wonderful city in their image, on their own terms.

It's "so Asian?" Just a few years ago, the pundits thought that the Asian population would soon be in a majority, but that's no longer true. In addition to the well-educated San Franciscans of all backgrounds—some 87% completed high school and about 55% hold college degrees—other young well-educated Americans are flocking here to join the tech industries and allied start-ups that need their expertise. Highly paid, these professionals are willing to spend their money to support their lifestyles—making the city even more, even better, even more interesting—but at the same time, driving prices up, in housing especially. Statistics say that an income inequality is forcing about 5% of the residents to leave the city each year—those whose education and earning power can't meet the rising prices. But the city is still gaining about 10,000 new residents a year, now primarily those young highly trained tech industry workers mentioned above.

In fact, San Francisco is a city of minorities, for no ethnic, religious, or societal group dominates. In addition to the large Asian and Latino communities, there are sizeable populations of African Americans, Russians, and Italians, and across all these ethnic groups, some 15% of San Franciscan identify themselves as gays or lesbians. This leads standard tourist guides to devote separate sections to Chinatown, Japantown, the Mission, or the Castro, describing them to people passing through. But no such delineation can really help you understand the populace, for these people and their areas are each just a part of the overall scene. Part of what makes San Francisco so interesting is that each separate residential area is open enough that anyone can feel welcome, but tight enough not to lose its sense of community and identity. Since its beginnings, San Francisco has embodied the country's vision of the "melting pot", where differing societal cultures and attitudes enrich the whole.

So, this is San Francisco—sometimes a puzzle for newcomers, but ultimately understandable, after all. For most of these people, no matter which category they fall in, have the commonality that San Francisco seems to be where they want to be. Whoever they are and wherever they have come from, or whoever they have decided to be, they are in love with their city, adore its views (visual, political, and social), appreciate its eclectic population, and in general are convinced they live in the best, most exotic city in the United States, if not the world. In fact, some people claim San Franciscans are snobs, and it may have some truth to it, but it's not about money or class. People here just have decided, for example, which beer they think is best, which sushi bar ranks higher for them than others, and how proud they are of their healthy lives, for which they have worked. (And, perhaps tediously, they never stop telling everybody so.) Some people joke that San Francisco—beautiful, varied, and charmingly unpredictable—is "49 square miles surrounded by reality," and maybe they have a point.

SO, WHAT ARE THEY LIKE?

Clearly, stereotyping does not work in San Francisco, but some generalities might prove helpful as you look around. The Chinese community—like other immigrant communities—tends to be close-knit, grouped in extended families, private (but not entirely closed toward outsiders), welcoming and friendly within. And, apart from the older generations, the children—born in San Francisco, most likely—on the buses on their way home from school might speak Mandarin to each other, but also shout in English, "See you tomorrow," as they get off the bus. The Latinos in the Mission seem to be, as one might expect of people coming from warm climates, more open, outside in the streets, laughing with friends. If you have something in common with any of these cultures—those of your heritage or outlook on life—you will understand them. But, what of the rest?

When people talk about what San Franciscans are like, they are generally referring to the people who work in the constantly-emerging technologies, on the expanding business of the Pacific Rim, to entrepreneurs who own shops, or those who create the superb cuisines and libations and particular services these demanding San Franciscans require. And if we are talking about them, then we can surely give some clues as to who they are.

If you have not noticed it by now, you will soon. San Franciscans like to play. They may well love their work and strive to succeed, but their lives outside their jobs also define who they are. Being fitness conscious, after work they may go to the gym (or take an aerobics or yoga class at lunch time), but they also enjoy happy hours with their friends or co-workers, and they eat out, often in some new trendy place they have just found. (They do not smoke, for the most part, and they will not hesitate to chide you if you do!) Weekends also see hiking, running or spending time in the beautiful parks. And these may be the evenings to try the craft cocktails or gastropubs that are proliferating. San Franciscans enjoy it all.

As already mentioned, the climate is agreeable year-round, the air clean, and the views are exquisite. Acquaintances are friendly and open, and the best of everything is not hard to find. No wonder people seem light-hearted and ready for themselves and everyone else to have fun. And they have come to the right city, for there is something about San Francisco itself that makes it all work. Newcomers are generally welcomed into the groups, when they have something in common: the workplace, the gym, or even their religion. Along with their strong opinions about "what's best", San Franciscans do love to talk about what's going on—in the world, in the country, and even more—in this city they have created and love.

A SENSE OF HUMOR

If Americans have found that it is easier to get along together by avoiding talk of politics, sex, and religion, San Francisco begs to differ. A sense of humor is important, and San Francisco encourages its admirers to think that anything—and anybody—can be teased, even themselves.

Where else would you have found the citizens of a city irreverently twitting a rather imperial mayor Willie Brown by referring to him as "His Williness?" And, where else would you find a group of gay men forming an "order" of nuns, "The Sisters of Perpetual Indulgence", with one of those men—Sister Boom Boom—running for a seat in the Board of Supervisors, as "nun of the above"? People voted for him, but not enough for him to

San Francisco's iconic Golden Gate Bridge, completed in 1937, a symbol of human ingenuity. With the Pacific Ocean to its west and the Bay to the east, it spans the Golden Gate, found by Spanish soldiers in 1769.

win. These both happened decades ago, but the stories have quickly gone into the city's legends and lore.

Should you find some of the humor distasteful, just roll your eyes and shake your head, for San Francisco's enjoyment of the outrageous goes far back and it has encompassed all strata of the city's society. Take the case of one Joshua Abraham Norton. Having left San Francisco in the mid-1850s a financial failure, he returned just a few months later styling himself as "Emperor of the United States and Protector of Mexico." His proclamations were published in the newspapers, and he became the "darling of everybody in town." For 20 years, Emperor Norton sported regal finery, was fed

It was Emperor Norton who first admonished the citizenry never to call their city Frisco. "Whoever after due and proper warning shall be heard to utter the abominable word 'Frisco,' which has no linguistic or other warrant, shall be deemed guilty of a High Misdemeanor."

for free at various establishments around the city, and pontificated at corporate board meetings. When he died in 1880, he was given a fittingly "royal funeral" to which some 10,000 of his "subjects" came.

GAYS IN THE CITY

In fact, San Francisco from its beginnings was a town of men: the priests and soldiers who adventured north to Alta California to settle the area two centuries ago, the Chinese men fleeing famine who sailed the Pacific to work in the mines or to build the railroads, and the adventurers who flocked to the California frontier in 1849 seeking gold. That the miners also sought booze and bawdy women convinced some moralists that the city should be punished, and after the 1906 earthquake they thought it had been. (Not likely!) But a port city it was and it remained, welcoming more sailors after the opening of the Panama Canal in 1914 and ship workers through World War II. During the war, San Francisco was a military port of embarcation, where eagle-eyed officers mustered out men who were homosexual, many of whom then decided to stay. By the 1960s, when it was said that the 70,000 gays who lived here frequented "decadent" gay bars, national newspapers stereotyped the city as a haven for sexual deviates. Far from having the desired effect, the news spread throughout the country that this was a place for gays and other iconoclasts to feel at home.

When gay San Francisco Supervisor and activist Harvey Milk was assassinated in 1978, the gay community mobilized itself and has since become a potent political force. Indeed, the city was in the forefront on affording equal rights to domestic partners of any persuasion, and it led the way for marriage equality, which is now the law of the land.

Again for tolerance of all, when some years ago a gay politician, Tom Ammiano, was sworn in as President of the Board of Supervisors, although his political acumen brought him to the office, with the sense of humor the city is known for, his predecessor gave him a tiara and feathered sceptre she had received at the beginning of her term, and declared him "queen of the realm."

If the city was once primarily the province of gay males—in the Haight and Polk Gulch, and of course the Castro—and lesbians were more prominent across the Bay in Oakland, this has been changing for some time. In recent decades, the lesbian community has been establishing itself solidly throughout the city, especially in the Inner Mission, Noe Valley, Bernal Heights, and Glen Park.

So here, gay life is like any other life. People work hard, they participate consciously in keeping their city prosperous and tolerant, and they play, in their own styles. This is San Francisco, after all.

MAKING IT WORK

So the City by the Bay is managing to triumph in its own unique way, and it's the populace that makes it so. The intensity San Franciscans bring to their lives translates into a civic activism that cuts through all levels of society. As that former Mayor Brown once said, "Here in San Francisco, you have more than 750,000 people, and each and every one of them is informed, interested, and has an opinion on everything." It is true. Residents volunteer at food banks that feed the homeless, at non-profit cultural institutions, for environmental and political causes, and at organizations for needy children. They form groups to protest injustice and to call for reform. They insist volubly on better transportation and more affordable housing. They vote in higher percentages than in most other major cities, and if it appears that San Francisco is at the far side of "liberal", look at the most talked-about issues and see that residents vote for the very things that make their city work: good social programs, preservation of cultural institutions, improvement of the downtown areas, and equality and tolerance for all. What is different about San Francisco is that each mini-society in its own way embraces this vision and is—at least for the most part and on most days—proud of it. Clearly, you will discover all this for yourself as you settle in. Look around. This eclectic population known as San Franciscans, whether they say so or not, hope—no, they assume—that you will find your place among them. And, no doubt, you will.

CHAPTER 4

FINDING YOUR
SOCIAL NICHE

> *I have always been rather better treated in San Francisco than I actually deserved.*
>
> **— Mark Twain**

FIRST ENCOUNTERS

Your own attitudes plus a bit of fortitude will play a large part in how your life in San Francisco unfolds. That is probably true in moving to any new city, but in this one, the myriad social structures and mini-structures—as open and deep as in many other cities combined—ensure that if you reach out, you will find the communities that suit you best. Yes, "communities" in the plural, for there is no reason to fit yourself into just one group. In this eclectic city, as we've already mentioned, groups manage to keep their identities while complementing, merging, and overlapping with others, forming that ever-fluid and delicious whole called San Francisco. But fortitude also plays a part. Assimilating and being accepted will require a conscious effort: the ability and willingness to look around and observe how each community functions within its own value system, to see how best you can fit in, and to patiently let time take its course as you interact.

Of course, knowing people from the same background or country who have already adjusted to the city's ethos but who still feel bound together can help you integrate and start feeling at home. Even if these people do not ultimately become your best friends, they will—either explicitly or not—show you the San Francisco ropes. And, if you do not know where to look for these welcoming folk, contact your consulate (or access its Internet site) and ask about cultural groups you might attend. There is no need—as the American saying goes—for you to "feel like a fish out of water" in San Francisco, even at the start.

Even with people from your own background, though, in whose homes you might think to expect the utmost in

Two friends enjoying some tortilla chips at a Mexican restaurant in the eclectic neighborhood of the Mission.

traditions, you will learn more. They too are living in San Francisco and have made adjustments to the culture, the climate, the seasons, and even the agricultural bounty (including the wines). So, as they have done, look around and see how each group comports itself, and then, to use a favorite American expression, "When in Rome, do as the Romans do." A good beginning, to be sure.

Civic Activism

But, if you do not know a soul when you get here, see page 104 to find a religious denomination listed that mirrors your own beliefs or attitudes. Even if you are not religiously observant, the congregants of any faith will be welcoming. Religious congregations in San Francisco certainly have worship services, but they also help feed the homeless and work with disadvantaged groups. They hold potluck suppers and conduct other social events, and they mix with different denominations' congregations, as well. They take part in city life, and there is no better way for you to do so, than to participate with these groups yourself.

Also look at the networking guides, on pages 257 and 292 for other networking groups. With non-profit associations, political groups, theater or music groups, surely any newcomer can find a niche, whether cultural or social, political or sportive, or—in other words—with activities that mirror your own interests. The groups in San Francisco cover just about anything the city enjoys.

Yes, San Franciscans are serious—when it suits them. They are serious about their work. They are serious about their social activism. And they are extremely serious about socializing with their likeminded friends. So, going to happy hour with your new colleagues or taking aerobics classes at the gym, going out to dance, or joining a hiking club, will also help you fit in. Walking your dog in your neighborhood will certainly attract new friends. Enjoy yourself, whatever you are doing, working or playing. San Franciscans do.

SOME HELPFUL HINTS

Expect the unexpected when it comes to fitting in with San Franciscans—no matter who they are or where they came from. Yet, there are, after all, some attitudes of the populace that translate into a cultural ethos. Perhaps they are not "rules" for behavior, but understandings that help people get along. Pay attention to how your new friends act, and after a while you will find that you are as flexible, adaptable, and easy-going about life in The City as anyone else.

Generally, San Francisco is an "early" town. Since stockbrokers and other financial types adjust their hours to the opening of the Stock Exchange in New York, they go to work sometimes before dawn and go to sleep early. If you go to the theater or a concert, you will no doubt notice people dining before, not afterwards. On weekdays, you may find people socializing right after work, gathering at a bar for a couple of drinks and snacks, hanging out together for a while, and then heading early for home. (Actually "happy hour" may last from 4:00pm until 6:30pm or so, making it a "happy" occasion indeed.)

If you are invited to someone's home, arrive close to the time specified. Being "fashionably late" may be the norm in some cultures, but not here. Depending on your hosts, bring a token of gratitude for the invitation: a bottle of wine, a box of artisan chocolates, a popular book you think your host might be interested in reading, something you have thought about and know your host will like. In some homes, pre-dinner hors d'oeuvres are served in the living room with a glass of wine or cocktail. At the table, praise the meal served, and feel free to accept seconds when offered. You will no doubt be served a California wine and also water. Savor the wine for the flavor but slake your thirst with the water. Then, take your cue from others—your hosts and other guests—as to how late to stay. Guests often linger over their coffees at the dining table, and shortly thereafter begin to take their leave.

If you go to a restaurant with friends, arrive at the time for which the reservation was made. When your meal arrives— each course that you have ordered—be prepared to offer a taste of yours to your dining partners and to taste their meals as well. This is normal in America. (But feel free not to taste something you do not want to.) Also, people like to share an appetizer or main course, either allowing them to eat less, or giving them the opportunity to sample several different dishes. Ordering two appetizers and no main course is also done.

If you have been invited to a particular function or party, understand that the bill may well be divided equally, even if your dinner cost less than the others. In a group, people some-times do look at each item on the bill to determine who pays how much more or how much less. But, if your friends have consumed a lot of alcohol and you haven't, feel free to remind them that you should pay less. Or just suggest gently that since you didn't drink, perhaps they would pay the tip.

If you are included at a weekend brunch, be prepared to stay for a while. Brunch? The word indicates a combination of breakfast and lunch, but what it means is a social occasion that might start with a mimosa (champagne and orange juice cocktail) and then continue with a specially-prepared traditional American breakfast, or any one of the exotic combinations that the trendiest multi-cultural eateries are concocting that day. People remain for hours over a weekend brunch, especially in a restaurant that has a view, that offers live music, or that has the "most" or the "best" of something that they want.

If you are with a group of sporty friends, you might go on a hike on the weekends, or take a bike ride together in the hills outside the city. Do not forget that your friends will probably work out in a gym during the week, or take a jog in the mornings before or the afternoons after work. Think about these things for yourself, for keeping fit; besides being good for your health, it will help expand your social horizons!

And on weekend evenings—especially Friday and Saturday nights—San Franciscans like to party. Each group will hang out with likeminded friends, doing whatever suits them best. Across the groups, however, they might like to try the newest eatery to appear on the scene, to drink the newest craft cocktails of the moment, to hear the hottest music, or even to bring a six-pack of beer to somebody's flat. And—early town or not—they stay out late. Enjoyment is what San Francisco is about.

CHAPTER 5

SETTLING IN

> **❝**Arrival in San Francisco is an experience in living.**❞**

> **— William Saroyan**

FORMALITIES FOR FOREIGNERS

Immigration

Perhaps the streets of the United States were not paved with gold as so many immigrants imagined when they came to these shores, but America has nonetheless been seen, since its earliest days, as a land of opportunity. Whether people came to escape poverty or persecution, America has always seemed to be—and often has been—the world's most beneficial haven. America, in fact, truly gained its strength by being a "melting pot" of cultures and becoming the world's most successful multi-ethnic nation.

Yet, although both American citizens and the government say they believe that diversity enriches society, the country has always had mixed feelings toward immigration. Thus, the subject of limiting immigration has always come up during economic downturns, for—whether true or not—it has been widely held that immigrants take jobs away from low-skilled American citizens.

Currently, immigration is being reviewed by the government; laws are changing and tightening considerably, and will no doubt remain complex. Thus, it's best to check the government websites for the most current information. It's also important to consult the American Embassy in your country (or the consulate nearest to you) long in advance of your desired trip (or emigration) and to receive the most up-to-date information.

One thing is sure: compile as much documentation as possible concerning your personal history, health, qualifications, financial condition, plans for your stay in the United States,

and any contacts or relatives you might have here. If you have a job you are coming for, your prospective employer should give you a letter of invitation. These are all sure to be carefully scrutinized. All people entering the United States must hold a machine-readable (biometric) passport. A biometric passport includes a digital photograph on the data page, plus several lines of machine-readable biographical information on the bottom of the page. The following are some websites for general guidelines.

- Entry into the United States: www.usa.gov/enter-us
- Entry and visas: https://travel.state.gov/content/visas/en.html
- Visa questions: https://travel.state.gov/content/travel/en/us-visas.html
- Biometric identity: www.dhs.gov.obim
- U.S. Citizenship and Immigration Services: www.uscis.gov/
- Customs and Border Protection (CBP): www.cbp.gov
- Visa Waiver Program (VWP): www.cbp.gov/travel/international-visitors/visa-waiver-program
- Student visas: https://internationalstudent.com/study_usa/preparation/student_visa/

USCIS

The San Francisco District Office of the Bureau of U.S. Citizenship and Immigration Services (USCIS) is at 444 Washington Street, near Sansome tel: (415) 375-5283); www.uscis.gov. Appointments are made through INFOPAS; http://infopass.uscis.gov. If you need a passport, immigration photographs, or fingerprint documentation, Leetone Photo Center, is nearby at 615 Sansome: tel: (415) 483-9727; www.leetone-photocenter.com/.

Foreign Consulates

All foreign embassies are situated in Washington, D.C., but some countries maintain regional consulates as well. They are most helpful during times of crisis: they replace lost passports and help in medical or legal emergencies by making referrals to appropriate doctors, dentists, or lawyers. They do not, however, help people get out of jail. Yet in all emergencies, if you have registered your presence and your next of kin with your consulate, they can act as liaison between you and your family at home. And, sometimes, consulates offer information on local services, including lists of doctors and attorneys who speak your language, as well as translators.

Find out when your consulate is open before going. It will no doubt be closed on the national holidays of both the United States and of your own country. Contact details of all embassies in Washington can be obtained at www.embassy.org/embassies. For consulates in San Francisco, see www.embassypages.com/city/sanfrancisco.

Bringing …
… Your Belongings

If your visa for residency is in order, you may bring your personal effects into the United States if you have owned them for more than one year. Your goods must be cleared through Customs at its first port of arrival. Customs does not notify you when the goods have arrived, so your mover must do so within 15 days of their arrival.

... Your Appliances

Electricity in the United States is 110–120 volts, 60 hertz. Importing European appliances may be more trouble than it is worth, for appliances—large and small—are fairly inexpensive in America, and discount shops are found in every city. To import appliances may mean dealing with converters and adaptors, and putting your appliances into spaces that were not designed for them.

... Your Car

All cars and vehicles coming into the country must conform to U.S. safety, bumper, and emission standards; bring written certification that the vehicle meets the set requirements before shipping. This may either be in the form of a statement from the Environmental Protection Agency (EPA), or a manufacturer's label in English that is affixed to the inside front door of the car. Check these websites: www.epa.gov/importing-vehicles-and-engines or www.cbp.gov/trade/basic-import-export/importing-car.

... Your Money

There is no limit to the total amount of money—cash, traveler's checks, or negotiable securities—that may be brought into the United States. But if you bring in more than $10,000 (or if you receive that amount), you must report it to the CBP.

... Your Medications

To bring any medications that contain habit-forming drugs or narcotics (prescription-strength cough medicine, diuretics, heart drugs, tranquilizers, etc.) into the country, make sure all are properly labeled and that you have a physician's prescription or written statement that the medicine is used under a doctor's direction. Bring an amount that will tide you over until you can get a new prescription in the United States.

… Your Pets
All dogs and cats being brought into the country will be examined at the port of entry. This also applies to pets that were taken out of the country and are being brought back in. Check the website of the Centers for Disease Control: www.cdc.gov/importation/bringing-an-animal-into-the-united-states/dogs.html.

INTO THE CITY

From the Airports
First, you have to get into the city. The area's two main airports are San Francisco International (SFO) and Oakland (OAK). There are both public and private transportation options from both, and your choice will depend on your budget and time constraints, how much luggage you are carrying and the degree of inconvenience you are willing to bear. Public transportation is efficient and the least expensive but may not be convenient. Shuttles—vans that are reserved in advance—carry a number of passengers together, and they are door-to-door. Ride-hailing companies such as Lyft and Uber (see page 137 below) can also be reserved in advance, and are reliable, and less expensive than taxis.

For the latest on all flights in and out of San Francisco, as well as ground transportation, and details on shopping, dining, and services at the airport, access www.flysfo.com.

Taxis into San Francisco are, of course, the most expensive; the meter may run as high as $60 plus tip. Yet they are the most easily arranged—just walk out the door of the airport and find the line. Take only taxis that are in the line and that are registered. If you arrive at one of the rush hours, taxis will join the seemingly endless lines of vehicles crawling toward the city, while the meter is clicking away merrily. Nonetheless, they are easy and convenient, depending on your circumstances.

Public Transportation
- BART (Bay Area Rapid Transit); about a 30-minute ride to downtown San Francisco, this is one of the cheapest and most efficient ways to get into the city, if you do not have a lot of luggage to carry; tel: (510) 989-2278; www.bart.gov. Fares vary according to the destination.
- At SFO, the BART terminal is located on the Departures level of the International Terminal. The inter-terminal AirTrain stops at the GarageG/BART Station stop. Consider how many people will be traveling and if you will need to take a taxi after exiting BART; it might be almost as economical—and easy—just to take a taxi or car company.
- At OAK, the BART station is just across from the terminal 1 baggage claim and not far from terminal 2.
- SamTrans (San Mateo County Transit); the SamTrans buses mostly serve San Mateo County, the peninsula: coastside and inland; tel: (800) 660-4287; www.samtrans.com. For areas served, check www.samtrans.com/schedulesandmaps/html.

Shuttles
Shuttles are generally efficient, on time, and relatively inexpensive. That they pick up passengers at different locations means that you may not be the first on or off. They charge by the passenger, so if you have a large family with you, it might be more economical to consider the shuttles' other options. Check their websites for prices and to reserve. For an overall look at airport shuttles, access www.airportshuttles.com/sanfrancisco.php. There are others, as well:
- Marin Airporter, tel: (415) 461-4222; www.marinairporter.com/. Servicing SFO and Marin.

- East Bay Shuttle, tel (925) 800-4500; http://eastbayshuttle. net/ Servicing both airports from the East Bay.
- Wingz, tel. (088) 983-0156; www.wingz.me. Servicing both airports.

FINDING YOUR NEST

Getting Started: Hotels

If you are coming to San Francisco for a visit, you will first need to find somewhere to stay. Even though San Francisco has more than 200 hotels and some 32,000 hotel rooms, it also has about 25 million visitors a year and is a favorite convention destination. So, finding a hotel that meets your needs and your budget should be an early priority of your travel planning. Book the accommodation that you want as soon as you can. That there are so many hotels doesn't mean they are inexpensive; some luxury hotels may charge as much as $500 per night, and the average is about $350. The city's moderate climate assures that tourism is not seasonal, so prices for hotel rooms do not fluctuate as much as they might elsewhere.

Nonetheless, even the most sought after hotels do offer special "packages", and you should ask about them. Check the Internet. If you call a hotel directly, you will be told the "rack rate" (the published price); inquire about corporate, family, or "special packages", and specify any discounts you might be entitled to: AARP, AAA, or your airline benefits, for instance. Your travel agent usually has access to the best deals and should tell you about them. When calculating costs, remember that taxes are not included in the price of the room: you will have to add 14 per cent state and city taxes, and if you will be parking a car, you will also have to add the hotel's fee, for its "valet parking" is charged on a per day basis. The motels on Van Ness or on Lombard Street are reasonably priced and have easier accommodations for an automobile.

Starting the Search

There are dozens of global websites such as www.expedia.com or www.opodo.co.uk, www.booking.com or www.trivago.com that price hotels all around the world. Be sure to check www.tripadvisor.com and www.yelp.com. Hotel chains—Holiday Inn, Best Western, Westin, Marriott and Hilton, for example—have several locations in San Francisco, with varying price rates and levels of service. Usually their website address is www.(hotel-name).com. The following sites are especially good, and you can put "10 best motels in San Francisco" into your browser, as well.

- San Francisco Travel Association: the city's visitors bureau: recommendations for some hotels and basic tourist information: www.sftravel.com
- California Hotels: www.californiahotels.com
- Joie de Vivre Hotels: a group of charming smaller hotels, including the Kabuki and the stunning Vitale on the Embarcadero: www.jdvhotels.com

Residence Hotels

Furnished suites generally combine the comforts of an apartment with the amenities of a hotel. Suites are of various sizes
and include cooking facilities. Prices vary, of course, but the
marginal cost of your stay, when taking into consideration the
number of nights you will actually be staying and the amount
saved from not having to eat every meal in a restaurant, will
generally be lower than at a hotel.

Wyndham hotels offers several suite-hotels, both downtown
and Fisherman's Wharf areas. www.shellhospitality.com

- Synergy Corporate Housing, 1161 Mission Street, tel: (800)
  600-1115; www.synergyhousing.com An international firm
  of short-term corporate apartments.
- Van Ness—The Kenmore, Residence Club: 1570
  Sutter Street, near Gough, tel: (415) 776-5815; www.
  kenmorehotelsf.com. Near the Civic Center. Breakfast,
  dinners and Sunday brunch included.
- Van Ness—The Monroe, 1870 Sacramento Street, tel: (415)
  474-6200; www.monroeresidenceclub.com. Just off Van
  Ness, offering full breakfasts and dinners six days a week;
  brunch on Sunday.

Other Options

- Bed and breakfasts have long offered a more intimate and
  less expensive experience than the more impersonal hotels
  (www.bbsf.com). Size, amenities and locations vary, and
  occasionally in addition to the breakfast included in the
  price, there is a cocktail hour at the end of the day.
- Airbnb offers rentals of rooms, apartments, or even
  houses, by private citizens through the airbnb company
  (www.airbnb.com/San-Francisco). Now some 40 million
  bookings a year in 190 countries of the world and 65,000
  cities are showing its popularity.

- Vacation Rentals by Owner offers lodgings by private owners through a central website, operated by Home Away (www.vrbo.com). Booking through the service offers a protective fraud guarantee. If payment is made directly to the owner, however, make sure all your questions are answered, and arrange some protection for your payment.
- Home exchange is the least expensive way to stay on a vacation. International home exchange companies list homes available worldwide online. Members pay to list their homes, specifying the dates available, and can search for themselves those in the city of their choice. You correspond with the people who respond to your ad and check recommendations of previous travelers before coming to an agreement. Again, ask questions ensuring your own priorities will be met.
  - Homelink International: www.homelink.org
  - Intervac U.S.: www.intervac.com
  - HomeExchange.com: www.homeexchange.com

The Long-term Housing Situation

The good news is that as small and compact as it is, San Francisco offers a wide range of housing, from elegant mansions and single-family homes with gardens to semidetached row houses; from high-rise complexes to low-rise apartments over neighborhood stores, to flats in two-story homes. Thousands of charming Victorian houses and small homes coexist peaceably with the modern high-rises, and each of the almost 30 distinct neighborhoods has its own eclectic blend. Housing, in all of them, when it becomes available, is both for purchase or rent. Actually, in general, San Franciscans are apartment dwellers. Of the more than 385,000 residential units in the city, about half are rentals.

But, unfortunately, San Francisco is a city whose boundaries are fixed by water, so until recently there seemed some limits to residential opportunities. Those limits, now—with the extensive development south of Market and mid-Market—have been erased, and with the vertical high-rises not taking up a lot of the available land space.

Also, the city is demanding that a percentage of new residential construction be assigned to "affordable" housing. This is crucial, as increasing demand over the last decades—with the presence in the Bay Area of headquarters of such mega-international corporations such as Apple, Twitter, Google, Salesforce Spotify, Uber, Yelp, Facebook and Oracle—has fueled a difficult income inequality situation, for many of the well-paid prefer to live in San Francisco and are willing to pay whatever it takes to do so whether for rentals or purchase (and the companies oblige by providing shuttles to their peninsula headquarters). All of this has pushed prices up to the point where the city is rated as the most expensive housing market in the country. Fortunately, thousands of new units are underway.

The Housing Problem

The problem began with the construction boom after World War II. High-rent commercial skyscrapers in the city were built during what critics called the "Manhattanization of San Francisco," which stopped (for a while) because people were concerned about the change of the downtown character, but also because there seemed to be no more space there. Small businesses were driven to the outer reaches, some lower-end apartments were demolished to build hotels or upscale apartments, and some former rental units themselves were converted to expensive condominiums. But finally, when the "downtown" expanded well to the south of Market Street the rental units and condominiums were generally offered at market price. So, the city acted. Not only did it step in to require units at affordable prices, the municipality itself is now buying properties to provide more reasonably-priced housing,

as well as support for the homeless. The current plans for the renovation of Pier 70, for instance, near Dogpatch, include affordable housing in addition to market-level units and commercial spaces.

Do not be shocked by prices, do not be upset. It is just the way it is. Finding the right home at the right price is not an easy matter, but eventually you will find one, especially if you understand that you will have to compromise. But do not expect to arrive in San Francisco and move into the perfect inexpensive apartment with a spectacular view after a short stay in a hotel of about two or three days. San Francisco does not work that way. Expect first to do your research with your company if one is bringing you, or on the Internet with relocation or real estate agencies.

Yet the news is not all bad. Although the cost of living in San Francisco is considerably higher than that of the United States average, income levels in the Bay Area are generally commensurate and the median income is much more than in most of the rest of the country. In other words, salaries are also higher here, too, although with the most desirable housing, they may not stretch far.

The old idea of "roommates" has now, 21st century style, evolved into "co-living", communes of young professionals renting rooms in large homes together and forming communities of their own. Rents are affordable and joint activities bring like-minded people together. Co-living in the city—whether short- or long-term—makes the city work more easily. Just put "co-living San Francisco" into your search engine and see what currently pops up.

Costs other than housing are not particularly high: the mild climate allows residents to spend less on household utilities than in some other cities, for instance, and San Franciscans are always happy to say how little they paid for something, whether clothing bought at a discount or a delicious meal in an Asian eatery. For cost of living comparisons, access any of the online "cost of living calculators, and find specific information about SF from the city's own websites:"
- www.bestplaces.net
- www.numbeo.com/cost-of-living/
- www.sfgov.org (click on "Residents").
- http://sfmohcd.org/
  finding-affordable-rental-housing-san-francisco

Rent Control
Fortunately, despite the high rents, renters do have some protection under San Francisco law. Apartment rental in San Francisco has been controlled since 1979, meaning that rents for tenants with leases may only be raised a certain percentage each year, determined by a formula tied to the Cost of Living Index. Currently, the rate of increase is 1.6 per cent. Rents may be raised to "market levels", however, when a tenant leaves and before a new tenant moves in.

Starting the Rental Search

You can begin to understand the San Francisco rental market in advance of arrival by looking online.

- Craigslist: https://sfbay.craigslist.org/search/sfc/apa.
- Apartments for Rent.Com: www.forrent.com.
- RentSFNow: www.rentsfnow.com.
- San Francisco Chronicle: http://sfgate.com.

The Apartment

San Francisco real estate makes a distinction between an apartment and a flat. A flat is an entire floor of a small apartment building or two-story house, and it has its own entrance. Thus, you might walk up an outdoor flight of stairs to your door, and inside, the entire floor is your own. An apartment, however, is one of several—or many—on a single floor. Foreigners should understand that, in the United States, the first floor is really the ground floor, and the second floor is the next floor up.

If you are bringing a car, pay attention to the parking situation. Although new buildings must include some off-street parking, older dwellings may have no garages, and parking in San Francisco is generally a problem in all but the western neighborhoods. If you intend to park your car on the street, you will probably need a city-issued parking permit (see Residential Parking below). You should also determine the closest access to public transportation. Even people with cars often take public transportation or walk to work.

Be prepared to provide official identification, a credit reference and the names of your past and current employers and landlords. Identification might include your driver's license, bank account numbers, and Social Security number. Many places do not allow pets, but it is illegal for a landlord to prohibit children.

Security deposits are used to cover or compensate for any damage to the apartment (deducted upon your departure).

Thus, when you are signing a lease, check for any irregularities in the apartment, and specify them in writing—every crack in the walls or chip on an appliance—so that upon leaving you will not be charged for the damage. If you are applying for a furnished apartment, inquire about some of the items you require, such as a desk, Internet access, or a microwave oven.

Apartment Complexes

Some large apartment complexes handle their own rentals. These generally have a management office on the premises, which—at least theoretically—should make it efficient for repairs and service. In addition to considering these for long-term leases (if there are apartments available), some offer short-term contracts that might give you a place to live while looking for permanent housing.

Trinity, at 1145 Market Street (tel: (415) 433-3333; www.trinitysf.com/), offers apartments throughout the city, handling both short- and long-term apartments, furnished and unfurnished. Its Trinity Place in Mid-Market will soon add much needed housing in this up-and-coming area.

- Embarcadero—The Gateway: 460 Davis Court, at Jackson, tel: (415) 434-2000; www.thegateway.com/. Luxury apartments and townhouses, with a fitness center, tennis courts, and a swimming pool. Garage.
- Embarcadero—Bayside Village: The Embarcadero at Brannan, tel: (844) 321-0439; www.baysidevillage.com. Studio to two-bedroom units, parking. Swimming pools and a fitness center.
- Lake Merced/San Francisco State—Parkmerced: 3711 19th Avenue, tel: (415) 301-5194; www.parkmerced. com. Moderately priced single-family townhouses and apartments in a large development near San Francisco State.
- SoMa—Marina Apartments: 2 Townsend Street, tel: (415) 495-4119, www.sbma-sf.com. One- and two-bedroom

apartments in two towers and a courtyard, a pool, sauna, tennis courts, parking.

- SoMa—Soma Square Apartments: One Saint Francis Place, tel: (415) 284-3000 or (888) 473-8617; www. SoMaSquare.com. Conveniently in the heart of downtown SoMa, the Square has luxury apartments, a pool and rooftop lounge.
- Western Addition—Webster Tower and Terrace: 1489 Webster Street, at Geary, tel: (415) 931-6300; www. webstertower.com. Modern studios to two-bedroom apartments and penthouses, both furnished and unfurnished.
- The New Fillmore—The Fillmore Center, 1475 Fillmore Street, tel: (415) 941-5747; https://thefillmorecenter. com. Studios to three-bedroom apartments, penthouse, townhouse. Health club on premises.

Purchasing a Home

Since most homes for sale are listed in the centralized database of the San Francisco Board of Realtors' Multiple Listing Service, brokers have access to the broadest range of available housing. Check all the websites you can to give you an idea of what's available, and to compare prices. Here are a few representative examples:

- www.realtor.com/realestateandhomes-search/ San-Francisco_CA
- https://sfbay.craigslist.org/search/sfc/rea
- www.ziprealty.com/homes/forsale/sf/city
- https://sf.curbed.com
- www.zillow.com/san-francisco-ca/

The "fair market value" of a home is what a buyer will pay and a seller will accept. Generally, a home lists at a price comparable with similar homes on the market in its area, and your real estate agent should be able to give you an estimate of what each neighborhood's homes are going for.

Be specific with your agent about your price limits and your needs; also indicate on which items you might be willing to compromise. Ask also about their relocation services. Visit "open houses" in the neighborhood you are considering, so you can understand property values and the types of property available.

Understanding the Market

Small, stucco single-family bungalows line the streets in the western sections of the city, and large, well-designed homes (some are really mansions) are found in the northern districts of Pacific Heights and the Marina, farther out at Seacliff, and in enclaves such as Cole Valley, Diamond Heights, and Sherwood Forest. There are low-rise apartment buildings (four floors with bay windows) in every area, high-rise apartment complexes in some, and some semidetached row houses in just about all.

The Victorians, famous and expensive as they may be, are not all the city offers. If you are interested in historic houses, look also for the Brown Shingles popular in the 1890s, single-family homes built in reaction to the ornate Victorians. Made of natural materials, used simply and liberally, with cedar shingles and window trims of plain broad planks, they were still fairly Victorian in attitude. It was not until the early part of the following century that the one-story Craftsman Bungalow led the city away from its previous era. By the twenties, the compact California Bungalow, with its front porch and stucco walls, had become predominant in the then-developing western portions of the city. All these interesting styles still exist in the city and are occasionally put up for sale.

Most apartments for sale are condominiums in which each unit is privately owned along with a percentage of the common space. Today, however, only a few of the condominiums may measure 2,500 square feet (232.3 sq m) in floor area, and in general a new one-bedroom apartment averages 800–900 square feet (74.3–83.6 sq m) and a two-bedroom about 1,200–1,300 square feet (111.5–120.8 sq m).

Since San Francisco rates among the country's most expensive housing markets, you should take into consideration where the best resale locations are in the city. Check out if they are in good school districts, in sunny areas, or in upcoming parts of the city, although these are the most expensive. Some districts—the Marina, Pacific Heights, Noe Valley, the Castro—are always in strong demand. Others continue in upward transition, both in atmosphere and price, especially those to the south in Bayview, Dogpatch, Hunters Point and Potrero Hill. Note that most neighborhoods have their own improvement associations—local residents who are vigilant about keeping the character of the area intact—which will, of course, maintain the value of real estate as well as that area's lifestyle. A general rule in the property market is "the better the view, the higher the price; the farther out into the fog, the lower the price."

Yerba Buena Gardens

There is no better place to alleviate the stress of settling into a new home than Yerba Buena Gardens, at Mission and 4th Streets (www.yerbabuenagardens.com.) No matter what makes you relax, you will probably find it here. Five and a half acres of meadows, trees, flowers, falling water, public art, and museums, plus entertainment for the whole family and small cafés. There is a striking waterfall memorial honoring Martin Luther King, and a beautiful wooden tribute to the Ohlone Indians that centuries ago might have lived on these grounds. The Rooftop of the Moscone Center, has a Children's Garden with 100,000 square feet (929 sq m) of gardens and streams, an antique carousel, a play circle, a labyrinth made of hedges, and an interactive play center—the Children's Creativity Museum and Learning Garden are here as well. The Center for the Arts has a gallery with changing exhibitions, and performances at the Center for the Arts Theater range from music festivals to operetta. So, come to Yerba Buena Gardens once—and then come back often again. Everyone does.

As of this writing, the median listing price for homes in San Francisco is $1.6million. The forecast is for a continual but gentler rise than before. Zillow maintains a website with available listings, but also comprehensive up-to-date statistics on both purchase and rentals: www.zillow.com/san-francisco-ca/home-values/. This also includes a helpful listing of neighbourhood values.

Making Yourself At Home

Now that you have found a place to live, you have to get your new home ready to move in. What comes next? Whether you have rented or bought a place, you will need to arrange for the electricity to be registered in your name, for your telephone service, and for your cable television and Internet access. In San Francisco, it is not difficult. You just have to know where to look. (For household furnishings and appliances, see pages 223–224.)

Electricity Voltage

In the United States, electricity is 110 volts, 60 hertz, and appliances brought from abroad that run on 220 volts will not work. Fortunately, all housing comes with major appliances such as refrigerators and stoves, and sometimes clothes washers and dryers are included as well. To have the electricity registered in your name, contact Pacific Gas & Electric: https://www.pge.com/.

Water

If you rent an apartment, the water will be turned on when you move in, and the utility cost is included in the rent. If you are purchasing a home, you will need to have the water service transferred to your name. Contact the San Francisco Water Power Sewer: http://sfwater.org.

Communications

Owing to inexpensive options and the advent of the Internet for cheap digital calling and communications, providers offer many options and promotions. This includes AT&T (see below), which provides local service, but which also offers competitive alternatives to its standard home service. Some bundle phone, Internet and television. Shop around until you find what you need and which will give you the best reception, depending on which side of which mountain you live.

Mobile phones in the United States use either CDMA system or GSM, which much of the rest of the world uses; quad-band unblocked mobiles should work. Ask your original provider if it has an agreement with an American company, and when you arrive, switch your settings to that partner. And ask about inexpensive plans for foreign travel and roaming costs.

As competition is fierce among service providers, and price plans can be inexpensive, some newcomers do not bother to hook up a landline, using only their mobiles. On the other hand, people who do not use their cell phones can often purchase a "pay as you go" option and pay only for the minutes used and topping up the prepaid account when it is low. For local companies, access www.whistleout.com/CellPhones/Guides/Best-Plans-In-San-Francisco. And see Xfinity, below.

- AT&T: tel: (888) 333-6651; www.att.com (GSM)
- MetroPCS: tel: (888) 863-8768; www.metropcs.com (GSM)
- Sprint: tel: (866) 275-1411; www.sprint.com (CDMA)
- T-Mobile: tel: (800) 866-2493; www.t-mobile.com (GSM)
- Verizon: tel: (800) 225-5499; www.verizonwireless.com (CDMA)

VoIP

Voice over Internet Protocol (VoIP) offers inexpensive calling: free anywhere to other users of that company, and with low costs to others.

- Skype: www.skype.com
- Vonage: www.vonage.com
- Magic Jack: www.magicjack.com

Area Codes and Dialing

The area code for the city and county of San Francisco is 415. For all other telephone numbers, you must dial the number 1 and then the area code before the telephone number itself. Calls to numbers that start with 800, 888, 877, 866, 855 and 844 are toll-free, but those starting with 900 charge by the minute. Some impose a minimal fee.

Internet

There are dozens of Internet broadband providers in San Francisco. One good website is https://broadbandnow.com/California/San-Francisco. Another popular locally-based popular provider is Monkey Brains www.monkeybrains.net/. Until you have connected your Internet at home, note that just about any café in the city offers free wireless access. Also, the city itself is making San Francisco a "wireless city"; currently, there is free Wi-Fi in various areas and parks around the city: http://sfgov.org/sfc/sanfranciscowifi.

Television and Radio

For television cable service—aside from some mentioned above—one option is XFinity, which also has digital voice and Internet services: www.xinfinity.com.

With some 80 radio stations in the Bay Area, you can probably find just what you are looking for, in whatever language. FM reception may depend on what side of a hill you are living on. AM reception is generally clear (www.radiolineup.com/locate/San-Francisco-CA). You can also find radio apps for your cell phone.

Getting the News

Aside from Internet and television, San Francisco has one daily newspaper, the *San Francisco Chronicle*, which is available for delivery or online (www.sfgate.com). Just about any international newspaper can also be read online.

- *Bay Guardian* (www.sfbg.com/): online liberal weekly covering issues of Bay Area interest, plus reviews events and cultural activities
- *SF Weekly* (www.sfweekly.com/): found in news boxes on street corners
- *San Francisco Examiner* (www.sfexaminer.com/): owner of the two above, is itself a full breaking-news newspaper
- *Korea Times San Francisco* (www.servage.net): San Francisco edition of a national newspaper
- *Niche Bei* (https://nichibei.org): Japanese-American news and culture
- *Sing Tao Daily* (https://www.singtaousa.com/sf/: Chinese publication has an extensive section on San Francisco
- *Tecolote* (http://eltecolote.org): English-Spanish biweekly publication for the Latino community.
- *San Francisco Bay View* (http://sfbayview.com/): national newspaper for the African-American community
- *Bay Area Reporter* (www.ebar.com): for the LGBT communities
- *San Francisco Bay Times* (http://sfbaytimes.com/): also for the LGBT communities.

Subscribe also to *San Francisco*, the city's monthly magazine for articles, reviews, and lists of upcoming performances and events (www.modernluxury.com/san-francisco).

Mail Delivery

The United States Postal Service delivers mail addressed to you at your new address without official notification, although you will have no doubt submitted a Change of Address card to your previous post office. There is one mail delivery per day, except Sundays and holidays.

Each postal "zip code" has a post office. For the post office nearest to you, access the website www.usps.com.

Household Insurance

If you are buying a home, homeowner's insurance is required as part of the process of obtaining a mortgage, but even if you are renting an apartment, you should consider homeowner's insurance to protect yourself against theft or liability if someone is injured in your home.

If you are insuring a car, then having both policies with one insurer may lower the cost. For information on home insurance, contact the California Department of Insurance, tel: (800) 927-4357; www.insurance.ca.gov.

Many Californians are members of the California State Automobile Association (American Automobile Association), https://calstate.aaa.com.

Earthquake Insurance

Homeowners may want to take out earthquake insurance as part of the homeowners' insurance policy. Check with your insurance agent or the California Earthquake Authority (CEA) for policies available (tels: (916) 325-3800; (877) 797-4300; www.earthquakeauthority.com).

Speaking of Earthquakes ...

On a practical note, no matter where you are in the Bay Area, you should keep a working flashlight in your home and perhaps some candles, a portable radio with extra batteries, a stand-ard, non-electric telephone, non-perishable food supplies, and a few gallons of water—just in case. Always keep enough medication and a small reserve of cash to tide you over. Stores around the Bay Area sell earthquake kits.

Identification Cards

For obtaining a California Driver's License, see page 139. If you do not intend to drive, however, you may wish to obtain a state identification card. Like drivers' licenses, these are issued by the Department of Motor Vehicles. Bring your birth certificate or passport, and Social Security or taxpayer identification number and proof of residence. www.dmv.org/ca-california/id-cards.php.

Opening a Bank Account

Opening a bank account is easier here than it is in some other countries. You will only need to provide a picture-identification, an address, and enough money to make your initial deposit.

Inquire as to all options open to you, especially their charges. You will be provided with a debit card to use in the automatic teller machines (ATM) and you will be asked whether you wish to apply for a Visa/Master Card. Inquire as to the rates of interest charged, for rates vary and low-interest cards are available. It is illegal in California for merchants to use your credit card as identification; they may not write its number down on your check. There are many banks and credit unions to consider. Here are a few of the most well-known.

- Bank of America: www.bankofamerica.com
- Bank of the West: www.bankofthewest.com
- Chase: www.chase.com
- Citibank: www.citibank.com
- Wells Fargo: www.wellsfargo.com

Currency Exchanges

If you need to exchange your foreign currency for dollars, you can use a "currency exchange," if that is your only option. You will get a better rate of exchange, however, if you have a debit card and can use an ATM. These are generally linked to your bank and give the bank's competitive rate of exchange. With currency exchanges, however, be sure to ask about fees and the rate for the amount you wish to exchange.

Taxes

If you are earning income in the United States, you will no doubt be required to file a tax return by April 15 of each year. This requires you to have a Social Security number (www.ssa.gov), or a Taxpayer Identification number. If you are from a country that has a bilateral agreement with the United States, a portion of your income may be exempt from taxes here. Contact the Internal Revenue Service (www.irs.gov) should you need answers to any questions.

As a resident of California, you will also have to pay California state tax. If you have questions, you can get information from the State Franchise Tax Board (www.ftb.ca.gov).

Storage Lockers

If your new home is smaller than you had imagined and you need to store some belongings, consider a self-storage locker. Sizes range from those that would hold a few items to those in which you might store all your furniture while looking for housing. In these dry, well-maintained warehouses, there is 24-hour security; you retain the key to your own locker and have daily access.

- Attic Self Storage: 2440 16th Street, tel: (415) 689-6570; www.atticselfstorageca.com/
- American Storage Unlimited: 600 Amador Street, tel: (415) 824-2338; www.americanstorage-ca.com/
- Public Storage: facilities throughout city; https:// www.publicstorage.com/storage-search-landing. aspx?location=San+Francisco
- SoMa Self Storage: 1475 Mission Street, tel: (628) 400-4990; www.somastorage.com

Trash Collection

Almost all apartments and houses have in-sink garbage disposal units to handle food waste. Recycling of waste is obligatory. For people living in large apartment buildings, both trash collection and recycling of paper, glass, and metal are taken care of by the management. In small buildings, tenants themselves are required to separate their wet garbage, recyclable materials, and other trash, and to put the containers at the curb on the days specified. If you live in a house, you will have to arrange for garbage collection: Recology Sunset Scavenger/Recology Golden Gate (https://www.recology.com/recology-san-francisco).

Finding Your Spiritual Home

Generally the city's religious congregations are welcoming of anyone, whether affiliated with that religion or not. San Franciscans practice their religion the same way they do everything else—according to their own reasons and tastes—and it is said that only some 35 per cent of the population identifies with a major religious denomination. Nonetheless, there are multilingual options for daily or weekly worship for just about any faith.

There are so many faiths that listing all of them here would be impossible: traditional denominations, evangelical, messianic, and those that worship in their own ways, such as the well-attended Church of Saint John Coltrane, an African Orthodox church that "preaches the gospel of jazz and love" in its liturgy: 2097 Turk Street, tel: (415) 673-7144; www.coltranechurch.org/.

No matter your traditions, you should know about Glide Memorial United Methodist Church: 330 Ellis Street, at Taylor, tel: (415) 674-6000; www.glide.org. In the heart of the Tenderloin, Glide is the city's most celebrated religious gathering place and Sunday services are always well-attended. This is the church most known in the city for social activism.

- Baptist—Third Baptist Church: 1399 Mcallister Street, tel: (415) 346-4426; https://thirdbaptist.org/. FirstSF Baptist Church: 22 Waller Street, tel: (415) 863-3382; http://firstsf. com. San Francisco Chinese Baptist Church: 1811 34th Avenue, tel: (415) 831-2313; http://sfcbc.org
- Buddhist—Zen Center: 300 Page Street, tel: (415) 863-3136; www.sfzc.org/. Also, San Francisco Buddhist Center: 37 Bartlett Street, tel: (415) 282-2018; www. sfbuddhistcenter.org.
- Catholic—Cathedral of Saint Mary: 1111 Gough Street, at Geary, tel: (415) 567-2020; www.stmarycathedralsf.org/. Mission Dolores; 3321 16th Street, tel: (415) 621-8203; www.missiondolores.org/. For information on the Catholic community: Archdiocese office: 1 Peter Yorke Way, tel: (415) 614-5500; www.sfarchdiocese.org.
- Christian Science—First Church of Christ, Scientist: 1700 Franklin Street, tel: (415) 673-3544; http://firstchurchsf.com/.
- Episcopal—Grace Cathedral: 1100 California at Taylor, tel: (415) 749-6300; https://www.gracecathedral.org/
- Greek Orthodox—Cathedral of the Annunciation: 245 Valencia, tel: (415) 864-8000; www.annunciation.org.
- Islam—The Islamic Society and the Masjid Darussalam Mosque: 20 Jones Street, tel: (415) 863-7997; http:// islamsf.org.
- Jewish (Reform) Congregation Emanu-El: 2 Lake Street, tel: (415) 751-2535; www.emanuelsf.org. (Orthodox): Adath Israel (www.adathisraelsf.org) and Keneseth Israel (www. kenesethisraelsf.org.): SF Hillel on university campuses (www.sfhillel.org/). The Jewish Community Federation: 121 Steuart Street, tel: (415) 777-1411; www.jccsf.org.
- Lutheran—Saint Mark's: 1111 O'Farrell, tel: (415) 928-7770; www.stmarks-sf.org.
- Methodist—In addition to Glide (above), Temple United Methodist: 65 Beverly Street at Junipero Serra, tel: (415) 586-1444; www.templeunitedmethodist.org/.

- Presbyterian—Noe Valley Ministry: 1021 Sanchez, at 23rd Street, tel: (415) 282-2317; www.noevalleyministry.org/.
- Quaker—Friends Quaker Meeting: 65 9th Street, tel: (415) 431-7440; https://sfquakers.org. Unprogrammed meeting.
- Unitarian—First Unitarian Universalist Church: 1187 Franklin Street, tel: (415) 776-4580. www.uusf.org/.
- Vedanta—The Vedanta Temple: 2323 Vallejo Street at Fillmore, tel: (415) 922-2323; www.sfvedanta.org.

Gay and Lesbian Worship

San Francisco's churches and synagogues are openly welcoming of the LGBT community. Yet, gays and lesbians are also forming supportive spiritual groups and worship sites of their own. They too are welcoming of whoever wants to participate.

- Catholic—Dignity San Francisco: 1329 7th Avenue at the Presbyterian Church, tel: (415) 681-2491; www.dignitysanfrancisco;org
- Interfaith Christian—Metropolitan Community Church: 1300 Polk Street, tel: (415) 863-4434; www.mccsf.org;
- Jewish—Congregation Sha'ar Zahav: 290 Dolores Street; tel: (415) 861-6932; www.shaarzahav.org;
- Evangelical—Freedom in Christ Evangelical Church, Fireside Cafe: 4248 18th Street, tel: (415) 662-8149; www.ficcsf.com.

A CHILD'S WORLD

Great for the Kids

San Francisco is great for kids. The area's moderate climate means that outdoor play is available just about any day of the year: parks and playgrounds dot the landscape, wide beaches offer endless play in the sand, and schools offer extensive extracurricular sports programs. The ethnic diversity of the city means that children will have a culturally stimulating environment in which to grow and learn. And the open friendliness of the city means a generally nurturing environment. Well-behaved children are welcome in most restaurants, and even the most elegant restaurants have booster seats. Theaters, museums, private organizations, and the city's Recreation and Parks Department have enriching programs for children. And the options for schooling, although seemingly complex and perhaps slightly discouraging at the outset, can offer a well-rounded education, especially when parents participate and pay attention. Whatever you want for your child, you will no doubt find it in San Francisco.

- Tourist Office: www.sftravel.com/article/10-free-things-do-san-francisco-families
- Parents' Press: informative and fun magazine about opportunities for children, including a helpful list of Bay Area schools: www.parentspress.com;

Thinking about Schools

Choosing a school in San Francisco, whether elementary, middle, or high school, is not as simple as showing up on the first day of school in your neighborhood and expecting your

child to receive a good education. In fact, it might be wise to consider the educational opportunities available while you are deciding on neighborhoods where you might want to live. With research and care, you should be able to find a good public school for your child, or you may choose a charter school or even a private school, if tuition fees that may run from $17,000–$25,000 per student are within your budget. Some of the private schools, however, do offer financial assistance.

If you can make a trip to San Francisco before your actual move, investigating schools should be among your priorities. Get advice from the Human Resources Department of your company, visit the San Francisco Unified School District (SFUSD) and then the schools you are considering, and if you can, talk with parents of children in those schools. Then, when you have found the schools appropriate for your children, follow carefully every procedure for application, for the most popular schools draw the most applicants, and acceptance to each of these is not always guaranteed.

School Match has detailed statistics on public and private schools across the country (tel: (614) 890-1573; www.school-match.com). After you detail your priorities, School Match will suggest schools in the area that match your preferences. Prices vary according to the information requested.

The Public School System

Choosing a school in San Francisco, whether elementary, middle, or high school, is not as simple as showing up on the first day of school in your neighbourhood and expecting your child to go to that school in your "attendance zone." The size of these zones vary according to the number of school-age children living in them. It would be ideal if popular schools were in each neighborhood and if each of them had schools to accommodate all the area's children, but this is not the case. Thus, parents must apply for the public schools they believe would be best for their children. The application process is crucial, so make sure you know all the current regulations by checking the SFUSD website.

Not all schools are the same, although every school provides a required core curriculum. Yet, schools at all levels offer differing educational themes and teaching approaches; some specialize in academic programs while others stress technology, and a few have language immersion programs. Some have better educational track records than others; for an idea of a school's performance, access the School Accountability Report Card on the SFUSD website.

Check out these resources:

- SFUSD: 555 Franklin Street; tel: (415) 241-6000; www.sfusd.edu. Download the Enrolment Guide for detailed information: www.sfusd.edu/en/assets/sfusd-staff/enroll/files/2017-18/2017-18_enrollment_guide_en_low_res.pdf

- SFUSD: Student and family handbooks: www.sfusd.edu/en/family-and-comMunity-support/parent-handbooks.html Things Parents Should Know: www.sfusd.edu/en/family-and-comMunity-support/parents-rights.html. Nutrition Services: www.sfusd.edu/en/nutrition-school-meals/nutrition-overview.html

- California Department of Education: All aspects of education and educational news. For general information, access the California Department of Education website (www.cde.ca.gov). Also download the CA Schools Mobile app: www.cde.ca.gov/re/mo/caschools.asp.

For Non-native English Speakers

SFUSD has dual language and immersion "pathway" programs for children whose native tongue is not English. Languages include Cantonese and Mandarin, Korean and Spanish: www.sfusd.edu/en/enroll-in-sfusd-schools/language-pathways.html.

Preschools

Preschooling has long been important in San Francisco, a city in which both parents are likely to work outside the home, and to which people migrate without having any family in the area to help take care of the kids. But preschool is important on other grounds; it is widely held that children who have been "socialized" when they attend preschools perform better in their early school years than children who have not. For a good discussion of preschools and links to resources, access the Bay Area Parent's primer: www.bayareaparent.com/Article/A-Preschool-Primer/

SFUSD's Child Development Program is for children aged three to five: 20 Cook Street (tel: (415) 750-8500); www.sfusd.edu/en/assets/sfusd-staff/programs/files/Early%20Education/Application%20-%20SFCEL.pdf.

More than a dozen Child Development Centers offer full- or part-day programs, for children who are toilet-trained. The highest priority for acceptance is for families with the lowest income per family size.

When investigating any preschool, consider only those that have been licensed by the State Department of Social Services. Licensing means that the facility has met the state's criteria concerning the physical plant (amount of fenced playground areas, number of toilets per child, safe food preparation area, and so on) and that the staff has met educational and experiential qualifications.

- Independent preschools are not affiliated with public or religious agencies. Many are neighborhood schools, serving the ethnic mix of that area. Some have bilingual programs, also depending on the neighborhood.
- Agency-affiliated preschools are sponsored by an organization, such as the Jewish Community Center (JCC) or the Young Men's Christian Association (YMCA). Each school sets its own approach; some have a religious component to the program, but others do not.

- Religious preschools are sponsored by a particular church or synagogue, and not by the agencies mentioned above.
- College and university preschools are sponsored by the city's institutions of higher learning, servicing their faculty and students. Inquire of the university.
- Montessori schools are all similar, using the philosophy of Dr. Maria Montessori, who advocated stimulating, non-competitive activities in a structured atmosphere while providing creative freedom for children.

Charter Schools

Technically, charter schools are district schools that receive state funding, but they are independently run and have greater flexibility than municipality-run schools. They have autonomy in management, in hiring of teachers, and in the development of curricula and enrichment programs. They must, however, adhere to public school norms. In San Francisco, there are eleven charter schools; the SFUSD website has details (www.sfusd.edu/en/schools/charter-schools.html).

Private Schools

Private schools have distinct advantages and you may find their education worth paying for. Although each has its own character, basically they are accredited and provide a high standard of education, have a smaller class size with a better teacher to student ratio, and give more individual attention to each child. They generally also provide enriching extracurricular activities, all in a nurturing and stimulating environment. There are a variety of schools in the city and in nearby towns, but all these advantages come with a price tag. Tuition and other fees at private schools in the Bay Area are high, but they are generally in line with similar schools around the country. Some schools have financial aid programs and some offer reduced tuition fees if there are siblings in the school. (Private School Review: www.privateschoolreview.com/california/san-francisco.)

Some of the schools outside the city, especially in Marin, are extremely popular (www.cde.ca.gov).

Child Care

One of the most widespread day-care and preschools is the non-profit Marin Day Schools, with its campuses around the Bay Area: 100 Meadowcreek Drive, Corte Madera (tel: (415) 924-7500; www.marindayschools.org).

- Children's Counsel of San Francisco: 445 Church Street, tel: (415) 276-2900; child care info tel: (415) 343-3300; www.childrenscouncil.org. The Council provides workshops and counseling for parents needing childcare and referrals to licensed child-care providers in San Francisco.
- Wu Yee Children's Services: 880 Clay Street, tel: (644) 677-0100; www.wuyee.org . Provides much the same services, with bilingual (Chinese) resources.

Recreation and Parks Department

Get to know the Recreation and Parks Department, Golden Gate Park at McLaren Lodge, 501 Stanyan Street (tel: (415) 831-2700; www.sfrecpark.org). After school activities in more than a dozen recreation facilities are both structured and fun. Rec and Parks also operates Camp Mather, a rustic summer camp in the Stanislaus National Forest which allows families to spend a week together swimming and playing sports, and participating in camp-like activities (http://sfrecpark.org/destination/camp-mather/).

Educational Entertainment and Fun

The following is a small but representative sample of the area's range of enriching and fun, locally-based opportunities for children (and their parents!). Others include Ripley's Believe it or Not! (www.ripleys.com/sanfrancisco) and Madame Tussauds (www.madametussauds.com/san-francisco/en/. For outdoor activities, make sure to bring a jacket for your child.

- Aquarium of the Bay: Pier 39, Embarcadero at Beach Street, tel: (415) 623-5300; www.aquariumofthebay. org. Visitors progress on a moving walkway through this wraparound aquarium to see marine life of the Pacific Ocean.
- Bay Area Discovery Museum: Fort Baker, 557 McReynolds Road, just over the Golden Gate Bridge, tel: (415) 339-3900; www.bayareadiscoverymuseum.org. Hands-on multi-building museum for the entire family, focusing on natural sciences, art and multimedia.
- California Academy of Sciences: 55 Music Concourse Drive in Golden Gate Park, tel: (415) 379-8000; www. calacademy.org. For details on this amazing institution, see page 190.

The Golden Gate Bridge

The spectacular, soaring Golden Gate Bridge, spanning the Golden Gate Strait, where the Pacific Ocean meets San Francisco Bay, is beloved by locals and tourists alike. Having taken four years to build, the bridge was completed in 1937, and at the time—with a 4,200 foot suspension—was the longest suspension bridge in the world. (Now it ranks seventh.) In today's dollars, it cost US$1.2 billion to build. Hundreds of men worked high above the choppy frigid waters, and although a safety net below saved most lives, ten men met their deaths when a scaffold broke and fell through the net. Currently, using modern safety equipment, dozens of ironworkers and painters work fulltime to make sure the bridge is well maintained and that it keeps its beautiful orange glow.

The International Orange color of the bridge, which enhanced visibility for ships, was also chosen to blend with the natural colors of the landmasses on either side and to contrast with the blue sky above and the dark waters below. Beginning in 1965 (a project that took thirty years), the original paint was replaced with modern synthetic materials that would resist rust and corrosion from the high salt content of the ocean winds. Think of the work! Each tower rises 746 feet (227 m) and has 600,000 rivets, and there is more than enough cable to circle the globe several times.

More than a billion vehicles have crossed the bridge since its opening, and now about 41 million cross it each year. In 1987, on the 50th anniversary, some 300,000 people crossed the bridge on foot, just 100,000 more than crossed it on its glorious opening day half a century before.

- Cartoon Art Museum: 781 Beach Street, near the Aquatic Park, tel: (415) 227-8666; www.cartoonart.org. Original art exhibits of cartoon panels, classic and comics. Fun for anyone young at heart.
- Children's Art Center: Fort Mason Center, Building C, tel: (415) 771-0292; www.childrensartcenter.org. Art classes for children, including after-school and mini-camp programs.
- The Children's Creativity Museum: 221 Fourth Street, tel: (415) 820-3320. https://creativity.org/: part of the Yerba Buena Gardens complex. Art and technology programs for kids from early-childhood on, and for families.
- Exploratorium: Pier 15, the Embarcadero & Green Street, tel: (415) 528-4444)/; www.exploratorium.edu. The spectacular hands-on, interactive Exploratorium is a "public learning laboratory" and is sure to educate and amuse parents as well as children.
- Golden Gate Fortune Cookie Factory: Chinatown at 56 Ross Alley, tel: (415) 781-3956. Watch fortune cookies being made, and then buy some.
- M.H. De Young Memorial Museum: Hagiwara Tea Garden Drive, Golden Gate Park, tel: (415) 863-3330; http://deyoung.famsf.org/families. The city's outstanding art museum has extensive educational programs for families and children.
- Musée Mécanique: Pier 45 at the end of Taylor Street, tel: (415) 346-2000; www.museemecaniquesf.com. Its large arcade of coin-operated and antique fun machines is sure to fascinate everyone, not just children.
- Randall Museum: 199 Museum Way, at Roosevelt, tel: (415) 554-9600; www.randallmuseum.org. A wonderful hands-on nature and history museum of the Parks Department, providing an educational platform for children to feed their curiosity.

Although Pier 39 may well be the most touristy attraction in the city, everybody should go there at least once (www.pier39.com). The exquisite view from the end of the pier may keep everyone in the family riveted for hours. The city's world-famous sea lions bask on their own pier on the northern side, occasionally barking loudly or swiping at each other, and always a delight to see. (Great photo-ops here!) The Aquarium of the Bay is fun, and children also love the carousel. There are rides, bungee jumps, and dozens of other attractions, casual eateries and good restaurants, all enough to keep the family browsing for half a day, and this is also the place to pick up the Blue and Gold Fleet for a cruise on the Bay or to Alcatraz.

- San Francisco Maritime National Historical Park: Hyde Street Pier, at the foot of Hyde Street, near Fisherman's Wharf, tel: (415) 561-7000; www.nps.gov/safr/index.htm. Explore historical ships and a World War II submarine in an extensive Aquatic Park, with events, hands-on projects, and a full calendar of activities for children.
- San Francisco Zoo: Sloat Boulevard at 45th Avenue, tel: (415) 753-7080; www.sfzoo.org. More than a conventional zoo, the daily activities are posted on their website, plus special exhibitions, and lots to do for children.

THE STUDENT LIFE

Opportunities Galore

The Bay Area has 35 degree-granting universities, colleges, and specialized technical schools, some the finest of their class in the country. Non-degree and certificate courses are also available in a surprising number of fields, and all can further enrich your life, or your lifestyle. Some representative samples of schools are listed below; their names should give an idea of what they are about and their websites should allow access to more substantive information.

If you are a foreigner, you will have to apply for a student visa and you will no doubt have to take the Test of English as a Foreign Language (TOEFL) as part of the application procedure. If you want to study in the United States, learn English first. For language schools, see below.

Student Visas

Some 480,000 foreigners—primarily Asians and then Europeans—are studying in the United States, the majority in California. Universities welcome foreign students, providing their credentials meet the institutions' standards and all immigration criteria are met.

If you are entering the United States as a tourist and are taking a short course of less than 18 hours a week, you probably do not need a student visa, but for educational courses that require more than 18 hours a week, you will need one of two types of visas.

- http://educationusa.state.gov/
- www.ice.gov/sevis/index.htm

Student Housing

If you are in San Francisco to study at one of the English-language schools, it will no doubt have a program for temporary housing. Also, universities have housing offices to help students find housing; some also have on-campus housing.

For temporary and inexpensive accommodations, San Francisco has several youth hostels that offer basic dormitory-style rooms at competitive prices. If you are bringing valuables such as computers or printers, inquire as to their safekeeping; some have provision for safe storage, others do not. Hostelling International membership is required, but may be purchased on-site (www.hiusa.org). The following three hostels in San Francisco are members of HI, but there are many others; see www.norcalhostels.org and put "hostels San Francisco" into your browser.

- HI Fisherman's Wharf, Fort Mason, Building 240, tel: (415) 771-7277
- HI Downtown, 312 Mason Street, tel: (415) 788-5604
- HI City Center, 685 Ellis Street, tel: (415) 474-5721

Studying English

English is the language of America and the official language of California. So, if English is not your native tongue, you should make every effort to learn—or improve—your English as quickly as possible. If you don't, you will certainly be at a disadvantage in business or in school, and you won't know as much as your neighbors as to the happenings in the city at any given time or even what opportunities are available for you. There are many registered English language schools in the Bay Area, choose one that suits your schedule and budget. For people who are going to apply for further study in the United States, the schools all offer TOEFL (Test of English as a Foreign Language) preparation.

City College of San Francisco offers free English classes for adults at its John Adams Campus, 1860 Hayes Street at Masonic; tel: (415) 561-1835; www.ccsf.edu/Departments/ESL/jad.html .

The private schools listed here differ somewhat in their offerings and prices. Generally, they have programs for students of all levels and needs. Some conduct evening classes and social programs, too. They should also assist with the necessary visas and temporary accommodations, if needed.

- American Academy of English: 530 Golden Gate Avenue, tel: (415) 567-0189; www.aae.edu
- Brandon College: 944 Market Street, 2nd floor, tel: (415) 391-5711; www.brandoncollege.com
- Saint Giles Language Teaching Center: 785 Market Street, Suite 300, tel: (415) 788-3552; www.stgiles-international. com/english-language-schools/usa/san-francisco

- Stafford House International: 417 Montgomery Street, tel: (646) 503-1810; www.languagecourse.net/school-stafford-house-international-san-francisco.php3

Most Americans speak what is called General American (also referred to as Standard Midwestern). As you meet people from different regions, though, you will hear different accents and occasionally a few different words, but if you listen hard, you will find that Americans actually speak the same language, no matter their place of origin. Even Americans can hear the differences in accents and sometimes must make an effort to comprehend: people from New Jersey often have a distinct accent, different from that of the Deep South. As you study English in a school in San Francisco, though, you will be learning the accent and pronunciation that are standard across America.

State-wide Education Systems

Four higher education systems are funded by the State of California. The most prestigious and stringent belong to the University of California system: in the Bay Area, its major campus is in Berkeley, and its medical and other health-profession schools are in San Francisco, as is its Hastings College of Law. Next come the California State Universities, which in the Bay Area are San Francisco State, Sonoma State, San Jose State, and Cal State Hayward. These are followed by the city and community colleges: San Francisco City College.

University of California

The University of California, Berkeley, is one of the country's finest teaching and research universities, as is the Medical Center in San Francisco with its Mission Bay hospital and research complex. Admissions are extremely competitive, and priority is given to California residents.

- University of California, Berkeley: 110 Sproul Hall, Berkeley 94720, tel: (510) 642-6000; www.berkeley.edu
- UCSF School of Medicine: 500 Parnassus, tel: (415) 476-4044; https://medschool.ucsf.edu
- University of California Hastings College of the Law: 200 McAllister Street, tel: (415) 565-4600; www.uchastings.edu

California State University

The widespread California State University system educates the bulk of California high school graduates. The admissions process is less competitive than the University of California system.

San Francisco State University: 1600 Holloway Avenue, tel: (415) 338-1111; www.sfsu.edu. This 30,000 student "commuter" university offers undergraduate and graduate degrees, a law school, and several certificate and credential programs.

City College

City College of San Francisco: 50 Phelan Avenue, tel: (415) 239-3000; www.ccsf.org. City Collee is a free-tuition community college that offers associate degrees and certificates, online certificates, and continuing education programs. Campuses and "instructional sites" are in several locations.

Private Universities

In a class by itself among private universities, the beautiful campus of Stanford University is located on the Peninsula, at Palo Alto, about 35 minutes south of San Francisco: Stanford University, Stanford CA 94305, tel: (650) 723-2300; www.stanford.edu. Its undergraduate application process is extremely competitive; less than 15 per cent of applicants are accepted. Located in San Francisco are:

- University of San Francisco: 2130 Fulton Street, tel: (415) 422-5555; www.usfca.edu. A Jesuit university founded 150

years ago, it offers undergraduate and graduate degrees in business, education, law, and many other fields.

- Golden Gate University: 536 Mission Street, tel: (415) 442-7800; www.ggu.edu. In the heart of downtown, Golden Gate offers undergraduate and graduate degrees, and a law school.

Specialized and Technical Schools

Specialized schools may offer full degrees or professional certificates and other credentials in particular fields. This should give you an idea of the range of education offered.

- Academy of Art University, 79 New Montgomery Street, tel: (800) 544-2787; www.academyart.edu. Focusing on the arts, communication and design, the academy offers undergraduate and graduate degrees, and certificate programs in campuses all around the city.
- San Francisco Law School, (Alliant International University), 1 Beach Street, tel: (415) 626-5550; www.alliant.edu/sfls/#tab-juris-doctor-program. Part of the

Alliant International University system now, this is a long-established law school.

- American College of Traditional Chinese Medicine, 455 Arkansas Street, tel: (415) 282-7600; www.actcm.edu . Acupuncture and Chinese medicine.
- San Francisco Conservatory of Music, 50 Oak Street, tel: (415) 864-7326; www.sfcm.edu. A world-class conservatory with a wide-ranging curriculum.
- Arthur A Dugoni School of Denistry, 155 Fifth Street, (415) 929-6400; www.dental.pacific.edu. Year-round accelerated three-year program, with DDS and graduate specialties.
- San Francisco Art Institute, 800 Chestnut Street, tel: (415) 771-7020; www.sfai.edu. Educating artists since 1871, the Art Institute's liberal arts curriculum focuses on fine arts, photography, sculpture, and filmmaking.

Part-time Work

Part-time work on campus may exist at some universities, especially for graduate students who may be offered teaching/research assistantships. For work and study programs, internships and seasonal work, contact the Council on International Educational Exchange (CIEE) or access their website for extensive information: 300 Fore Street, 3rd Floor, Portland Maine, tel: (207) 553-4000; www.ciee.org

TO YOUR HEALTH!

Medical Care in San Francisco

The quality of medical care in San Francisco is excellent. Practicing physicians who are also researchers at the area's major medical research centers and hospitals bring cutting-edge knowledge and techniques to their patients, assuring them of the best of care. There is a question, however, as to accessibility—how much access any individual has to this care—and this is most often determined by finances and health insurance. Health insurance legislation is currently being debated in the Congress; keep up to date with the news in the various media.

If You Become Ill

All public hospitals have 24-hour emergency rooms, and many of them have bilingual staff (Spanish, Russian, or Chinese). All emergencies are treated, regardless of a person's ability to pay; once in stable condition, however, the patient may be transferred to a different facility. Each hospital has its own procedures for payment or insurance reimbursement. If you are covered by insurance in another country, you may be required to pay in advance and submit the itemized bill to your own provider.

> For all dire health emergencies, call 911. For emergencies requiring police attention, call (415) 553-0123. For more emergency numbers and procedures, see Chapter 10, Resource Guide.

Travelers are not required to have health insurance when in the United States, but as health treatment is costly, it's best to have coverage. If you do not have health insurance in your home country, inquire if your travel agent sells temporary travel policies when booking your ticket. Even people with health insurance should inquire of their carriers about the documents needed and which receipts to keep in order to be reimbursed for any financial outlay.

Health Insurance

Private insurance is available, provided you can pay for it. Workers may be covered through their employer's health plans. While discussing health benefits with your future employer, ask what the company's plan covers; not every possibility is

covered by every carrier. Small businesses may not offer health insurance, and employees must thus find coverage elsewhere. It's not wise to be without insurance.

Even among individual plans there are differing options. Not all insurance plans provide the exact same coverage, not even within the same company. It is best to compare plans and prices, but not to take too long, for people without insurance are at great financial and health risks.

• The Healthy San Francisco program makes basic and ongoing medical care accessible and affordable to residents who do not have health insurance, and who earn up to $54,000 (tel: (415) 615-4555; www. healthysanfrancisco.org/visitors/). Availability is regardless of immigration or employment status, or even pre-existing medical conditions. Check the website for eligibility.

San Francisco Hospitals

Zuckerberg San Francisco General Hospital and Trauma Center, the city's public hospital, is one of UCSF's primary teaching hospitals, working with the city's Department of Public Health: 1001 Potrero Ave; tel: (415) 206-8000; https:// zuckerbergsanfranciscogeneral.org. A new research building on this campus is scheduled to open in 2019.

Some major medical groups have several specialized treatment centers and hospitals around the city.

- California Pacific Medical Center (tel: (415) 600-6000; www.cpmc.org/) is a major conglomeration of the hospitals and medical services of Sutter Health, with four extensive campuses: in Castro/Hayes Valley, Pacific/Presidio Heights/Inner Richmond, Mission/Bernal Heights, and Fillmore/Lower Pacific Heights/Western Addition.
- Kaiser Permanente, a nationwide multi-lingual health organization, has about ten locations in the city and more in the Bay Area; its full-service hospital is at 2425 Geary Boulevard; tel: (415) 833-2200; www.kaiserpermanente.org
- UCSF Medical Center: www.ucsfhealth.org. The University of Calfiornia has major presences in the public hospital described above and its own hospitals on Parnassus in the Sunset District, Mount Zion (off Divisidero), and its state-of-the-art hospital and research complex in Mission Bay. Other locations also offer primary, paediatric and geriatric care. For the Betty Irene Moore Women's Hospital, see Women's Health, below.
- Dignity Health Medical Group: www.dignityhealth.org/bayarea/medical-group/san-francisco operates two hospitals: St. Mary's Medical Center at 450 Stanyan Street; tel: (415) 668-1000; www.stmarymedicalcenter.org; and Saint Francis Memorial Hospital: 900 Hyde Street; tel: (415) 972-2249; www.saintfrancismemorial.org.
- San Francisco VA Medical Center: Veterans may use the services of the Veterans' Administration; contact the San Francisco Veterans' Affairs Medical Center, at 4150 Clement Street; tel: (415) 221-4810; www.sanfrancisco.va.gov.

Women's Health

The Women's Health Resource Center of University of California at San Francisco (UCSF): 2356 Sutter Street (tel:

(415) 353-2667; www.whrc.ucsf.edu/). Comprehensive health-care for women. The Women's Health Library and Resource Center offers information and classes on women's health, including a Centering Pregnancy Program.

The UCSF Betty Irene Moore Women's Hospital is part of the ultramodern UCSF Medical complex at Mission Bay: 1855 4th Street, tel: (415) 353-1664; www.ucsfmissionbayhospitals. org/women/. Treatment for the "whole woman" in a specially-designed area with green space, light-filled private rooms, a state-of-the art Birth Center.

The Womens Health Resource Center of California Pacific Medical Center at 3698 California Street also supports and treats all aspects of women's health (tel: (415) 600-0500; www. cpmc.org/services/women/whrc/) .

Natural Resources: 367 Valencia Street, is a pregnancy, childbirth, and parenting center that provides excellent resources for expectant mothers and new parents, in a shop that sells supplies for new babies (tel: (415) 550-2611; www. naturalresources-sf.com).

HIV/AIDS

It has now been more than 30 years since the first outbreak of HIV/AIDS. Unfortunately, San Francisco was hit particularly hard by the epidemic—some 20,000 people have died from it here, and there is still no cure. Fortunately, however, new medications are extending the life—and quality of life—of many HIV/AIDS patients, and San Francisco has extensive public resources for testing and care.

San Francisco General on its Ward 86 has a well-known AIDS clinic (see above) and the San Francisco City Clinic at 356 7th Street tests and treats sexually transmitted diseases at low cost or for free: tel: (415) 487-5500; www.sfcityclinic. org/.

For comprehensive information, access the website for the California HIV/AIDS Service Referrals: https://npin.cdc.gov/ca/.

- University of California San Francisco: HIV/AIDS Program: 350 Parnassus Avenue, Suite 908, tel: (415) 353-2119; https://www.ucsfhealth.org/clinics/hiv_aids_program/\. Comprehensive AIDS treatment in their "360:Positive Care Center."
- AIDS/HIV Nightline; Emotional support hot-line that is open 5:00 p.m–5:00 a.m daily; tel: (415) 434-2437.

Alternative Medicine

San Francisco is one of the foremost cities in the United States in the practice and development of alternative medicine, including Eastern techniques and homeopathic healing. Traditional Western physicians in San Francisco are open-minded, probably to a greater degree than those in other American cities.For the most part, they are willing to discuss non-traditional techniques and remedies with their patients, as well as to consider a variety of options. Some hospitals also have Eastern-oriented medical clinics, and the major insurance companies accept claims for acupuncture. Licensed acupuncturists work on their own or in conjunction with Western colleagues, and herbalists and homeopaths prescribe natural remedies. Therapeutic massage of varying internationally recognized techniques is available, as are classes for yoga and other relaxation methods.

Acupuncture, considered an alternative medicine in some countries, is considered mainstream in the United States, and chiropractic treatments for muscular and skeletal difficulties are also generally covered by health insurance carriers, depending on the condition. There are many licensed Doctors of Chiropractic in the city; it is best to ask among your friends and colleagues for a recommendation.

- American College of Traditional Chinese Medicine, 450 Connecticut Street; tel: (415) 282-9603; www.actcm.edu/. The clinic of this well-known school offers acupuncture and Chinese herb treatments.

- The Osher Center for IntegrativeMedicine: 1545 Divisadero Street, 4th floor, tel: (415) 353-7700; www.osher.ucsf.edu/. The Osher Center of UCSF provides modern care for the modern person: healthy living, for mind, body, and spirit.

Pharmacies

When you first arrive in San Francisco, have with you enough medications to tide you over until you have found a doctor and pharmacy (usually called drugstores) of your own. Foreigners should understand that many medications that are over-the-counter in other countries might require a doctor's prescription here. Ask your physician to write new prescriptions using both the trade and generic name of the medication. Bring a copy of your eyeglass prescription and an extra pair of glasses as well.

Drugstores also carry over-the-counter medications, vitamins, and familiar brands of health- and beauty-related items, plus foods, cold drinks, magazines, candies, and more. Neighborhood drug stores stay open late, depending on the traffic in their area, sometimes until 8:00 pm or 10:00 pm. The city's chain drugstores are open on Sunday, although small neighborhood pharmacies may not be. The major chain in San Francisco is Walgreens.

In the United States, when you take your prescription to a pharmacy to be filled, it is that same pharmacy that will refill it when you need a new supply. Although in some countries, the prescription is returned to you and you can refill it at any pharmacy you choose, this is not the case in America. So, make sure that the drugstore you go to is convenient for you in the future, should your prescriptions need to be refilled.

Dentists

If you don't already know dentists in San Francisco, it's best before moving to have any remaining dental work done, and bring with you current x-rays and copies of your dental records.

Until you have found a dentist of your own, you might try the clinics of the dental schools in San Francisco. Both schools listed below offer inexpensive dental care by students under the supervision of faculty dentists who have first evaluated the condition and recommended the treatment.

- University of California School of Dentistry, 707 Parnassus Street, tel: (415) 502-5800; https://www.ucsfdentalcenter. org/
- University of the Pacific Arthur A. Dugoni School of Dentistry, 155 5th Street, tel: (415) 929-6400; www.dental. pacific.edu

UP AND DOWN THE HILLS

Understanding the City

The city plan of San Francisco should not be difficult to understand. Streets are laid out in a more or less grid-like pattern, except where one of the city's 42 hills intrudes; on either side of a hill the name of a continuing street is most likely different. To understand the city, first take into consideration the role of the diagonal Market Street, which starts at the bay and cuts southwest through much of the city. North of Market, the streets are named; south of Market, the streets are numbered.

North of Market, the street names have no particular order to them; you just have to learn them. South of Market, the north/south streets start with First Street and continue regularly to 30th Street, where Twin Peaks and then Mount Davidson loom above. At Twin Peaks, Market Street changes its name to Portola, and as it winds toward Ocean Avenue, the names and contours of streets follow no system or plan.

This network of numbered streets south of Market should not be confused with what are called "The Avenues." These begin at Arguello (north of Golden Gate Park) and Stanyan (south of the park). These straight avenues run north/south from Second Avenue (there is no First Avenue) to 48th Avenue, at the edge of the sea. And intersecting with them, making orientation easier, are alphabetically consecutive streets (running east/west), starting with Anza and Balboa, and—after jumping the Park—continuing to Wawona.

If none of these make sense at first, take heart; most intersections throughout the city have large green signs above them, indicating the cross street, which is helpful when driving, for street signs may occasionally be missing or hidden by foliage. And, if you call someone for directions, ask what the "cross street" is, so that on a long street you can more easily pinpoint your destination. House numbers start with 1 at the beginning of each block. So the first building in the 1700 block of Geary might be 1701, and the first building on the next block, the 1800 block, will be 1801. Across the street will be 1702 and 1802, respectively. Even numbers are on one side of the street, odd numbers on the facing side.

Thinking about Transportation

Transportation is an important issue in San Francisco. The population of this small city swells enormously each workday, when more than 200,000 commuters file into the city—in vehicles, on ferries, on trains. Rush hours may be among the busiest in the country, as vehicle access into the city is limited to two bridges and two major highways coming up from the Peninsula. Traffic problems are further complicated by the many tourists who come to the Bay Area every year, who either bring their own cars or rent one to go out into the countryside. Thus, if you decide to live in a suburb and commute daily to the city, you will have to think strategically. In the city itself, driving and parking in the city center are difficult, depending on time of day and the number of delivery trucks double-parked—and how many of the Uber or Lyft cars are circulating. There are, however, numerous parking lots, but on a daily basis, they are also costly to use. Many people walk or use bicycles to get to work, and buses have bike racks on them. Also, banks of parking meters downtown are designated for motorcycles. Parking meter fees are due to rise, as the city is currently considering a new plan for rates.

Walking Safely

San Francisco, despite its hills, is a walking city, and people walk whenever and wherever they can. In fact, some 30,000 people walk to work each day.

According to California law, all vehicles must stop for a pedestrian in a crosswalk. (Jaywalkers in the middle of a block do not have the right of way, but this does not mean that a driver has the right to hit them.) Surprisingly, for the most part,

drivers actually obey the laws but it's still important to pay attention to traffic and cross when it is safe. Obey the traffic signals and the "Walk" or "Don't Walk" signs. Many of these signs now also blink how many seconds remain until the light changes to red, informing both drivers and pedestrians of how much time they have left to get out of the intersection.

When crossing the street, watch out for cars that are turning right on a red light, which is legal. Be sure to pay attention to cars that dash through the intersection just after the light has turned red. This has been a major problem in San Francisco, but it has abated somewhat after serious accidents happened. Do not assume that the instant the light has turned green in your direction, it is safe to cross. Be vigilant. Your safety is your own concern.

Bicycling

San Francisco rates among the top ten urban centers in the country for bicycling. The city encourages bicycling for daily transportation, and more than 35,000 San Franciscans commute regularly to work by bike. The San Francisco Municipal Transportation Agency (SFMTA) offers information on its bike share network: www.sfmta.com/getting-around/bike/bike-share.

The Ford GoBike bike-share has thousands of bikes in the Bay Area for inexpensive short-time use (www.fordgobike.com/).Join or buy one of several single passes, unlock a bike from its docking station and return it to a docking station near your destination. Get the Ford GoBike app, making it easy to know the location of the docking stations with available bikes.

The San Francisco Bicycle Coalition promotes bicycles in everyday life, and has regular meetups and events. Its website keeps cyclists up to date on all aspects of bicycling in the city (www.sfbike.org).

Electric Scooters

Note that dockless electric scooters are now in the process of acquiring permits for circulation. Companies such as Uber, Lime, Lyft, Bird are all interested in putting e-scooters on the streets. In addition to the permits and regulations, problems with docking and disposal have been cropping up, but no doubt will be solved as this new and easy transportation method takes hold.

Public Transportation

The SFMTA (generally known as "the Muni") accommodates more than a half-million passenger rides each day (info tels: 311 & 511; https://www.sfmta.com). Muni is responsible for the buses (diesel) the trolley buses (electric), the cable cars, vintage streetcars, and the city's light rail streetcars known as Muni Metro. Download the SFMTA app to keep current on transportation issues and buy your tickets.

The Fares

For a single trip, exact fare is required; if you plan another trip within 90 minutes, ask for a "transfer" while paying your fare.

Transfers to another bus, which are free, allow two additional trips within the time limit marked on them, usually about 1½ –2 hours. There are no transfers on cable cars.

For regular use of Muni, it is best to buy a refillable Clipper Card (www.clippercard.com/ClipperWeb/index.do). The card holds transit passes for the Bay Area, including BART, SamTrans and Caltrain, plus the ferry services. Add money when needed or sign up for Autoload. The card can also be linked to the Ford GoBike program.

Tourists should inquire about the various travel passes (City Pass, GoCard) that highlight the major tourist attractions, all at one price: www.sftravel.com/attraction-passes.

The Cable Car

Cable cars—a registered national landmark since 1964—contribute much to the city's charm, for tourists and locals alike. Everyone loves them: www.sfcablecar.com.

One of San Francisco's beloved cable cars with a stunning view of the glistening surface of the bay and Alcatraz Island in the background.

Although an omnibus system of horse-drawn carriages was in operation in the city by 1851, the horses could not climb the steep hills, so the summits remained out of reach as residences. Thus, the availability of sturdy, mechanized transportation affected the development of the modern city as much as its geology. In their heyday at the end of the 19th century, some 600 cable cars traversed more than 100 miles (160.9 km) of tracks, transforming the rocky heights—Nob Hill, Russian Hill—into areas of prime real estate.

Today, the cable cars continue to clang charmingly above their underground cables at just under 10 miles (16.1 km) per hour. The 40 little cars with their brass and wood fittings run for 12 miles (19.3 km) on three lines—the Powell/Mason and Powell/Hyde lines, which begin at Powell and Market and head toward Fisherman's Wharf, and the California Street line, which begins at Market and California and terminates at Van Ness. The gripman rings the bell to alert pedestrians and traffic of the cable car's arrival, and to signal a stop coming up. (If you are near Union Square in July, perhaps you will hear the gripmen's bell ringing contest!)

Wait on the sidewalk, signal the gripman to stop, and board only when the car is fully stopped. Theoretically, automobiles are supposed to stop to allow people to cross to the cable car, but they do not always, so watch carefully when stepping off the sidewalk to board. During the height of the tourist season it is hard to find a seat inside. Generally, it is the tourists who like to hang on outside in the fog and the wind, while the locals head for the inside seats.

Heritage Streetcars

And there is still more charm. When the freeway that ran along the Embarcadero was demolished in the Nineties, the entire waterfront was refurbished into the beautiful stretch it is today. This allowed the completion of a project already started, the building of a streetcar service using restored antique streetcars from the 1920s on a light rail system. Now the brightly colored streetcars are in service along the Embarcadero with the F-Market and Wharves lines running from the Castro to the Embarcadero, and along the Embarcadero to Fisherman's Wharf. The streetcars run from about 6:00 am to about 1:00 am. Along with the cable cars, they make public transportation in San Francisco fun.

The Buses

Buses run from about 5:00 am until 1:00 am (www.sfmta. com/). In the early morning hours (1:00–5:00 am), the city is serviced by its Owl Network with twenty routes connecting AC Transit, SamTrans, and the Golden Gate Bridge. (www.sfmta.com/getting-around/muni/routes-stops/muni-owl-service-late-night-transportation).

The front of each bus displays the route number/letter and name, destination, and type of service: black/white lettering indicates local buses with many stops, green/white lettering indicates limited stops, and red/white lettering means express service. Buses are numbered with their routes (e.g. 38-Geary), and streetcars are lettered (e.g. J-Church). The bus stops themselves indicate which buses/streetcars stop there and their schedules. Buses stop only at designated bus stops, and not even in the pouring rain is the driver likely to open the door for you one inch away from the bus stop.

BART

BART (Bay Area Rapid Transit) is a six-line, 121-mile commuter railway that stops at some 46 stations on its route between the East Bay and the Peninsula; info tel: (415) 989-2278; www.bart. gov). Efficiently run, BART accommodates more than more than 400,000 passengers each week—up to 129 million trips annually. Bus lines are set up throughout the Bay Area to take people directly to the BART. The service starts around 4:00 am (later on weekends) and shuts down around midnight and 1:00

Taking BART makes commuting into the city easy.

am on some routes. Check the schedules, for on weekends the service period is somewhat reduced. See also page 83 for airport transportation.

Taxis

Although some taxis roam the streets, it is still best to call a cab well in advance if you need one at an appointed time. Some hospitals, hotels, and apartment complexes have direct lines to the taxi companies, and any restaurant will call a taxi for you when you are ready to leave.

For a complete list of taxi companies, access the Muni's website (www.sfmta.com/getting-around/taxi/taxi-companies). These are generally popular:

- Flywheel Taxi (de Soto), tel: (415) 970-1300; www. flywheeltaxi.com

- Luxor Cab, tel: (415) 282-4141; www.luxorcab.com
- Green Cab, tel: (415) 626-4733 www.greencabsf.com
- Yellow Cab, tel: (415) 333-3333 http://yellowcabsf.com/

Ride-Hailing Companies

Private ride-hailing companies such as Uber and Lyft are providing efficient and more affordable options than taxis. This makes them extremely popular with the public (although not with taxi drivers) for they generally arrive within minutes of an Internet call, have options for private or the cheaper shared ride, charge much less, and are generally more pleasant. Chariot is a van commuter service that is also reliable and inexpensive.

- Uber: www.uber.com
- Lyft: www.lyft.com
- Chariot: www.chariot.com

Sharing

Owning a car to get around the city may not be the best solution, given not only the congestion and parking problems, but also economically, depending on your usage. Like the bike and e-scooter sharing programs, there are currently several on-demand car share options. And soon to be on the streets are two-seater electric "pod cars" as well.

- Zipcar: www2.zipcar.com/san-francisco
- Get Around: www.getaround.com/san-francisco

Driving Safely

Some 700,000 cars move around this small city each day, so the most important thing about driving in San Francisco is to drive defensively. The congested downtown streets, the few major arteries, and the hills and the sun in drivers' eyes all contribute to a fairly high rate of accidents.

Do not let the hills intimidate you. People drive up and down the hills every day, and some major routes go over the steepest of hills. When stopping at a traffic light while driving up a hill, leave at least ten feet between you and the car ahead, in case that car rolls back a little when starting up again. On some steep hills, you may have to downshift to maintain the car's power level, and some streets are marked with the percentage of grade and warnings to trucks not to attempt them. Make sure you have sunglasses when you drive, for at times—especially when maneuvering the hills—the sun can be blinding.

When parking on a hill, "curb your wheels." This means if your car is heading down a hill, turn the front wheels toward the curb, to keep it from rolling. If your car is heading up a hill, turn the back part of the front wheels toward the curb to keep it from rolling back down. This is a law: your car will be ticketed for not curbing your wheels. Worse, if your car rolls down a steep street, it could hurt someone.

Some downtown streets have "diamond lanes," reserved for buses and for cars turning right at the next corner. Cars may turn right on a red light, after having come to a complete stop; some streets, however, have signs saying "no turn on red." Left turn on red from a one-way street and into another one-way street is permitted under the same conditions.

Rush hours in San Francisco are generally 7:00 am–9:30 am and 3:30 pm–7:00 pm and traffic out of town is slow until early evening. Local radio and television stations report traffic conditions every few minutes during rush hours and regularly throughout the day; many have apps you can download.

Last, all car passengers must wear seat belts, and occasionally a ticket will be given for failure to do so. Babies must be strapped in a car seat in the back of the car, and children under four years of age and under 40 pounds (18.1kg) must wear a child restraint.

The Parking Problem

There may be about 800,000 cars moving around in the city each day, but there are fewer than half as many parking spaces, so parking is a major concern of residents. The closer to the bay, the harder it is to find a parking space. Downtown, parking is scarce, and the few metered spaces are generally reserved until 6:00 pm for commercial vehicles to load and unload merchandise. Do not assume that parking is free on holidays, especially in tourist areas, and do not even think about parking in a bus zone. It's best to use a parking garage—under Union Square or at Sutter/Stockton, for example.

Making the problem even worse, some major arteries prohibit parking during morning or evening rush hours; for infractions, your car will most likely be towed. These streets are usually marked with the hours you may not park, and the indication that it is a "tow-away zone." Most downtown and neighborhood streets are cleaned on certain regular days. So, you may not park there on those days. If you do, or if you forget to move your car, it will be been towed. (If you see a street on which no one is parked, do not thank your lucky stars that you found a parking space: look to see if this is street cleaning day.)

Generally, if you can avoid driving downtown, do avoid it. Take public transportation, a taxi, or one of the ride-hailing services.

Driver's Licenses and Car Registration

Residents of San Francisco—defined as people who are making their home here or who have taken a job here—must within 10 days of establishing a residence apply to the DMV (California Department of Motor Vehicles) for a California driver's license: 1377 Fell Street (tel: (800) 777-0133; www.dmv.ca.gov). If your license is from another country, you will have to take the written and practical driving test. Proof of residency is a requirement.

When you have established residency, you will need to register your car within 20 days. Details can also be had from the DMV online: www.dmv.ca.gov.

If you are staying in California for only a short time, you do not need to register your car and may drive with your own state's license plates. This may pose a problem if you are living in a neighborhood which requires parking permits to park on the street; you cannot get a permit for a car not registered in California. In this case, it is best to rent a space in a garage nearby, or to make sure in advance that your apartment has a garage space.

Automobile Insurance

California state law requires that all drivers be financially responsible for their actions while driving and for the vehicles they own; if you have an accident not covered by your insurance, your driver's license may be suspended. In fact, car dealers do not permit you to take possession of a new car without proof of liability insurance; make sure to arrange for it in advance.

If you are bringing a car with you, you may be able to transfer your policy if the company does business in California; talk in advance with your carrier. Rates vary considerably, so its best to browse car insurance companies for the details important to you.

- Allstate: www.allstate.com/auto-insurance/california-auto-insurance-coverages.aspx.
- California State Automobile Association (AAA): calstate.aaa.com.
- Farmers: www.farmers.com/california/.
- Geico: www.geico.com/information/states/ca/.
- State Farm: www.statefarm.com/.

Residential Parking

Once you have found your home, and you have registered your car, you will need permanent parking. The large apartment complexes offer parking spaces; these generally cost extra and are not included in the rental lease. In some residential districts, however, residents may park indefinitely on non-metered streets with a permit issued by Muni's Department of Parking (www.sfmta.com/services/permits-citations/parking-permits). You must have proof that the car is registered in California and that you live where you say you do. Street signs indicate the permit needed for that area, and they also specify how long non-permit cars may park during certain hours.

Accessibility

San Francisco is basically wheelchair friendly. For hills that would be difficult to navigate in non-motorized wheelchairs, transportation is easily available. Buses have operator-assisted ramps for wheelchairs, all BART stations are wheelchair accessible, and curbs throughout the city are cut to a slope for easy access to sidewalks and crosswalks. All streetcar stations are wheelchair accessible, although cable cars are not. Hotels, restaurants, and most public rest rooms have wide stalls that will accommodate wheelchairs, and most taxi companies have cabs that can accommodate wheelchairs. Check San Francisco Local Paratransit (www.sfparatransit.com).

- Golden Gate Transit has extensive information on accessibility: http://goldengatetransit.org/accessibility/.
- Access Northern California, a non-profit association that facilitates accessible travel, has information about access in Northern California: www.accessnca.com.
- The Wheelchair Travel Organization gives helpful information about getting around San Francisco: https://wheelchairtravel.org/san-francisco-ca.
- BART (Bay Area Rapid Transit) has information about its accessible services: www.bart.gov/guide/accessibility
- Muni also has information about its accessible services: www.sfmta.com/accessibility.
- Muni's Paratransit program arranges reasonably priced van taxi transportation for people who can't use public transportation: www.sfparatransit.com.

Drivers with physical disabilities may apply to the DMV for a permit to park in any of the blue-marked parking spaces reserved for drivers with disabilities. Your doctor should have a form that entitles you to such application. When accepted, you will receive a blue placard to hang on the rear-view mirror of your car.

The Call of Nature

It should not be hard to find a clean public bathroom in San Francisco. In addition to large hotels, department stores, shopping centers, supermarkets and drug stores, the city's Department of Public Works administers a network of 25 self-cleaning public toilet kiosks: www.sfpublicworks.org/services/public-toilets. These are accessible for people with disabilities.

Fast-food restaurants, bars, and coffee shops may expect you to purchase at least a cup of coffee to use their rest rooms, and some small restaurants on the tourist path have clear signs indicating that rest rooms are for customers only. Rest rooms at service stations may require that you ask the attendant for an access key. In most places, if you ask to use a rest room, you will not be refused.

Shops, restaurants, and a spectacular bay view please the crowds at Pier 39, near Fisherman's Wharf.

CHAPTER 6

FOOD LOVERS' HAVEN

You can't have a bad meal in this town.

— Emeril Lagasse

GASTRONOMIC SUPERLATIVES

San Francisco—The Best?

San Franciscans believe their city to be the gastronomic capital of America. Residents of a few other American cities may dispute this, of course, but the seemingly endless numbers of people who reserve their tables two months in advance at the city's finest restaurants and the repeated rankings by national magazines tend to confirm that San Francisco's offerings rise to the top. But how has this come to pass? The answer is itself a stew, combining the city's particular geography, climate, history—and attitude.

Begin with the ingredients: the region's moderate climate and the city's proximity to lush, fertile, agricultural lands, to the Pacific Ocean, and to the country's top wine-producing region. See the fishing boats coming in early each morning to the piers off Jefferson Street, and you will never doubt that the fish is fresh, year-round. Drive south or east, passing the rich vegetable farms and flourishing orchards that supply the city's restaurants directly, and you can tell what is in season and what will be on the menu at that time. Or pass the miles of grape-laden vines as you head up to warm, sunny Napa or Sonoma—just an hour north of the city—and then don't be surprised to find outstanding wines produced by those vineyards in restaurants all over town.

Now stir in a bit of history. From its earliest days, San Francisco was a town where people ate out. It started with the Gold Rush, when thousands of miners with gold nuggets in their pockets, came down from the hills for a taste of "civilization" and "home cooking". Even at that time, the cooks were immigrants—Italians, Hungarians, French, and then Chinese—melding their own cooking traditions with the ingredients locally found. After the flurries of the Gold Rush and the Silver Rush died down, eating establishments remained.

Since then, each wave of immigrants has added to the aromas of the city. Today, with categories more specific, you'll hear appellations such as "East Meets West", Cal-Asian, "contemporary American", "Indian-Mexican" or "modern Moroccan". What matters, no matter the definition—even the slightly passé term "fusion"—is that each flavor contributes to the overall dish served, yet is identifiable in itself. In fact, fusion of cultures, cuisines, and traditions without losing any of them is what has always defined the city itself.

Food here can be high art. What was first known as California Cuisine originated at Berkeley's Chez Panisse, which continues to epitomize this trend. Emphasizing regional, in-season ingredients, California Cuisine—or Modern California as it's coming to be called—presents a beautiful yet simple-seeming and healthy effect, although the exotic combinations of ingredients and presentation may not be simple at all.

In fact, San Francisco's ground-breaking restaurants have moved into exquisite new territory, with elaborate tasting menus that demonstrate what the chef can create with locally-sourced ingredients and wholesome combinations, Some don't even bother to distinguish the names of courses (appetizers, entrees, etc), as this staid tradition may no longer fit the sequence of the offerings.

Attitude of San Franciscans

Adding spice to the answer of why San Francisco's restaurants are so exceptional is that San Franciscans demand it. San Franciscans love to eat out—at restaurants of all levels—and with a median household income hovering around $100,000, residents spend about 10 per cent per year eating out. Thus, no one needs to settle for just a "good dinner". Although it is not true that San Francisco has more restaurants than people, it may well have more restaurants per capita than other cities. Thus, diners get to choose and set the tone. In fact, the city works on the premise that the entire experience of eating should mirror the city's image. San Franciscans consider eating out to be one of their major cultural experiences, and they demand and get the best.

"The best" does not necessarily mean the most expensive or those that are lavishly reviewed—although those may be truly awesome. A Thai restaurant out in the Avenues might have the "best" lemongrass soup or garlic noodles, and an otherwise undistinguished-looking Italian storefront might well have outstanding calamari. Other places may tickle diners' fancy with their imaginative decor, and many now are providing entertainment of one sort of another along with the dining experience. San Francisco Travel Association has an interesting list of restaurants by neighbourhood: http://www.sftravel.com/article/san-franciscos-iconic-eats-every-neighborhood.

Also, particularity rules. Gone are the days when Italian food meant spaghetti with tomato sauce; choose among Ligurian, Roman or Tuscan-style. No longer does Chinese food mean Chicken Fried Rice; now San Franciscans pick carefully among Hunan, Chiu Chow, Cantonese or the extra-spicy Hunan cuisines. San Franciscan restaurants demonstrate a strong sense of place.

But even the cuisines do not tell the entire story. San Franciscans demand that the food they eat should be healthy and well-presented, whether it is a luxurious dinner in a beautifully designed restaurant, a casual meal in a neighborhood gastropub, or—the current trend—a tasting menu. What San Franciscans want, in short, is everything all at once: appetising and healthful food imaginatively prepared, a splendid view, an attractive space, and friendly service. If San Franciscans, as some people claim, "want everything now", at least in terms of dining out, they seem to be able to get it.

Resources

Checking the restaurant reviews and diners' comments on the Internet is helpful, and websites of the various restaurants not only describe their offerings, they often note any culinary events they may have in the offing, and some describe their sister restaurants; the Big Night group, for example, contains Marlowe, Petit Marlowe Wine Bar & Oysterette, Leo's Oyster Bar, Park Tavern, Marianne, and the Cavalier, every one of them worth exploring (www.bignightgroup.com). The Hi Neighbor Group is in four different neighborhoods (www.hineighborsf.com), and some have multiple locations, such as the Delfina Restaurant Group, serving some of the tastiest pizza in town (www.pizzeriadelfina.com). For news, the Daniel Patterson Group has several restaurants and more to come: www.dpgrp.co/.

Bon Appetit!

Of the more than 4000 eating establishments in this gastronomic heaven called San Francisco, only about 150 could be described in these several sections devoted to nectar and ambrosia. Alas, there is not enough room. So, think of the pleasurable exploration you have in store, and start the process.

Many restaurants have their own websites, usually displaying the menus, and hundreds have been reviewed by such media as Yelp or Trip Advisor or Zagats. And Internet lists of the 10 or 20 "best" in every category abound. So, when you hear of a place that interests you, head for your browser before you head out the door. Consider subscribing to some of the email free subscriptions for news of openings and closings of restaurants.

- www.zagat.com/san-francisco.
- www.tablehopper.com/
- www.sfgate.com/food
- https://sf.eater.com/
- www.theinfatuation.com/san-francisco
- www.thrillist.com/san-francisco
- www.sftravel.com/explore/dining
- www.happycow.com
- www.vegsf.com.

Note that all eating establishments here are mentioned by location, so they're easy to find. And see the entries with the ✦. They each have something that makes them particularly interesting, whether the food or the ambience.

Reserving a Table

Most restaurants require reservations some as far as one or two months in advance, and if you do not call exactly when specified, you might be too late. As a general rule, the better the restaurant, those with a view, or ones that have special events, the longer in advance you should book.

Of course, you can make reservations directly from the website of most of the restaurants. Yet, reserving online is an easy option. Choose the restaurant you are interested in, and the day and time you want. You will find out immediately whether there are any tables available and, if not, when the next one will be.

- www.opentable.com
- www.exploretock.com
- www.reserve.com
- www.yelp.com

Yet, tables may be available at off-hours, such as 5:45 pm or 10:00 pm. And there is no harm in calling the restaurant itself to see whether there has been a cancellation. Some restaurants reserve a few tables for "walk-ins," and many serve at the bar.

Most neighbourhood restaurants can accommodate you if you reserve the day before or even on the same day; but even if you don't reserve, you can wait for a table to be vacated. Restaurants generally figure 90 minutes for a couple to remain at a table and two hours for a party of four. When you put your name on the list, the maître d'hôtel ("maitre d'") will be as honest as possible—given the unpredictable time a party may linger—in assessing the wait time.

Dress is generally casual, and it is rare to find a man wearing a suit. In the most fashionable restaurants, a man might wear a sports jacket and women either a dress or slacks and a fashionable top. In any case, it is always good to dress appropriately to the establishment and the occasion. One casual

East Bay establishment once humorously advertised, "food so good, you might want to wear your nice jeans."

Opening Times

Most of the large restaurants serve dinner every day, although some close one day a week. Many restaurants don't open until 5:30 pm, skipping lunch altogether, and others may serve lunch only on weekdays. Check the websites for the opening times of a restaurant that interests you.

San Francisco is an "early town". As the Pacific Time Zone is three hours behind New York's financial markets, financial workers start their day before dawn and eat lunch and dinner early, and because people most often dine before performances, not after, do not expect to get into restaurants around the Union Square or Civic Center in the early evening (or on days when there are matinees), unless you reserve in advance. On the other hand, you can generally get a table if you are willing to eat a little later, after a performance has started.

Restaurants start to serve breakfast around 6:30 am and begin lunch at 11:30 am, some closing for a while between lunch and dinner. Dinner service starts at 5:30 pm, taking last orders around 10:30 pm.

For a young and more flexible population, however, more restaurants of all levels and cuisines are beginning to stay open late, at least until 1:00 am, some until the wee hours. https://sf.eater.com/maps/best-late-night-food-restaurants-san-francisco.

The Menu

The menu depends on the season. Some restaurants print their menus daily, and in others, servers recite the list of that day's special dishes. These invariably reflect the fishermen's catch and fresh, seasonable produce, as well as what is most environmentally-friendly and locally-sourced. See the box on page 157. And for menus of dozens of San Francisco restaurants, access www.allmenus.com/ca/san-francisco/.

Do not hesitate to ask how a dish is prepared, and in the case of an oral recitation of the specials, to ask the price, if the server omits it. This includes asking the price of the wine even if you just order a glass of the house wine. It is best not to be surprised.

If you have dietary restrictions, specify them when you make the reservation or to the server when ordering so that you can be assured of eating a meal that is appropriate for you. Many menus now are indicating with a small symbol which dishes are gluten- or lactose-free, and a few—like the interesting pan-Asian E&O Kitchen at 314 Sutter Street—have special gluten-free menus. Ask your questions when ordering, for in general, you send back a meal only if it is not cooked properly or if it is different from its description on the menu.

Order only as much as you want. Restaurants are used to people ordering two appetizers, to splitting appetizers and main courses, or just an appetizer and a dessert. And every establishment, from the grungiest dive to the fashionable temples of gastronomy, will wrap your leftovers to take home.

Although many countries would roll their eyes at this, coffee here may be served at any time during daytime meals and at dinner generally with the dessert, not after. Tea drinking is becoming trendy, so your restaurant may show a box with a selection of teas and herbal infusions.

Happiest of Hours

The "happy hour" is a crowded few hours at the bar of many restaurants of all levels, offering lower-priced drinks and a selection of the restaurant's specialties for snacking. Many people meet after work for a convivial time together, eating and drinking well, while paying less and getting home at a reasonable hour. The restaurants' websites generally announce the times for the happy hour.

In restaurants, wine is sold by the glass and by the bottle (usually 750 ml). Depending on how much you drink, it can make economic sense to order a bottle of wine for two people, as there are four 6 oz. servings in a bottle, and the cost is perhaps 20 per cent less than four single glasses.

What Will It Cost?

Prices vary wildly, from perhaps $30 for two to up to well more than a thousand. As with most things, you get what you pay for. Asian eateries may list a nourishing and pleasant lunchtime special of soup, a main course with plenty of rice, plus tea for about $10. The same holds true in the Latino eateries, although not in the more "Modern Mexican" restaurants. At the far distant end of the scale, however, an outstanding, memorable experience may cost upwards of $500 per person.

Do not, however, be discouraged: most prices are definitely in between. An average two-person three-course dinner tab is currently about $80, on a par with New York; for that price you will get a high-quality meal with the freshest of ingredients, no doubt well-prepared and nicely presented. What matters to San Francisco diners is value for the money, and in general, eating out in San Francisco is an affordable and delectable pastime. The menus on the restaurants' websites generally give the prices for each dish.

Yet, even that is not all there is. Throughout the chapter look for the "fast food" sidebars, the "three B's": burritos, banh mi, and burgers. Order them the way you like them, eat in or on the go, and you won't stretch the budget. Even fast food here can be special.

Credit Cards/Tipping

All major restaurants accept credit cards. Visa and MasterCard are the most widely accepted, along with American Express. In the United States the tip is generally not included in the bill, although some restaurants avoid the question by including the tip in the bill. Some will add 15–20 per cent for a party of at least six people. A few, like Zazie (see page 167) have foregone tips entirely. Yet, the standard tip is 15–25 per cent, depending on level of service; 20 per cent is generally common for good service. Look at the bill carefully: the sales tax added at the bottom is 8.5 per cent, and many people don't tip on that portion of the bill.

It is best not to assume that the small Asian eateries accept credit cards. Even some of the local neighborhood restaurants do not, so call ahead or carry enough cash. In some Chinese eateries, you may not understand the bill because it is written in Chinese on a small slip of paper only somewhat resembling a bill. On the other hand, the amount may be so cheap—about $22 for two people—that a rarely-made mistake of a few cents wouldn't matter much, and arguing probably wouldn't get you very far.

THE CITY'S SPECIALTIES

Dungeness Crab

The season (November–May) for the sweet, meaty Dungeness crab is eagerly awaited, and people keep track of the weather, for stormy weather makes for a bad catch. Cracked crab, served cold with a cocktail or butter sauce, or the beloved Crab Louie, a Dungeness crab salad with a Thousand Island-type dressing, are the well-deserved standards. Asian restaurants serve well-sauced crab dishes, and the three establishments below are often seen as among the best for roast crab. And pay attention to the various crab fests when Dungeness crab is highlighted in restaurants all around the city.

- Polk Gulch—Crustacean: 1475 Polk Street,
  tel: (415) 776-2722
- Outer Sunset—Thanh Long: 4101 Judah Street,
  tel: (415) 665-1146
- Outer Richmond—PPQ Dungeness Island: 2332 Clement Street, tel: (415) 386-8266

Cioppino

If every fishing port has its favorite seafood soups, San Francisco's is cioppino, a hearty fish stew based loosely on the Ligurian ciuppin. Basically, cioppino features locally-caught crab in season, other fresh shellfish and fish, all stewed in a spicy tomato broth. ✦ Worth a visit is The Old Clam House: 299 Bayshore Boulevard at Oakdale Ave, tel: (415) 826-4880. The Old Clam House has been serving its oysters, clam chowders and clam bake since 1861, including its own delectable cioppino. Other than the three listed below, dozens of others, of course, have their own tasty versions.

- North Beach—Sotto Mare: 552 Green Street,
  tel: (415) 398-3181.
- Lower Pacific Heights—Woodhouse Fish Co: 1914 Fillmore Street; and 2073 Market Street, tel: (415) 437-2722.
- Wharf—Cioppino's: 400 Jefferson Street, tel: (415) 775-9311.

Hangtown Fry

Few restaurants serve this San Francisco specialty that dates back to the Gold Rush days when miners wanted a dish that could be made in one pan: an omelette stuffed with oysters and bacon. Now, often the oysters are breaded and fried first and then folded in, and other ingredients might be added. No matter, it's still Hangtown Fry.

- Dogpatch—Just For You Café: 732 22nd Street; tel: (415) 647-3033. Open for breakfast and lunch and a well-known Sunday brunch, the cinnamon raisin bread alone is worth the trip. Just For You does a good Hangtown fry, and there's other unusual breakfast fare such as catfish or pork chops—and the mimosas—keeping all comers happy.
- Fi-Di—✦ Tadich Grill: 240 California Street, tel: (415) 391-1849. Hangtown fry is a speciality in this restaurant dating back to 1849, making it the oldest in the city. Seafood dishes include a mouth-watering Crab Louie and an excellent cioppino. Reserve or be prepared to wait or eat at the bar.
- Union Square—John's Grill: 63 Ellis Street, tel: (415) 986-0069. John's Hangtown fry goes well with its oldtime, retro ambience, as does the "Joe's special" another popular omelette made with ground beef, spinach and mushrooms. Dashiell Hammett ate here, and the Sam Spade lamb chops are a specialty.

Sourdough Bread

During the Gold Rush and silver mining years, bakers discovered that their bread tasted different—slightly sour—and everyone liked it. The yeast starter—now officially labelled L.sanfranciscensis—is used today and has become part of the city's lore. Today's San Franciscans love their sourdough, they know which of the crusty outside and softly-dense inside loaf is their favourite, and they line up at the city's bakeries to get it—warm and fresh. Boudin Bakery & Café, at 160 Jefferson Street, in business since 1849, is a well-known tourist spot for its clam chowder in a sourdough bowl; if it's not always rated at the top anymore, it's nonetheless worth a trip for the old-time flavour, and fun. Some of the city's current favorites—and rightly so—are:

- Alamo Square—Josey Baker Bread at the Mill: 736 Divisadero Street, tel: (415) 345-1953

- Mission—Tartine: 600 Guerrero Street, tel: (415) 487-2600
- Noe Valley—Noe Valley Bakery: 4073 24th Street,
  tel: (415) 550-1405

It's It Ice Cream Sandwich

Almost a century ago in a small shop in San Francisco, a scoop of vanilla ice cream was placed between two large oatmeal cookies and then dipped in dark chocolate. The "It's It" was born and has ever since been a favorite of San Franciscans, and now others worldwide. Today, you can find It's It in the city's supermarkets, but there are other local ice cream purveyors that now draw the aficionados, with unusual flavors and combinations fit for this century's crowds:

- Hayes Valley—Smitten: 432 Octavia Street,
  tel: (415) 863-1518
- Mission—BiRite Creamery: 3692 18th Street,
  tel: (415) 626-5600
- Mission—Humphry Slocombe: 2790 Harrison Street,
  tel: (415) 550-6971 and the Ferry Building
- Russian Hill—Swensen's: 199 Hyde Street,
  tel: (415) 775-6818
- SoMa—Coletta Gelato: 685 Harrison Street,
  tel: (415) 795-3170

Chocolate

Ghirardelli Chocolate has been a San Francisco staple for 150 years, first in a small store on the Barbary Coast, and later in its own large building that now is the landmark Ghirardelli Square. Their scrumptious chocolates became known nationwide, and in 1999 the company became part of the Swiss company Lindt & Sprungli, bringing about a worldwide success. Ghirardelli keeps its original Ice Cream & Chocolate Shop at Ghirardelli Square and some outlets around the city, but new local chocolatiers are taking over the forefront with San Franciscans. Their modern and unusual "bean-to-bar" and boxed artisanal combinations are definitely hard to resist. (And why should we?)

- Ferry Building—Dandelion: Kiosk in the Ferry Building Marketplace, and 740 Valencia Street (at 18th), tel: (415) 349-0942
- Ferry Building—Recchiuti Confections: Ferry Building, tel: (415) 834-9494; and 801 22nd Street, tel: (415) 489-2281
- SoMa—Socola Chocolatier: 535 Folsom Street, tel: (415) 400-4071
- North Beach—XOX Truffles: 754 Columbus Avenue, tel: (415) 421-4814

WHAT'S HOT—OR COLD

If you are someone who tends to look for what's new—what's the hottest San Francisco trend—you'll find that here the search never ends. But "trendy" lasts longer than "new," so even if a guidebook can't show the newest of the new—which change with the wind—it can show the trends that have taken hold. These few examples in single categories may indeed overlap with other categories, for restaurateurs realize how eclectic are the tastes of their diners, and they work to provide always what's freshest, different and special. Places noted for brunch may also have great dinners; in fact, many restaurants—no matter their category—may also highlight their craft cocktails. So these few examples—among the qualified thousands—are only meant to be representative of concepts to be found throughout the city. For diners' updated "hottest" restaurants at any time, access www.zagat.com/l/the-10-hottest-new-restaurants-in-san-francisco.

Spectacular Views

First, understand that San Franciscans never tire of looking at the water, whether it be the bay or the ocean. Clearly, in a city with water on three sides and hills that soar, there is a view wherever you go. In many places, the food is as good as the view. Be sure to reserve, especially at places with patios—so coveted on warm sunny days—and enjoy the food while feeling a true San Franciscan. For panoramic views, some of the major hotels—the Mark Hopkins, the Fairmont, the Hyatt—have rooftop bars and restaurants, exquisite at night.

- Oceanside—Beach Chalet: 1000 Great Ocean Highway, tel: (415) 386-8439. This micro-brewery overlooking the ocean waves serves casual New American food. First look at the beautiful murals from the 1930s on the ground floor, and then go up to the restaurant with its sampler of house-made brews.

- Oceanside—Cliff House: 1090 Point Lobos, tel: (415) 386-3330. Rebuilt several times since 1863, the Cliff House has the closest ocean view in town. Casual or formal restaurants, a Sunday champagne buffet, jazz on Friday nights—the Cliff House can be all things to all people.

- Embarcadero—The Ferry Building right on the bay has both fine and fun restaurants, for an afternoon by the water. Check out the shops and among the eateries, the splendid Hog Island Oyster Bar (tel: 415-391-7117) where you will no doubt have to wait in line, and the noted Vietnamese restaurant Slanted Door where you can reserve in advance (tel: 415-861-8032).
- North Embarcadero—Pier 23 Café, tel: (415) 362-5125. This longtime casual bar is a must all day long. Tables outside, live music in the evenings, and a good weekend brunch. On sunny, warm days sit outside for the crab cakes, fish tacos and clam chowder.
- North Embarcadero—✦ La Mar: Pier 1½, tel: (415) 397-8880. Striking upmarket Peruvian seafood restaurant, with its Latin interpretations, plus a dynamite Pisco cocktail, served too at the happy hour. Patio right by the bay.
- South Embarcadero—✦ Waterbar: 399 the Embarcadero, tel: (415) 284-9922, A view, a terrace, and smartly-prepared sustainable seafood and oysters galore. If it's full, eat at the bar, with its own classy view of the bay.
- South Embarcadero—The Ramp, 885 Terry Francois Street in Dogpatch, tel: (415) 621-2378. At the city's working port, this more-than-casual eatery and bar is beloved by locals. Burgers, salads, a crab sandwich and its famous Bloody Mary. Enjoy live music on weekend afternoons, along with their special barbeque,

Organic

For healthy eating for people and the planet, diners are looking for signals on the menu such as "organic, locally-sourced, no genetically modified foods (non-GMO) Paleo diet, low-fat, gluten- or lactose-free, or vegan. For a sampling of the city's truly excellent vegetarian/vegan restaurants, access www.sftravel.com/article/best-spots-san-francisco-vegetarian-diningwww.sftravel.com. ✦ Greens: Fort Mason, Building A, tel: (415) 771-6222. In this San Francisco classic, the outstanding vegetarian creations all have a "Zen" flavour, enhanced by the floor-to-ceiling windows overlooking the Bay.

The Plant Café has several locations (www.theplantcafe. com). Serving 100% organic American food with some Asian influences, the Plant Café uses sustainable seafood and meats from local sources and ethical farms.

- Mission—Gracias Madre: 2211 Mission Street, tel: (415) 683-1346. All organic, locally-sourced and plant-based Mexican food.
- Mission—Shizen Vegan Sushi and Izakaya: 370 14th Street, tel: (415) 678-5767. Fish-free sushi. A minimalist atmosphere, plus the friendliness of the Izakaya, give the same detail you'd expect in a regular sushi bar.
- Nopa—Nopa: 560 Divisadero, tel: (415) 864-8643. Organic, sustainable, and a weekly-created menu of wood-fired seasonal ingredients draw people for the generous portions at dinners and Sunday brunch.

Wagyu beef

Again for healthy eating, add the current focus on Wagyu beef from Kobe, Japan. Wagyu has more monounsaturated fats and omegas 3 and 6 than normal beef. The fat is softer, rendering the meat tender and rich in flavor. Some sushi bars also serve Wagyu beef.

- FiDi—Akiko's Restaurant and Sushi Bar: 431 Bush Street, tel: (415) 397-3218. Excellent sushi with an omekase option, and tender Wagyu beef dishes in the heart of the Financial District. Rated one of the best.
- ✦ South Embarcadero—Epic Steak: 369 the Embarcadero, tel: (415) 369-9955. Superlatives only for this restaurant with its sourced ingredients, beautifully prepared. Its best Wagyu beef cuts are both wholesome and wonderful, all served with a splendid view of the bay.

- ✦ Jackson Square—5A5 Steak Lounge: 244 Jackson Street, tel: (415) 989-2539. Combining traditional methods with contemporary presentations at this superb steakhouse. Steak cuts from around the world—including those of the highest quality A5Wagyu—are popular, as is its happy hour, an opportunity to taste its upscale offerings.

Crudo

People are enjoying more their food raw—with sushi and raw bars, carpaccios, tartares, raw fish salads, and other raw—or marinated—dishes. Some of the seafood restaurants have extensive raw bars with succulent oysters, the most coveted. Japanese restaurants, of course, have other raw dishes as part of or outside of their normal sushi menus. And poke (see below), is a recent welcome addition. But for oysters, Franciscans know where they come from, which selections are in season at the moment, and where to get them. Of course the Hog Island Oyster Bar and the Waterbar, mentioned above are remarkable, and oysters feature in some happy hours. ✦ Farallon is one of the city's top seafood restaurants with an oyster selection at happy hour: 450 Post Street, tel: (415) 956-6969.

- Bernal Heights—Red Hill Station: 803 Cortland Avenue, tel: (415) 757-0480. More than a neighbourhood eatery, Red Hill Station's seafood draws a crowd for its oyster shooters, tartares, pot pie samplers, and its mouth-watering cioppino.
- Nopa—Bar Crudo: 655 Divisadero Street, tel: (415) 409-0679. Raw bar at its best, with oysters, shellfish and combinations deliciously imagined, hot dishes, and a seafood chowder that's a more-than-satisfying meal in itself.
- Polk Gulch—Swan Oyster Depot: 1517 Polk Street, tel: (415) 673-1101. Lunch only at the counter of this

revered family-owned century-old fish market. Watch the oysters being shucked, and order a bowl of the outstanding chowder or one of its various seafood salads. A San Francisco institution, to say the least.

- The Castro—Anchor Oyster Bar: 579 Castro Street, tel: (415) 431-3990. Marvellous oysters, chowders and cioppino in this small restaurant that has become a classic.

Poke

Poke (pronounced poh-keh) is a Hawaiian newcomer, with cubed raw and marinated fish topping a bowl of rice, with various vegetable and sauces. Find poke in restaurants and in some of the small take-out eateries downtown for a fast, healthy lunch. The Market in the Twitter Building on Market Street, for example, has a poke stand with several choices.

✦ For an authentic Hawaiian ambience, try the Liholiho Yacht Club, at 871 Sutter Street on Lower Nob Hill (tel: (415) 440-5446. Known for its poke and its ohana family-style menu. Bar seating is first-come first-served.

- Duboce Triangle: I'a Poke: 314 Church Street, tel: (415) 829-8030. Excellent and varied poke bowls, interesting sushi burritos, and even a Hawaiian spam musubi. Other addresses.

IS YOUR CRAB HANDLING A LITTLE RUSTY AT THE START OF THE SEASON?

Dungerness crab is a popular delicacy served at San Francisco's Fisherman's Wharf. Watching the chefs prepare the dish is a tourist attraction in itself.

- Inner Sunset—Poke Origin: 716 Irving Street, tel: (415) 702-6328. Choose your own base and mix-ins, add your protein and toppings, however you like your poke.

Seafood

Living on the Pacific, people love fish, but only the freshest and sustainable. Here, categories definitely overlap—with sushi bars, restaurants with views, Chinese restaurants with crab and fish specialties, raw bars, and more. But look for the popular seafood restaurants in the local neighborhoods:

- Castro—Catch: 2362 Market Street, tel: (415) 431-5000. A casual and varied menu at lunch, and at dinner a well-prepared fresh seafood selection with a Mediterranean attitude.

- FiDi—Sam's Grill: 374 Bush Street, tel: (415) 421-0594.
  For well more than a century, Sam's has served fish, all
  wild and all fresh—try the rex sole and their Crab Louie.
- Outer Richmond—Pacific Café: 7000 Geary Boulevard,
  tel: (415) 387-7091. It may look old-fashioned, but the fish
  dishes are up-to-date, fresh, and they always hit the spot.
  A longtime neighbourhood favourite.
- Western Addition—Alamo Square: a Seafood Grill: 803
  Fillmore Street, tel: (415) 440-2828. Fish any way you like
  it at this French seafood bistro near the famous Painted
  Ladies and the refurbished Alamo Square Park.

Tasting Menu

The tasting menu has moved on from the "tapas" small-plate
concept. Not for sharing, the prolific "tasting menu," prepares
for each diner a small portion of many of its daily-chosen ingredients, combined by the chef into innovative creations. The
number of dishes can range from four to fifteen, depending on
the restaurant. The fixed-price varies according to the level of
the restaurant; with the Michelin three-star restaurants listed
below, for example, if you add the carefully-chosen "wine pair-
ings"—the appropriate wine for each type of dish—the price
can seem astronomical. But you're getting a true look at the
quality of the restaurant and the originality of the chef. See
"The Stars," below.

- Fisherman's Wharf—Gary Danko: 800 North Point Street,
  tel: (415) 749-2060. New American Cuisine in one of the
  first of the luxury restaurants with a quality tasting menu.
  Although there are no pretensions here, it is more casual
  at the bar.
- The Mission—Prubechu: 2847 Mission Street,
  tel: (415) 952-3654. This authentic Guamanian
  establishment features the country's Chamarro food,
  and its reasonably-priced tasting menu demonstrates
  its variety. Good list of microbrews.

The Burger

It wouldn't be San Francisco if it didn't have its own take on America's much loved hamburger. From the McDonalds-type chains to the elegant restaurants, burgers are a must, one time or another. Even the most upscale restaurants have their special burgers, and neighborhood eateries satisfy their regular customers who know which ranch the beef comes from, which cheese suits their tastes, the kind of bun they like, and the add-ons and sauces they prefer. Don't forget the fries—regular or sweet potato.

- Cow Hollow—Maybeck's: 3213 Scott Street, tel: (415) 4000-8500.
- Ingleside: Beep's Burgers: 1051 Ocean Avenue, tel: (415) 584-2650
- Marina: Roam Artisan Burgers: 1785 Union Street, tel: (415) 440-7626
- Mid Market—✦ Zuni Café, 1658 Market Street; tel: (415) 552-2522.
- Outer Richmond: Bill's Place, 2315 Clement Street; tel: (415) 221-5262.
- SoMa—Marlowe: 500 Brannan Street, tel: (415) 777-1413.
- Western Addition—4505 Burgers & BBQ: 705 Divisadero, tel: (415) 231-6993.

- The Mission—✦ Californios: 3115 22nd Street, tel: (415) 757-0994. In this Michelin-starred intimate Mexican restaurant, the 15 course tasting menu is locally-sourced and remarkable.
- Pacific Heights—SPQR: 1911 Fillmore Street, tel: (415) 771-7779. Five innovative pasta dishes to taste in this excellent Italian restaurant, with other well-created dishes and an interesting wine selection.

Omakase & Kaiseki Sushi

With the Japanese *omekase* fixed-price tasting menu, the sushi chef prepares his own personal creations, again from carefully sourced and selected ingredients. Kaiseki continues the small plate concept, Japanese style. Omakase at its best features chef-selected freshest, seasonal ingredients of the day in an extensive presentation. For a unique Tokyo-style experience: the Michelin-starred Sushi Hashiri; 4 Mint Plaza, tel: (415) 908-1919. But many others that couldn't be mentioned serve excellent *omekase*. If you reserve, be sure to arrive on time.

- FiDi—Kusakabe: 584 Washington Street, tel: (415) 757-0155. Two seatings at this traditional sushi restaurant that highlights its seasonality and harmonious creations.
- Inner Richmond—✦ Wako Omakase: 211 Clement Street, tel: (415) Small, welcoming and upscale sushi bar, offering omakase small plates, in modern-Japanese style.
- Western Addition—Ju-Ni: 1335 Fulton Street: tel, (415) 655-9924. An innovative cross-cultural omekase experience from an American-born modern chef.

The Mission

Once patronized only for its Mexican street food, the Mission has become a permanent fashionable destination for much more. For taquerias, see the box on page 173.

- Delfina: 3621 18th Street, tel: (415) 552-4055. Small, reasonably priced, and friendly restaurant serving simple yet elegant Tuscan specialties.
- El Nuevo Frutilandia: 3077 24th Street, tel: (415) 648-2958. In this Cuban/Puerto Rican eatery, it's worth a visit for the ceviche, empanadas, alcapurrias (yucca and ground beef), and more Caribbean specialties in this perennial favorite.
- Loló: 974 Valencia Street, tel, (415) 881-0590. Specializing in recipes from Jalisco on the Pacific. All the foods and craft cocktails use seasonal ingredients, with well-concocted tequilas and mezcal drinks.
- Panchita's Pupuseria No2: 3091 16th Street, tel: (4150 431-4232) Here are the corn pupusas of El Salvador, with a variety of fillings of your choice. And there are others, such a yucca root with port, and plantain pies.
- Lolinda: 2518 Mission Street, tel: (415) 550-6970. Modern Argentinian steak house, with excellent meats wood-fired on the grill, with Latin and California flavors. The modern and classic cocktails bring the same sensibilities.

- CatHead's BBQ, 1665 Folsom, near 12th Street;
tel: (415) 861-4242. Southern country cooking in the Inner
Mission (or outer SoMa). Tender ribs, Pulled pork, biscuits,
and a smoked lamb shoulder.

Pizza

Once you've tasted the pizza in San Francisco, you'll see why
it's listed as trendy. Exotic toppings mirror San Franciscans'
tastes; pizza is definitely a "go-to" destination. ♦ Some Italian
restaurants such as A16 in the Marina offer Neapolitan pizzas
every bit as delicious as their other courses: 2355 Chestnut
Street, tel: (415) 771-2216.

- Dogpatch—Long Bridge: 2347 3rd Street, tel: (415) 829-
8999. Thin-crust pies, and an outstanding meatball sub.
- Glen Park—Gialina Pizzeria: 2842 Diamond Street,
tel: (415) 239-8500. Neapolitan pizzas with seasonal
toppings, gluten-free crusts.
- Mission—Pauline's: 260 Valencia Street, near 14th,
tel: (415) 552-2050. Here, the pesto pizza here has long
been an insider's favorite.
- North Beach—Tommaso's: 1042 Kearny Street, tel: (415)
398-9696. The city's oldest pizzeria and some say still the
best.
- North Beach—Golden Boy Pizza: 542 Green Street,
tel: (415) 982-9738. Doughy squares of Sicilian pizza.
No atmosphere and no amenities. Just go for the pizza.
- North Beach—Capo's Pizza: 641 Vallejo Street, tel: (415)
986-8998. Deep dish or pan pizza, or "cracker thin," plus
Chicago-style Italian dishes.
- Potrero Hill—Goat Hill Pizza: 300 Connecticut at 18th
Street, tel: (415) 641-1440. A decades-long favorite:
crunchy sourdough crust pizzas and all you can eat on
Monday nights.

Breakfast and Brunch

During the week, restaurants serve breakfasts. But the Sunday brunch is a city-wide social occasion that draws crowds to restaurants that strive to entice with their exotic eggy combinations, their craft cocktails, and a fun atmosphere—all intended to make Sunday morning as "San Francisco" as can be. ✦ For a great Irish breakfast, including corned beef hash and an Irish bacon & eggs sandwich, try the Chieftain. Basically an Irish pub, with its libations it also creates a formidable lamb chilli. 198 5th Street, tel: (415) 625-0436.

- Cole Valley—Zazie: 941 Cole Street, tel: 564-5332. No tips here in this employee-friendly French bistro with a garden patio. Serving brunch daily, its differing versions of Eggs Benedict can be served on gluten-free muffins.
- Outer Sunset—Outerlands: 4001 Judah Street, tel: (415) 661-6140. Bringing crowds to the fog belt for dinners, but even more for its the weekend brunch, with its homemade pastries and organic fare.
- Polk Gulch—Brenda's French Soul Food: 652 Polk Street, tel: (415) 345-8100. New Orleans dishes—Creole, French, and Southern—are happily featured here, with Brenda's signature beignet, for a remarkably tasty brunch.

Ramen

It may seem passé, but with all its varieties and tastes, ramen is clearly back in fashion. Traditional and regional recipes mixed with delicious ingredients, ramen hits the spot, especially on those foggy and windy San Francisco nights. The specially-seasoned broths are the base, varying according to the different eateries, as do the artisan noodles and the type of meat—the succulent pork, chicken or seafood (and even vegetarian options), plus the other ingredients added in. Some of the izakayas serve ramen, and of course, other Japanese restaurants do, too. Although you'll find satisfying ramen throughout the city—in the izakayas as well—The Japantown mall is a good place to start. ✦ Marufuku: 1581 Webster Street, (415) 872-9786. One of the best—be prepared to wait in line.

- Bernal Heights—Coco's Ramen: 3319 Mission Street, tel: (415) 648-7722
- FiDi: The Ramen Bar: 101 California Street, tel: (415) 684-1570
- Lower Haight—Iza Ramen: 237 Fillmore Street, tel: (415) 926-8173
- Japantown—Hinodeya Ramen: 1737 Buchanan Street, tel: (415) 757-0552
- Mission—Orenchi Beyond: 174 Valencia Street, tel: (415) 431-3971
- Tenderloin—Mensho Tokyo SF: 672 Geary Street, tel: (415) 800-8345

Izakaya

It's hard to know where to list the *izakayas*. Traditionally a Japanese-style pub where people could linger to enjoy the sakes and snacks, San Francisco-style means there's going to be excellent and modern wholesome food in addition to the various drinks. Small plates, grills, ramen—but mostly a place to settle in with friends and have a relaxing time, plentiful drinks, and a satisfying meal.

- Inner Sunset—Izakaya Sozai: 1500 Irving Street, tel: (415) 742-5122
- Mid-Market—Izakaya Roku: 1819 Market Street, tel: (415) 861-6500
- Mission—Rintaro: 82 14th Street, tel: (415) 589-7022
- SoMa—Okane: 669 Townsend Street, tel: (415) 865-9788

Food Trucks

If you can't go to a restaurant, one can come to you. Food trucks—offering just about any cuisine a San Franciscan might want—can be stationary, they can move around, or for a fun social occasion, they can be grouped for a picnic with friends and entertainment. Do you want soup or a curry, a slice of pizza, or even just a grilled cheese sandwich? Look to see where you favorite food trucks might be. And pay attention to their special weekend events.

- www.somastreatfoodpark.com/
- https://offthegrid.com/
- https://roaminghunger.com/food-trucks/ca/
  san-francisco/1/

Pop Up

Temporary restaurants stay in a particular place for a specified amount of time. They're fun, usually highlighting a particular's chef's specialties. Generally, they're mentioned on social media or heard of by word of mouth. Don't hesitate—some don't stay around long. For current news, check http://sf.eater.com/pop-ups.

Bubble, rooibos and matcha teas

San Franciscans have discovered the Taiwanese bubble teas. Made with a base of tea plus fruit or milk, to which tapioca "pearls" are added, these drinks are also called "boba." Rooibos (or "red" tea) is a plant that hails from South Africa, and the leaves can be mixed with spices and dried fruits to make succulent flavors. Not officially a 'tea," roobibos is considered to have some health benefits. Another tea that is gaining popularity is "matcha," a green tea that is powdered, so the tea leaves themselves are drunk. It, too, is thought to have health benefits—but also a higher percentage of caffeine. The tearooms below have several locations for trying their well-crafted teas. ✦ In Chinatown, don't miss Red Blossom Tea Co: 831 Grant Avenue, tel: (415) 395-0868. It's not a boba establishment, but stocking at least 100 different teas and with a deep understanding of tea culture, it's one of the best places for tea lovers.

- Boba Guys. www.bobaguys.com.
- Super Cue: www.supercuecafe.com.
- Samovar Tea: www.samovartea.com
- Steap Tea Bar: www.steapteabar.com

Coffee

San Franciscans are just as particular about their coffee as everything else. In the cafés they know exactly the bean they want and how it should be ground. And they get it. Starbucks has several locations, but popular as it is, it isn't a local coffee roaster. Thrillist posts a rating of the best coffee roasters in the Bay Area. (www.thrillist.com/drink/san-francisco/the-definitive-top-11-bay-area-coffee-roasters.) Some of the best have several locations, and their websites offer tips on brewing, mention their community activism, and special events. Don't forget that North Beach is known for its cafés and coffee roasters. ✦ Caffe Trieste: 601 Vallejo, tel: (415) 392-6739. For more than a half-century, the city's first espresso coffee house is still revered for its atmosphere as well as its coffee.

- Blue Bottle Coffee: https://bluebottlecoffee.com/
- Graffeo: www.graffeo.com
- Andytown: www.andytownsf.com
- Sightglass Coffee: https://sightglasscoffee.com/

The Stars

So, what makes a restaurant so special that you're willing to reserve two months in advance, drive an hour to get there, and then pay hundreds of dollars a person for a meal? The Michelin Guide rates its best restaurants (from one to three stars) according to the quality of the food's ingredients and how the cooking techniques master the flavors through the creative personality of the chef. Value for the money—no matter the price—and consistency among visits round out the list. In 2018, four San Francisco restaurants rated three stars (seven in the Bay Area) and another 30 were rated one or two stars, themselves outstanding and worth a trip. This doesn't mean that you won't find your own "best" hot and sour soup in a local restaurant down the block; it just means that meeting every one of the Michelin criteria plus a lovely ambience and superb service makes for an unforgettable experience. Eater San Francisco publishes a list each year of the Michelin rated restaurants in the Bay Area: https://sf.eater.com/maps/san-francisco-bay-area-michelin-restaurants-stars-2018. Although some other starred restaurants are mentioned in this chapter, here are the current three-star restaurants.

- FiDi—Benu: 22 Hawthorne Street, tel: (415) 685-4860; www.benusf.com
- Jackson Square—Quince: 470 Pacific Avenue, tel: (415) 775-8500, www.quincerestaurant.com
- North Beach—Coi: 373 Broadway, tel: (415) 393-9000, www.coirestaurant.com
- SoMa—Saison: 178 Townsend Street, tel: (415) 828-7990, www.saisonsf.com

An International Town

Whatever you're craving at the moment, whether comfort food from your original home or an exotic exploration of international cuisines, it's probably somewhere in San Francisco. Herewith only a miniscule sampling of what's available. For the ubiquitous Asian restaurants, see below.

- FiDi—✦ Le Central: 453 Bush Street, tel: (415) 3391-2233. For more than four decades, Le Central has epitomized classic French cuisine. Filet mignon au poivre, mussels with fries, escargot bourguignon, and onion soup—all in a bistro atmosphere.
- Hayes Valley—Suppenküche: 525 Laguna Street, tel: (415) 252-9289. German pub and wursthaus serving a fine pea soup, sausages, sauerkraut, and a selection of German beers.

- Hayes Valley—Cala: 149 Fell Street, tel: (415) 660-7701. The menu might mention the typical tostadas or quesadillas, but the quality and inventiveness of the chef are not typical at all. This is Mexican seafood—no meat here—at its finest.

- Jackson Square—Kokkari Estiatorio: 200 Jackson Street, tel: (415) 981-0983. An elegant Mediterranean/Greek restaurant with an impressive list of grills, and fish dishes. Wonderful avgolemeno soup, moussaka, and braised lamb.

- Mid-Market—Destino: 1815 Market Street, tel: (415) 552-4451. Latin American influenced small plates, terrific South American cocktails (the mojitos!), and a festive ambience.

- The Mission—Bissap Baobab: 3372 19th Street, tel: (415) 826-9287. Traditional Senegalese food in a small and enjoyable restaurant. Part of the community, there are special events, DJ parties and dance performances.

- Nob Hill—Keiko á Nob Hill: 1250 Jones Street, tel (415) 829-7141. Delicate French-Japanese tasting menus and their wine pairing, plus an a la carte menu, equally impressive.

- North Beach—Albona: 545 Francisco Street, tel: (415) 441-1040. Although Italian restaurants of all levels and regions dot the city, Albona's unusual spices from the Istrian region on the Adriatic make its Croatian/Italian flavors stand out.

- Polk/Van Ness—✦ Acquerello: 1722 Sacramento Street, tel: (415) 567-5432. Luxurious Michelin-starred restaurant, with northern Italian specialties, homemade pastas, and delicious antipasti, plus a seasonal tasting-menu.

- SoMa: ✦ Mourad: 140 New Montgomery Street, tel: (415) 660-2500. The Michelin-starred Mourad offers an exceptional Moroccan/California cuisine, including a multi-course tasting menu and family-style dinners for two-to-four diners.

THE BURRITO

In San Francisco, don't ignore the burrito, an all-in-one Mexican sandwich that you can eat on the run and feel satisfied—for quite a while. Fortunatel:y, with more than 150 taquerias, there is no lack of places to search out your own best burrito. Don't expect fancy service or a charming atmosphere. Taquerias are about food and the price—cheap. Just be happy if you get two napkins. You may need both.

So, what is a burrito? It is a large flour tortilla stuffed with a number of ingredients, heated, and then folded over so you can eat it (you hope) without it bursting and spilling everything down your shirt. Actually, there is a knack to eating a burrito, which you have to figure out for yourself. But it's the ingredients that count, of course. And you can chose which among them you want.

Start with the melted cheese that—again, one hopes—holds in the other ingredients. And then there's the meat, rice and beans, guacamole or avocado slices, tomato, sour cream, cilantro, and, of course, the salsa. (Many burrito purists disdain adding shredded lettuce.) After choosing the ingredients, there's the salsa: red, green, picadillo, or mild. And vegetarians can get the same quality burrito without any meat or cheese at all.

It is hard to find a truly bad burrito. But there are some taquerias that burrito aficionados rate highly. Most of the places are plain and basic—and others are more upscale. What counts in any place, however, is the burrito itself.

- El Farolito: 2779 Mission Street
- Papalote, 3409 24th Street and 1777 Fulton Street
- ✦ La Taqueria, 2889 Mission Street
- Taqueria El Castillito, 136 Church Street and 2092 Mission Street
- El Burrito Express, 1601 Taraval Street and 1812 Divisadero
- Taqueria Cancun, 2288 Mission Street; Street
- Pancho Villa: 3071 16th Street

- Van Ness/Polk Gulch—Helmand Palace: 2424 Van Ness Boulevard, tel: (415) 345-0072. If you have never thought of Afghanistan as a country for good food, The Helmand will change your mind. Its fine Kabul cuisine offers hints of aromas from India and the Middle East.

Eating Out in Asia

If it is all just Chinese food to you, it will not be after you have lived in San Francisco a while. Differing aromas from the

hundreds of Chinese, Vietnamese, Thai, Korean, and Japanese restaurants permeate the city, satisfying the Asian population and just about everyone else. Each neighborhood has its Asian eateries, and some areas cater to particular nationalities: Japantown and Chinatown of course, but also Larkin Street in the Tenderloin for Vietnamese, Clement Street for a lively mix of Asian establishments, and Irving Street in the Outer Sunset for its own eclectic mix from the Far East.

Chinese

Chinese restaurants are in the majority. The food is both complex and subtle: in a society not rich enough to offer a slab of meat or a quarter-chicken to each person, Chinese cooks have based their dishes on the inexpensive rice or noodles, topped with the region's vegetables and a flavored sauce. To this might be added some meat or poultry, or along the coast, fish. For thousands of years this method of cooking has provided a nutritious diet of carbohydrates, vegetables, and an adequate amount of protein, at low cost.

With Chinese restaurants, you can't judge the quality of the food by how the place looks. Some unpretentious, basic-looking dives serve the best food in their class and some of the most reputable-looking places may not be as good. ✦ For an upscale Chinese experience, there's the Michelin-starred Mr Jiu's at 28 Waverly Place, tel: (415) 857-9688.

- Chinatown—China Live: 644 Broadway, tel. (415) 788-8188. Showcasing Chinese cuisine, its history and culture, and with a retail marketplace and bar, it's a destination in itself.

- FiDi—R&G Lounge: 631 Kearny Street, tel: (415) 982-7877. Because Canton (now Guangzhou) was an international trading port, its offerings varied more than in other inland districts. Fresh fish with sauces—hoisin, oyster sweet and sour sauces—enliven the dishes, while keeping the original flavour, and with light, natural ingredients. At R&G, the ground floor is more casual and the upstairs a bit more sophisticated. Salt & Pepper Crab and the R&G Special Beef are highlighted.

- Inner Sunset—San Tung, 1031 Irving, tel: (415) 242-0828. In the north, where rice does not grow plentifully, dough dishes such as noodles or dumplings and pancakes provide the major starch. Because Peking (now Beijing) was the capital of the empire, some delicate dishes were created for the Mandarins who ruled. In fact, Peking/Mandarin cuisine offers some of China's more imaginative dishes. San Tung in the Sunset features excellent dumplings and noodles.

- Jackson Square—Hunan Home's: 622 Jackson Street, tel: (415) 982-2844. The Chinese in the hot south believe that spicy food keeps people cool internally, encouraging people to drink more tea, to stay hydrated and to eat less of the expensive meat. Spices also help preserve food so it lasts longer. Hunan Homes serves extremely spicy dishes (that can be modified to your taste). The hot and sour soup seems like Chinese "comfort food" and dishes such as Hunan Spiced Garlic Prawns or Sizzling Beef show the cuisine at its best.

- Mid-Market—Tēo: 1111 Mission Street, tel: (415) 626-8366. Chiu Chow cooking from the eastern part of the southern Guangdong Province is—like Guangzhou—known for its healthy fresh vegetable and seafood dishes, but also for its Teo Chew hot pots with their succulent broths. Tēo uses locally sourced products, grass-fed beef meatballs, and a full menu of balanced dishes.
- Outer Richmond—Ton Kiang: 5821 Geary Boulevard, near 22nd Avenue, tel: (415) 752-4440. Hakka means "guest families." The Hakka were wanderers who adapted their own cuisine to the regions where they stopped, incorporating those regions' cuisines into their own. Here, try the creative dumplings, the clay pot dishes, and the salt-baked chicken, all traditional Hakka traditions. And some of the city's best dim sum, any time of day.
- Outer Sunset—Old Mandarin Islamic: 3132 Vicente, tel: (415) 564-3481. Muslim Chinese cuisine dates from the seventh century, when Arab and Persian merchants first came regularly to China. Here in this small Halal eatery there are no pork dishes and the specialty is the Mongolian fire pot, in which you cook your own meal in boiling broth from fresh raw ingredients you have chosen. Also sometime try the Mandarin lamb and onion pancakes.
- SoMa—Yank Sing: 49 Stevenson Street; tel: (415) 541-4949: and 101 Spear Street, tel: (415) 781-1111. "Dim sum" means "small bites," and generally features rolling carts with many dishes to choose among. Dim Sum places are often full on Sunday mornings, so be sure to reserve. Yank Sing is a downtown favourite, but there are others, such as the bakery Good Mong Kok at 1039 Stockton Street, tel: (415) 397-2688.

Japanese

The delicate Japanese cuisine emphasizes harmony, and dishes are arranged to be as pleasing to the eye as to the palate. Japanese cuisine features rice, low-fat fish, gently sauced dishes, braised meats, tofu, fresh vegetables, several types of noodles, and, of course, sushi. Sometimes it's hard to categorize: do the food and drink make it *omekase*, an *izakaya*, or a traditional or fusion restaurant? No matter, find what you like: there's much to choose from. ✦ For outstanding *omekase* and the Michelin-starred Sushi Hashiri, see page 164. But as you'll see, Japanese cuisine is also much more.

- Cow Hollow: Zushi Puzzle, 1910 Lombard Street, tel: (415) 931-9319. Sushi fused with art: imaginative, original rolls and combinations.
- Laurel Heights—Tataki: 2627 California Street, tel: (415) 931-1182. Sustainable fish for its sushi in this small but excellent neighbourhood sushi bar.
- Mission—Blowfish Sushi: 2170 Bryant Street, tel: (415) 285-3848. Some of the city's best sushi, plus a well-created larger menu. Hectic, noisy, young, and fun, with anime visible and (very) audible anywhere you sit.
- Mission—Yuzuki Japanese Eatery: 598 Guerrero Street, tel: (415) 556-9898. Historically traditional Japanese dishes from local sources, plus a mouth-watering sake selection.
- Mission—Cha-Ya Vegetarian Japanese: 762 Valencia, tel: (415) 252-7825. This cosy restaurant satisfies the vegan taste for no-fish sushi and other Japanese favorites, plus several soba, udon and harusame options,
- SoMa: Ozumo, 161 Steuart Street, tel: (415) 882-1333. Ultra-modern Japanese restaurant spread across several different dining areas. Extensive sake bar, a robata room for grilling (with another bar), and a main dining room and sushi bar for intriguing chef-inspired creations.

Burmese

A fusing of Thai, Chinese and Indian spices and approaches, Burmese dishes culminate in a delicious melange of Asian textures and flavors. Samosas, fish cakes, curries, and noodle dishes all have their distinctive flavors. ✦ The oldest and still worth a trip is Mandalay at 4348 California Street, tel: (415) 386-3895. Coconut curry noodles are featured, as is the Burmese curried catfish.

- Mission—Burma Love: 211 Valencia Street, tel: (415) 861-2100. Specialties are impressive rainbow tea-leaf salads, a comfort-food vegetarian samosa soup, traditional Burmese curried dishes, and a five-spice braised lamb.
- SoMa—Golden Burma restaurant: 15 Boardman Place, tel: (415) 735-8282. An inexpensive gem near 6th Street, serving authentic Burmese dishes, such as the tea-leaf salad and catfish noodle soup.

Banh Mi

Banh Mi in San Francisco has its devotees. A Vietnamese "street food," this large sandwich on a crunchy baguette—like the burrito described above—can be ordered with a choice of fillings. And it, too, is delicious, fast, and cheap. Whether from an eatery in the Tenderloin, an upscale version in a restaurant, or even at a stand at the airport, banh mi satisfies.

It may sound simple: bread, meats, vegetables, and mayonnaise. But each ingredient has dozens of varieties, and each eatery has its specialties. Start with the warm baguette: crispy outside and a soft, chewy inside. Move on to the roasted meat: different versions of succulent pork, including the tender roasted pork belly and smooth paté, or chicken—or for the non-meat eaters, sardines, tuna, tofu or Portobello mushrooms. Add your veggies and flavors: pickled vegetables, carrots, chilies, onions, daikon, jalapeños, cucumber, cilantro, mint, and others. Hold it all together with a flavored mayonnaise. Fillings are generous: ask for an extra napkin or two.

- Castro—Dinosaurs Sandwich: 2275 Market Street
- Embarcadero—Slanted Door: Ferry Building
- Mission—Duc Loi: 2200 Mission Street
- Outer Sunset: Que Huong Vietnamese Deli: 2138 Irving Street
- SFO, Terminal 3: Bahn Mee
- Tenderloin—Sing Sing Sandwich Shop: 309 Hyde Street
- Tenderloin—✦ Saigon Sandwich: 560 Larkin Street
- Tenderloin—L&G: 602 Eddy Street

Indian

Indian restaurants with regional dishes appeal to San Franciscans who look for intense flavors and pungent sauces. Curries are the most known, but Indian cooking is much more than that,and can be combined with other cuisines to make unusual but happy combinations. ✦ Try the Michelin-starred Taj Campton place, which offers a refined Cal-Indian cuisine. Locally-sourced ingredients combined into aromatic Indian dishes, have created a fusion that has awarded the restaurant its star: 340 Stockton Street, tel: (415) 955-5555.

- Civic Center—August 1 Five: 524 Van Ness Avenue, tel: (415)771-5900; Modern Cal-regional Indian dishes using locally sourced ingredients and contemporary methods. The cocktails also use Indian spices and herbs.
- Cow Hollow—Viva Goa Indian Cuisine: 2420 Lombard Street, tel: (415) 440-2600. Goa, long ruled by Portugal, offers a different-yet traditional—Indian cuisine. Fish and prawns in aromatic curries both Indian and Goan.
- Japantown—Dosa on Filmore: 1700 Fillmore, tel: (415) 441-3672. Dosa uses sustainable ingredients known from South Indian regions; "home-style cuisine," in curries and dosas—Indian-style wraps—with a variety of fillings.

Korean

The highlight of Korean restaurants in San Francisco is the bulgogi, marinated meats or fish that are grilled at the table on a fiery brazier or served on a sizzling plate, accompanied by rice and banchan—small side dishes to enhance the flavors: pickles and salads. Bibimbap is a full meal in a rice bowl, covered with vegetables, meat and sauces. ✦ For just one of the authentic experiences, try Brother's Restaurant, 4128 Geary Boulevard, in the Richmond, tel: (415) 387-7991.

- Inner Sunset—Manna Korean BBQ: 845 Irving Street, tel: (415) 665-5969. Classic BBQ grills with an impressive menu of meats, tofu stews and pancakes.

- Outer Richmond—Han Il Kwan: 1802 Balboa Street, tel: (415) 752-4447. Among the grilled meats is a tender pork belly that keeps San Franciscans coming, plus its own bibimbap.
- Inner Richmond—Dancing Bull: 4217 Geary Boulevard, tel: (415) 221-5227. All you can eat bulgogi, plus a highly-prized shabu shabu hotpot.

Thai

Thai food emphasizes sweet and spicy seafood dishes and soups, curries with coconut, sticky rice, and lots of aromatic lemongrass. ✦ For a memorable experience, try Michelin-starred Kin Khao: 55 Cyril Magnum Street, in the Parc 55 Hotel, tel: (415) 362-7456. Seasonally fresh and Thai-sourced condiments, this is true Thai cuisine.
- The Haight—Thep Phanom: 400 Waller Street, tel: (415) 431-2526. Curries, pad-Thai, sticky rice, and more in this restaurant with costumed wait staff.
- Mission—Farmhouse Kitchen: 710 Florida Street, tel: (415) 814-2920. Yellow and green curries, beautifully spiced dishes, from Thai street food to graceful creations.
- The Tenderloin—Pak Nam: 655 Larkin Street, tel: (415) 872-9398. Splendid traditional noodle soups and standout spicy curries in an area with many Asian eateries.

Vietnamese

Vietnamese cuisine has its own characteristics, but it also often incorporates French nuances, from when Vietnam was a colony of France, and from China to the north. Three of the city's most well-known Vietnamese restaurants have already been mentioned: Crustacean and Thanh Long (see page 153) and The Slanted Door in the Ferry Building. But of course there are many more than the two below: And for the hearty banh mi, see page 153.

- Mid-Market—Tú Lan: 8 6th Street, tel: (415). Imperial rolls are a favorite here in this little off-Market dive that has no ambience but a loyal following.
- Chinatown—Golden Star: 1 Walter Um Place on Clay, tel: (415) 398-1215. In the heart of Chinatown, Golden Star is known for its excellent pho, creations, and other spicy noodle dishes. Egg rolls and Vietnamese lunch plates.

Gourmet Dining at Home

After all this, would you rather just have your favorite meal come to you? Delivery services from many restaurants allow you to order your favourite meals online and then have the hot dishes delivered to your home.

- www.trycaviar.com/san-francisco
- www.doordash.com/food-delivery san-francisco-ca-restaurants/
- www.grubhub.com/Online-Ordering/San-Francisco
- www.seamless.com/browse/ca-san_francisco
- www.postmates.com
- www.ubereats.com

THE MARKETS

If you are at all concerned about your budget or your waistline, you will not dine out every day of the year. Fortunately, you can eat as well at home in San Francisco as in a restaurant, whether you want to cook or not. So, knowing how and where to shop for food will be on your mind as you begin to settle in. Wide-ranging options include buying fresh ingredients and starting from scratch or moving up to the artistically prepared meats from the butcher that are ready to cook, adding potatoes and vegetables already cleaned. You can also buy delicious entire freshly-cooked meals from supermarkets or specialty groceries, or even high-quality frozen meals.

Farmers' Markets

Outdoor markets, often called "farmers' markets," are held on particular days in different districts of the city, and along with selling the region's freshest seasonal produce, meats, cheeses and dry-good items, they are often—as you might expect—social occasions. Some may offer tastings or seating to eat a prepared meal, and others might have live music. But all of them offer produce that is usually of better quality and often at lower cost than that of standard supermarkets. Note that markets are not open on Monday. http://projects.sfchronicle.com/2017/farmers-markets/map/.

The Ferry Building Marketplace

In addition to trying its popular eateries, for a one-stop market experience, the Ferry Building Marketplace is for you. Pick up your ingredients or an already-prepared dinner. Find shops of all sorts here lining a long central corridor. Then stop at Peets for a cup of coffee and pick up a book at Book Passage. And, of course you can always watch—or catch—one of the ferries leaving the port.

The outdoor market is on Tuesday, Thursday, and Saturday. There are tables for eating and conversation, live music, and a convivial atmosphere. Check for current merchants at the Ferry Building on its website—some don't last, but many stay and more always come (www.ferrybuildingmarketplace.com/).

The Supermarkets

Safeway is the city's major general supermarket chain (www.safeway.com/shopstores/tools/store-locator.page). It offers high quality products of all sorts. Other supermarkets may stand out for their particularly fine selections. And some, such as Cal-Mart at 3585 California Street, in Laurel Village, are appreciated as a destination for the neighbourhood residents: tel: (415) 751-3516.

• Bi-Rite Market: tel: (415) 626-5600; www.biritemarket. com. Two outlets for this popular local market. The Bi-Rite Creamery at 3692 18th Street offers ice creams with unusual flavors; don't overlook the baked products.
• Outer SoMa—Costco, 450 10th Street, tel: (415) 626- 4388; www.costco.com. Warehouse chain with most items in bulk: Packaged and fresh foods, frozen items, alcoholic beverage, clothing and dry goods. Small annual membership fee.

- Lucky: https://www.luckysupermarkets.com/locations/ca/san-francisco. Only a few outlets, but inexpensive, well-stocked and preferred by many locals.
- Mollie Stone's: www.molliestones.com. Small chain of outstanding markets.
- Trader Joe's: www.traderjoes.com. Several locations for this chain of stores, with an extensive selection of healthy packaged and frozen goods, dairy products, snack foods, bakery items, and spirits.
- Whole Foods: www.wholefoodsmarket.com/stores/list. Sophisticated health food supermarkets, with just about anything you want, including artistically prepared meats to take out, fresh fish, bakery and an always-crowded take-out deli counter.

Shopping in Asia

Asian markets carry goods from their own countries, and they often stock items from other Asian regions. Shopping in Chinatown can be an otherworld experience, especially on Saturday and Sunday. Crowds of people carrying overflowing bags bump into each other as they push their way down Stockton, Powell, or the side streets, looking for the freshest (and cheapest) fish and produce. Because signs are in Chinese and not all personnel speak English, shopping is sometimes a challenge. Nonetheless, Chinatown is the place to shop if you are not faint of heart. Parking is impossible, so either hoof it or take public transportation. But remember that Asian shops are located throughout the city, many in the Inner Richmond on Clement.

- Chinatown & The Richmond—Lien Hing Supermarket: 1112 Stockton Street, tel: (415) 986-8488. Finding your way along the crowded aisles—you will eventually find what you want at prices so low that you will keep coming back. Also at New Lien Hing at 400 Clement Street, tel: (415) 386-6333.

- Inner Richmond- -First Korean Market: 4625 Geary Boulevard, tel: (415) 221-2565. Fresh and packaged Korean items: kim bap, fresh kimchee, bahn chan and other authentic, locally-made Korean classics.
- Inner Richmond—New May Wah Supermarket: 707 Clement Street, tel: (415) 221-9826. Largest and one of the best of the Richmond's Asian supermarkets, New May Wah's international selection draws the crowds.
- Japantown—Nijiya Market: 1737 Post Street, in the Kinetesu Mall, tel: (415) 563-1901. Branch of an extensive chain of Japanese shops, with bento boxes, organic rice, and more, often rated as one of the excellent Asian markets in the city.
- Mission & Bayview—Duc Loi: 2200 Mission Street, tel: (415) 551-1772. Among the top Asian markets with its hearty banh mi, it's basically Vietnamese and with other Asian products. Also at 5900 3rd Street, tel: (415) 349-4988.

THAT'S THE SPIRIT!

The Attitude

San Franciscans like to drink. This doesn't mean that they are drunk. It only means that they approach enjoying good wine, interesting brews, and the most recent cocktail craze with the same intensity that they do everything else (see page 196). Learning how the drinks are made and going to the wine tastings, for instance, are pleasures San Franciscans cherish. For the equally-sought after artisanal microbreweries and their pubs, see page 199. Supermarkets stock hard liquors and wines, and wine shops also sell stronger spirits. Little in San Francisco is hard to find.

The Fruit of the Vine

Wine, like the best food creations, is an art. California produces more than 90 per cent of the wine bottled in the United States. There is nothing to say about California wines except that many of them are spectacular and if you are a wine aficionado, you are going to enjoy yourself here. And if not—at least not yet—you have a treat in store. The more you learn about them, the more you will be able to distinguish each nuance and overtone in their wide range of tastes, colors, and textures.

- California wine industry: www.discovercaliforniawines.com.
- San Francisco Wine School: https:// sanfranciscowineschool.com/.
- Wine Events in the city: www.localwineevents.com/.

Do not forget, though, that the whole point of drinking wine is to enjoy it. No matter the current popularity of certain wines, the superior attitude of wine snobs, and even the authoritative stance of shop proprietors—everybody has different tastes, so if you do not like a particular wine, it is not for you.

Purchasing Wine

Wine prices run the gamut from the cheap-but-good to the astronomical and heavenly. The type of wine, the vineyard, the number of bottles produced, and the particular year the grapes were harvested all contribute to how a wine is priced. But good wines, reasonably-priced, are available, and the average price in 2018 was just about $15 per bottle, so it isn't necessary to spend a fortune on wine. (Unless the heavenly is on your mind.) It all just takes know-how: knowing what you like, when to shop for special offers, talking with the knowledgeable staff, attending the tastings, and joining the wine clubs many of the sellers offer. Some merchants are wine bars, and wine bars sell bottles.

- Dogpatch—The Wine House: 829 26th Street, tel: (415) 355-9463. For 40 years, the Wine House has highlighted its wine clubs, case specials, European, South African and New World Wines, and small producers as well.

- Ferry Building—Ferry Plaza Wine Merchant, tel: (415) 391-9400. A tasty selection in an unbeatable ambience. Boutique wines, and table service.
- Hayes Valley—True Sake: 560 Hayes Street, tel: (415) 355-9555. Like wines, Japanese sake has different qualities and tastes, many of which can be found here for exploring.
- Hayes Valley—Arlequin Wine Merchant: 384 Hayes Street, tel: (415) 863-1104. A broad international selection, with wine clubs for limited production wines.
- Mission—Ruby Wine: 1419 18th Street, tel: (415) 401-7708). Both Old- and New-World small producers, and natural and organics.
- Polk Gulch—Biondivino: 1415 Green Street, tel: (415) 673-2320. Italian small producers and wines from Eastern Europe are different from the norm.
- SoMa—Wine Club: 953 Harrison Street, tel: (415) 512-9086. Large selection of wines. Friday happy-hours draw wine lovers to the warehouse-style ambience.
- SoMa—Terroir Natural Wine Bar & Merchant: 1116 Folsom Street, tel: (415). 558-9946. Natural and organic wines, and traditional European wines.
- Union Square—Napa Valley Winery Exchange: 415 Taylor Street, tel: (415) 771-2887. Learn everything about the famous Napa Valley and its range of producers.

CHAPTER 7

ENJOYING THE GOOD LIFE

> *When you get tired of walking around San Francisco, you can always lean against it.*

— Unknown Wit

CULTURE—HIGH AND LOW!

From world-class opera, ballet, and symphony, to live theater, to American and international films, to rock concerts that host thousands, and to cabaret, dance and comedy clubs—San Francisco has something for everyone. Restaurants offer jazz, jazz clubs serve food, art galleries and museums serve wine and canapés at their exhibit openings, bookstores host readings by famous authors, and in general, you can find something interesting to do just about any time of day—or night.

Museums of all specialties dot the city, although many are clustered downtown. And almost every district has something special that enlivens the mood of the area. The Civic Center is a hub for opera, classical music concerts, and ballet, as well as the spectacular Asian Art Museum. Just off Union Square is the Theater District with its Broadway focus. North Beach is known for its coffeehouses, Nob Hill for its plush piano bars. SoMa—down to China Basin—also has trendy eating places and offbeat nightspots and dance clubs; the area around MoMa and Yerba Buena hums day and night. The Castro, of course, is known for its gay hangouts, although gay-friendly entertainment can be found throughout the city, and even in the Castro, many venues appeal also to people who aren't gay. And the Mission, while remaining distinctly Latino, is definitely reflecting an expanded popularity, with something new cropping up on almost every block—especially around Dolores Park and the Valencia Corridor. The "avenues" are certainly coming up with their own identities, no longer just neighbourhood hangouts, with—in addition to a major university and conservatory, a world-class museum, panoramic views and hiking trails—shops, restaurants and bars that continually pull in the local crowds.

The Museums

With some 65 museums of one sort of another in San Francisco, they cannot all be listed here. So, this sampling below can just give an idea of the diversity of the offerings. Some museums offer one free day; days differ: http://sf.funcheap. com/city-guide/monthly-free-museum-days/. Museums are wheelchair-accessible.

- The de Young Museum: Golden Gate Park, 50 Hagiwara Tea Garden Drive, tel: (415) 750-3600; https://deyoung. famsf.org/. The spectacular de Young and the Legion of Honor museums are together the Fine Arts Museums of the city. The De Young's building is amazing in itself; its permanent collections of American and international artworks, sculptures, and furniture are outstanding.
- California Palace of the Legion of Honor: Lincoln Park at 34th and Clement, tel: (415) 750-3600; https:// legionofhonor.famsf.org/. Outside, the imposing neoclassical-style museum overlooks the Golden Gate Bridge. Inside, there is a wondrous collection of three millennia of history and European art.
- Asian Art Museum: 200 Larkin Street at Civic Center Plaza, tel: (415) 581-3500; www.asianart.org/. More than 15,000 artwork spanning 6,000 years of Asian art history: paintings, textiles and furniture, armour, and more, with programs showing artistic cross-cultural connections. Excellent Asian café.
- California Academy of Sciences: 55 Music Concourse Drive, Golden Gate Park, tel: (415) 379-8000; www. calacademy.org/. One of the country's outstanding treasures, this is a stunning state-of-the art interactive natural history museum, with an aquarium, an all-digital planetarium, a 2.5 acre living roof, and a 4-story rain forest.

Even the café with its multi-cultural menus and the upscale
Terrace Restaurant draw San Francisco crowds.
- San Francisco Museum of Modern Art (MOMA): 151 3rd
Street, tel: (415) 357-4000; www.sfmoma.org. In the heart
of SoMa, this world-class dramatically-modern art museum
displays the best of European and American artists,
including many abstracts, an outstanding photography
collection, and interesting traveling exhibits.

Specialized Collections

- The Museum of the African Diaspora (MoAD): 685 Mission
Street, tel: (415) 358-7200; www.moadsf.org/. From the
origins of African roots to the modern diaspora—the
impact of people of African descent on contemporary life
in cultures around the world.
- Cable Car Museum: 1201 Mason Street, tel: (415) 474-
1887; www.cablecarmuseum.org/index.html If you've
ridden the cable car, it's fun to go to this little museum that
looks at the century-old history of the system and shows
how it works.
- The Contemporary Jewish Museum: 736 Mission Street,
tel: (415) 685-7800; www.thecjm.org/. Created around an
old power station, this soaring museum shows Jewish art
and history, music, films, events, and special programs.
The Wise Sons Deli downstairs serves California-style
"Jewish comfort food".
- Museum of Gay, Lesbian, Bisexual, and Transgender
History: 4127 18th Street, tel: (415) 621-1107; www.
glbthistory.org/archives/. Celebrating a century of gay life
in San Francisco, the archives contain primary source
material, works of artists and writers, documents from
leaders of the movement. The Archives and Research
Center is at 989 Market Street, tel (415) 777-5455.
- Precita Eyes Arts Center: 2981 24th Street, tel: (415)
285-2287; www.precitaeyes.org/. Offering both guided and

self-guided tours in the Mission, of more than 200 murals depicting the life and achievements of Mexicans in the Mission and elsewhere.

- Mission Dolores: 3321 16th Street, tel: (415) 621-8203; www.missiondolores.org/. The oldest structure in San Francisco, the four-foot thick adobe walls, tiled roof and façade are typically "Mission style." See also the adjacent basilica with its stained glass windows.

Events—Getting Tickets

Buying tickets directly from the websites of the events you are considering often gets you good prices and special offers on season subscriptions. Also, try the ticket sellers that list various events, especially for last-minute sales. For discount and pre-mium tickets for the performing arts, try Tix Bay Area, a small installation nestled toward the west side of Union Square, tel: (415) 433-7827; www.tixbayarea.org/.

- Ticketweb: www.ticketweb.com.
- City Box Office: www.cityboxoffice.com.
- Ticketmaster: www.ticketmaster.com/ search?q=san+francisco+ca.

Theater

As you would imagine, San Francisco's theater scene is wildly diverse, from Broadway musicals that stay around for years, to free Shakespeare in the Park, and to impressive experimental efforts in tiny, offbeat venues all around town. Visiting shows and performances generally sell out quickly. For current infor-mation on performances, theaters and tickets, you can get the TodayTix and Ticketmaster apps (and others) for your mobile, or access the links below. Also check BayStages on Facebook. Pay attention to the offerings of the smaller non-traditional theaters, as well; San Franciscans do:

- https://en.wikipedia.org/wiki/List_of_theatres_in_ San_Francisco.

- www.theatrebayarea.org.
- www.san-francisco-theater.com/.
- www.sfgate.com/entertainment/.

MUSIC

Any day, any night, any time of year, there's music in San Francisco. For traditional performance venues, street fairs and festivals, for church concerts, or for free in the parks—search what you're looking for and you'll be sure to find it. From classical to rock, from religious to EDM, from dance to dance-along, and at Christmas a sing-along Messiah, San Franciscans are sure to be seeking it out and standing in line—or buying tickets in advance. So join them, and don't miss out. Check the websites below.

Tried and True

- San Francisco Symphony: Davies Symphony Hall, 201 Van Ness Avenue at Grove, tel: (415) 864-6000; www. sfsymphony.org/. World class concerts from September to June, plus a summer season.
- San Francisco Opera: War Memorial Opera House: 301 Van Ness Avenue, tel: (415) 864-3330; https://sfopera. com/. Lavish productions that begin in mid-September.
- Opera Parallèle: 44 Page Street, tel: (415) 626-6279; https://operaparallele.org. Contemporary opera and new music.
- San Francisco Ballet: War Memorial Opera House, tel: (415) 865-2000; www.sfballet.org/. Classical and new works, plus special events such as the ballet's annual December performances of Tchaikovsky's Nutcracker Suite.
- San Francisco Performances: Herbst Theater, 401 Van Ness; tel: (415) 392-2545; https://sfperformances.org/. The major Bay Area independent presenter of chamber music and dance. Other venues, as well.

- San Francisco Conservatory of Music: 50 Oak Street; tel: (415) 864-7326; https://sfcm.edu/. An outstanding music conservatory, presenting a full and varied performance schedule each year by its talented students
- SFJAZZ: 201 Franklin Street, tel: (866) 920-5299; https://sfjazz.org/. Hundreds of concerts with visiting artists and promoting jazz through Family Matinees with live performances, interactive family workshops and a wide-ranging roster of educational programs.

Arena and Hall Concerts ...

It has been a long time since the Grateful Dead played in San Francisco or Jello Biafra of the punk-rock Dead Kennedys ran for mayor. But you will not have to wait long for a touring group to turn up somewhere in the Bay Area. As usual, tickets sell out almost immediately, so check the websites often.

- www.bandsintown.com/cities/san-francisco-ca. nhttp://sanfrancisco.eventful.com/events/categories/music
- http://sanfrancisco.giants.mlb.com/sf/ballpark/information/index.jsp
- www.thefillmore.com
- www.billgrahamcivicauditorium.com/
- http://sfmasonic.com /
- www.thewarfieldtheatre.com/

... and Around the Bay Area

Most arena concerts around the Bay Area are easily accessible by public transportation, but they also have extensive parking facilities for those who drive.

- Oracle Arena: in Oakland, www.oraclearena.com/
- SAP Center: in San Jose: www.sapcenter.com/.
- Concord Pavillion in Concord: www.livenation.com/venues/14806/concord-pavilion.
- Cow Palace: Daly City; www.cowpalace.com.

- Shoreline Amphitheater: www.mountainviewamphitheater. com/.
- Zellerbach Hall· University of California:,Berkeley; www. calperfs.berkeley.edu.

Smaller Settings

New venues for listening to music and just hanging out are opening all the time, but fortunately, the classic stick around. For any of the clubs, check the websites frequently, and make sure to get your tickets well in advance.

- Union Square—Slim's/Great American Music Hall: 859 O'Farrell Street, tel: (415) 885-0750; www.slimspresents. com/.
- North Beach—Bimbo's 365 Club: 1025 Columbus, tel: (415) 474-0365; www.bimbos365club.com/.
- Potrero Hill—Bottom of the Hill: 1233 17th Street, tel: (415) 621-4455. www.bottomofthehill.com/.
- SoMa—Hotel Utah Saloon: 500 4th Street, tel: (415) 546-6300; www.hotelutah.com/.

Drinking and Driving

The drinking age is 21 in California, and it is enforced. You may be asked for your identification in any place you try to purchase alcohol (called "being carded"), even if you are well over the minimum age. Just take it as a compliment. Do not drive even if you have had only a couple of drinks. DUI (Driving under the Influence) laws are strict, and the police department is not lenient with offenders. It is illegal to drive with a blood alcohol level of 0.08 or more; you will not know your level, but the police will. And they will test you on the spot. So, for a night on the town, it is best to ask someone in your group to be the "designated driver" and not drink. Or be wise and take a cab or a car service home.

If you are stopped for DUI, never try to bribe a police officer. You will only make matters worse. If you are convicted of DUI, you might go to jail for up to six months, you will no doubt pay a fine, your license may be restricted or suspended, and you might have to successfully complete a treatment program—all depending on the circumstances. So, be prudent. Do not drink and drive.

- Union Square—Biscuits and Blues: 401 Mason Street, at Geary; tel: (415) 292-2583; https://biscuitsandblues.com/.

Bars & Such

Bars come in many shapes and forms: the romantic lounge with a spectacular view atop a tall hotel, the loud sports bar with television screens visible in every corner, the gentle wine bar, the neighborhood lounge, or that funky bar that you love but might not take your mother to. And, as usual, categories overlap: cocktail bars and wine bars, microbreweries, gastropubs, izakayas, and even restaurants with their own idea of what the best drinks would please their clientele. They all have their devotees. One favorite is the Comstock Saloon: 155 Columbus, tel: (415) 617-0073. A vintage look here, with classic drinks and excellent grub.

- Beautiful bars: www.thrillist.com/drink/san-francisco/the-15-most-beautiful-bars-in-san-francisco
- Classic bars: www.sftravel.com/article/oldest-bars-san-francisco-neighborhood
- Happy hour bars: https://sf.eater.com/maps/best-new-happy-hours-san-francisco-oakland-berkeley
- Romantic bars: www.sftravel.com/article/6-romantic-places-sip-san-francisco
- Sports bars: https://sf.eater.com/maps/best-sports-bars-san-francisco
- Weird bars: www.upout.com/blog/san-francisco-3/11-weirdest-bars-san-francisco
- Wine bars: https://sf.eater.com/maps/best-wine-bars-san-francisco

Craft Cocktails

Craft spirits—the staple for the creative cocktails that are so predominant now—begin with the distilleries. Craft-spirits are developed in several distilleries around the Bay Area, and if they're not all available for tasting on their premises, they are sold in bottles and used in the craft cocktail bars, as well. These have tasting opportunities: https://www.bayarea.com/drink/local-liquor-5-bay-area-distilleries-offering-tastings-tours/.

The bars for the best craft cocktails—hand crafted recipes with specially-selected spirits and syrups and often with artistic decorations and presentations—are serious evenings' destinations; San Franciscans, of course, are as partial to their "mixologist" as to anything else. For the current favorites, access https://sf.eater.com/maps/best-new-bars-cocktails-san-francisco. ✦ Trick Dog, at 3010 20th Street in the Mission, for example, has a changing cocktail menu that describes the alcohol and the seasonal ingredients, plus an interestingly created bar menu, including its own Trick Dog. Open late nightly, it's always packed with aficionados; no off-hours here, tel: (415) 471-2999.

- Duboce Triangle—Blackbird: 2124 Market Street, tel: (415) 503-0630. The seasonal cocktail menu ensures that ingredients are the freshest in this rustic neighbourhood bar that also pours artisan brews.
- Fort Mason—The Interval at Long Now: 2 Marina Boulevard, Building A, tel: (415) 496-9187. Bar, café, museum, library and excellent crafted drinks, owned by the Long Now Foundation, promoting conversation about "long-term thinking" for the next thousands of years.
- Mission—ABV: 3174 16th Street, tel: (415) 406-4748. Small but well-designed local bar, serving an eclectic menu of snacks and a great burger in addition to its tequila- and mezcal-based crafted specialties.
- SoMa—Bar Agricole: 355 11th Street, tel (415) 355-9400. Always appreciated, serving traditional cocktails made modern, natural wines, and locally sourced ingredients for its Northern California cuisine.

Gay and Lesbian Watering Holes

Make no mistake. Gays and lesbians are welcome in any bar and in any club in any neighborhood of the city. San Francisco is a gay friendly town. But many bars and clubs throughout the city are known as catering to the LGBTQ communities— and non-gays are generally welcome, as well. For the newest favourites, plug "best bars in the Castro" into your browser.

The clubs—classic or new—tend to have it all: dancing, games, exotic cocktails, patios. Some are good for cruising, others for conversation, and all are good for hanging out. Some have a mixed clientele, others have ladies' nights. ✦ The SF-Eagle is a class unto itself, at 398 12th Street, tel (415) 626-0880. For more than 30 years, this biker bar in outer SoMa has survived—and thrived. Everyone in the LGBT communities comes for the Sunday Beer Bust and live music.

- Bernal Heights—Wild Side West: 424 Cortland Avenue, tel: (415) 647-3099. One of the oldest lesbian bars, this low-key institution welcomes the community to its patio and garden, its sports TVs, and friendly atmosphere.
- Castro—The Café: 2369 Market Street, tel: (415) 523-0133. Always crowded with its three bars, a large dance floor, shows and weekly events.
- Castro—Twin Peaks: 401 Castro Street, tel: (415) 864-9470. One of the classics, a small quiet tavern in the heart of everything, to see and be seen near its full-length windows.
- Haight-Ashbury—Trax: 1437 Haight Street, tel: (415) 864-4213). Both gays and straights have been hanging out since 1940 in this comfortable, typically Haight bar.
- Mid-Market/SoMa—The Stud: 399 9th Street at Harrison, tel: (415) 863-6623. This old bar has been around more than 50 years and is going strong with its good drinks, dancing, shows, burlesque, karaoke, and more.
- Mission—El Rio: 3158 Mission Street, tel: (415) 282-3325. A mixed clientele here dances to live music with a distinctly

Latin rhythm. Sunday afternoons are a highlight.

- Polk Gulch—Cinch Saloon: 1723 Polk Street, tel: (415) 776-4162. Great saloon with theme nights, holding its own after some 50 years. Dance, drink and hang out.

On to the Hops

Microbreweries rule! San Franciscans appreciate their brews the same as they do anything else. There are more than 100 breweries in the Bay Area, meaning that months of enjoyable experimenting are in store: www.liquidbreadmag.com/breweries/. Most of the breweries serve their own innovative recipes, and are eager to describe them to all comers. But there are many others—some called "gastropubs" for their fine food offerings as well—that serve a variety of draft beers from the region's breweries. And, pay attention to the annual Beer Week, when all San Francisco appreciates its brews in various locales: https://sfbeerweek.org. Meet other beer aficionados and try the city's most delicious brews.

Actually, the craft beer industry may have begun in San Francisco. Since 1896, the famous Anchor Steam has been the mainstay for craft-beer drinkers in San Francisco—and beyond: Anchor Brewing Company, at 1705 Mariposa Street, tel: (415) 863-8350; www.anchorbrewing.com. Anchor is now owned by the Japanese company Sapporo, which intends to continue its traditions. The Anchor Public Taps has opened its large tasting room for its seasonal brews across the street, at 495 De Haro.

Most microbreweries mentioned in the links have their own pubs, serving their own brews. The excellent Fort Point Brewery in the Presidio has its taproom in the Ferry Building (www.fortpointbeer.com).

- Beer tour: www.sfontaptours.com/?
- Brewers Guild: http://sfbrewersguild.org/
- Breweries and pubs: www.beeradvocate.com/place.

For pubs with extensive draft options—to sample different brews in one place—San Francisco's pubs oblige: https://www.thrillist.com/drink/san-francisco/42-san-francisco-bars-you-need-to-drink-in-before-you-die-bucket-list.

- ✦ The Haight—Don't miss Toronado: 547 Haight Street, tel: (415) 863-2276. Almost a legend, this pub in the Haight offers more than 40 brews on tap and an enormous list of bottles and casks. If you're hungry (or even if you are not), go next door and buy a delicious sausage from the Rosamunde Sausage Grill. A typical Lower Haight experience.

- ✦ Tenderloin/Union Square—The same is true for Mikkeller Bar: 34 Mason Street, tel: (415) 984-0279. Originally Danish, pouring more than 42 brews on tap plus interesting international bottles—and a cellar specializing in Lambic and sour brews. Leave room for the go-with New American gastropub food.

Irish Pubs

Of course, as there would be, there are more than one hundred Irish pubs, and this is important for on Saint Patrick's Day on March 17th, the city turns green. Irish or not, people wear green, they sport shamrocks, and, without doubt, they drink. Irish lager, stout (Guinness, most likely), ale, whiskies, and ciders rule the day, and to round out the festivities, there's the annual Market Street parade: www.thrillist.com/drink/san-francisco/the-best-irish-bars-in-san-francisco. ✦ The Buena Vista Café: 2765 Hyde Street, tel: (415) 474-5044. Not technically a pub or a bar, The Buena Vista is the home of the first Irish Coffee in the United States—a cup of cream-frothed coffee happily laced with whiskey—and it serves hundreds of its specialty every day. American food is served, but always can be served with a cup of the Irish. On Saint Patricks Day, the celebrations go on and on.

- FiDi—The Irish Bank: 10 Mark Lane, Bush Street near Kearny, tel: (415) 788-7152. Wonderful block party around Saint Patrick's Day at this cosy Irish bar downtown.
- Inner Richmond—Plough and Stars: 116 Clement Street, at 2nd Street, tel: (415)751-1122. This neighbourhood Irish pub still appeals after forty years.
- SoMa—City Beer: 1148 Mission Street, tel: (415) 503-1033. A good place to start understanding the city's offerings. Mix and match among the 300 brands for sale, or sit down for a cool one from its taps.
- SoMa—The Chieftain Irish Pub & Restaurant: 198 5th Street, tel: (415) 615-0916 Friendly Irish bar and restaurant, with everything: Guinness, Irish food, theme nights, live music, and a haven for international sports matches on its large screens.

Wanna Dance?

From salsa to swing, you can dance in venues all around the city, whether live to a band or with a DJ. When you check out dance clubs, find out the days, for some clubs are open or have events weekends only.

Would you like to dance the Nutcracker, yourself? You've got your chance at the annual Dance-Along-Nutcracker, put on by the San Francisco Lesbian/Gay Freedom Band (www.sflgfb.org). You do not have to be gay, of course, for anyone who has ever had a yen to dance comes and does so.

For information on Latin rhythms in particular, check www.salsabythebay.com/salsa-dancing-san-francisco/. Access also the Fuego Club, open weekends, with three rooms for different dance styles: www.fuegoclubsf.com/.

- Union Square—Starlight Room at Sir Francis Drake Hotel, tel: (415) 395-8595. www.sirfrancisdrake.com/san-francisco-nightclubs/. A splendid view and mellow music for dancing in a more formal (and romantic) setting.

- SoMa—1015 Folsom: 1015 Folsom Street, tel: (415)991-1015.. http://1015.com/. Five different rooms each with its own DJ and a live events calendar.
- Mission—Bissap Baobab Village: 3372 19th Street, tel: (415) 826-9287; www.bissapbaobab.com/. Senegalese/ restaurant (see page 172) , but with a full events calendar and dance parties.
- SoMa/Mission—DNA Lounge: 375 11th Street, tel: (415) 626-1409. www.dnalounge.com/. Always trendy locale, cutting-edge live music with three floors for dancing. One of the best.
- Mission: Roccapulco: 3140 Mission Street, near Cesar Chavez, tel: (415) 648-6611. www.roccapulco.com/. Salsa is the beat in this large two-story club, performed by visiting international groups.
- SoMa—The Endup: 401 6th Street, tel: (415) 646-0999; http://theendupsf.com/. An after-hours party destination for great entertainment, live music and dance—and after 40 years here, it's a constant for the late-night crowd.

FILMS

Films play a major part in the entertainment life of San Franciscans. If you are looking for a film, you will have lots of choices: first-run American movies and revivals, major foreign films in their original language (with English subtitles), and independent art films, often by local filmmakers. Cinema is not inexpensive, so look for when the festivals are held, and some theaters have a bargain matinee, with slightly cheaper tickets for the first daily showing of a film.

The major multiplex chains—AMC, Cinemark, or Landmark, for example—screen their films in different locations at different times, and have many screens. The AMC Metreon, for example, has 16. The few examples below are among the many different types of cinemas in tune with San Francisco.

- Japantown—New People: 1746 Post Street, tel: (415) 525-8600, www.newpeopleworld.com/. This 20,000 square foot entertainment complex is a one-stop destination showing Asian culture through film, art, shopping, dining, and more.
- Inner Mission—The Roxie: 3117 16th Street, tel: (415) 863-1087; www.roxie.com/. A non-profit film organization, the Roxie takes independent cinema to deeper levels, with invited guests interacting with the public, membership programs, and a community of film lovers for support.
- Mission—Foreign Cinema: 2534 Mission Street, tel: (415) 648-7600; http://foreigncinema.com/. For several decades, San Franciscans have enjoyed a California-delicious meal while watching a movie on the big screen. Sunday brunch is also popular. Check the website for the movie schedule. Adjacent is Foreign Cinema's bar Laszlo, with its own set of drinks, food, and music: www.laszlobar.com.
- Mission—Alamo Drafthouse/New Mission: 2550 Mission Street, tel: (415) 549-5959; https://drafthouse.com/sf. A nationwide cinema chain with a modern twist. Full-course menu and craft beers delivered to the seat you've reserved in advance.
- The Castro: 429 Castro Street, tel: (415) 621-6120; www.castrotheatre.com/. Built in 1922 and now a protected Landmark, the Castro mirrors the lively spirit of its neigbhorhood with special film events and a calendar of fun films.
- Balboa: 3630 Balboa Street, tel: (415) 221-8184. www.cinemasf.com/balboa/. Now part of the CinemaSF organization, this historic Outer Richmond theater shows Hollywood favorites, indie films, and special screenings.

Film Festivals

There are film festivals almost every month, some lasting a few days, or one week or even two. Some lure the entire city to major movie houses, some are revivals shown in smaller venues. Foreign language films, international films, an Urban Film Fest, Black films, documentaries, and GLBT and transgender Film Festival—are only a few that San Franciscans flock to. Although there are many festivals, they are often sold out, so buy your tickets well in advance. San Francisco Travel posts a guide to film festivals month by month: www.sftravel.com/article/guide-film-festivals-san-francisco-month-month.

And Last, Just for Fun

Not all culture is serious, yet not everything serious is culture, either. Laughter and a general fun time rule! Comedy clubs, karaoke, and more—each performance or venue tries to be more innovative than the other. Most of the comedians often poke fun—serious or not—at local and national politicians, and the audience eats it up.

Around 1st October, Comedy Celebration Day takes place at Robin Williams Meadow in Golden Gate Park. And, from July to September, the San Francisco Mime Troupe puts on performances in public parks around the Bay Area: www.sfmt.org/index.php. Think, too, of Clusterfest, a full weekend of comedy and music at the Civic Center: www.clusterfest.com.

- Beach Blanket Babylon, 678 Beach Blanket Babylon Boulevard (Green Street), tel: (415) 421-4222; www.beachblanketbabylon.com. A totally zany musical spoof of pop culture (and local celebrities) which has been keeping people laughing for 40 years, changing its content to fit the times.

- Cobb's Comedy Club, 915 Columbus Avenue, tel: (415) 928-4320; www.cobbscomedy.com. Both local and visiting comedians keep this place at the top of most lists for laughs. Visit their other club as well, for different performers, also local and nationally-known: The Punchline: 444 Battery Street; tell: (415) 397-7573; www.punchlinecomedyclub.com/.

- Festa Wine & Cocktail Lounge: 1825A Post Street; tel: (415) 567-5866; http://festalounge.com/. Among the dozens of karaoke establishments, this upscale Japantown bar offers thousands of songs—including those in Chinese, Japanese, Spanish and more.

THE SPORTING SCENE

All Year 'Round

The Bay Area's moderate climate allows outdoor activity on just about any day of the year. Access to outdoor sports, in fact, is a main reason for people moving to the Bay Area. San Francisco itself has more than 120 parks (many with miles of hiking trails), over 70 playgrounds, five golf courses, 100 tennis courts, nine swimming pools, almost six miles of ocean beach, several lakes, fishing piers, fly-casting pools, and a marina with a small craft harbor. Private facilities throughout the city offer rowing clubs, full-service gyms, and martial arts dojos. The Bay Area also has famous national baseball and football teams to root for. What more could one want?

Spectator Sports

San Franciscans are avid sports spectators. Seats for the major games are often sold out long in advance, but the city's sports bars provide large-screen TVs for viewing of just about any popular match. Tickets for all sporting events are available from the team's online box office or from ticket agencies.

Baseball

The San Francisco Giants belong to the National League; ticket office tel: (415) 464-9377; www.mlb.com/giants. The team plays in AT&T Park, in warm, sunny China Basin. Seating

Aerial view of AT&T Park, home to the San Francisco Giants baseball team. The 48,000 capacity waterfront stadium helped revitalize the South of Market area that was destroyed during the 1906 earthquake.

41,000 people, the ballpark can be reached by bus, train, streetcar, and ferry. You can also drive and try and park in public parking or at an expensive private parking lot.

AT&T Park is interesting in itself. Walk around the stadium and see the statues to former Giants greats: Willy McCovey who hit 521 home runs in his time; the beloved outfielder Willy Mays, and spectacular pitcher Juan Marichal. Fans will be more than happy to regale you with stories about their sports heroes.

The Oakland team, The Oakland Athletics (The A's), belongs to the American League: tickets tel: (877) 493-2255; www.mlb.com/athletics). The team currently plays at the McAfee Coliseum, at Interstate 880 and Hegenberger Road, but a move to a new stadium is currently being negotiated. You can drive or take BART to the Coliseum Station.

Football

Overlapping the summer baseball season, the football season begins in late August and culminates with the Super Bowl in

January of the following year. There are currently two Bay Area teams. Both are among the top in their respective "conferences"; the rivalry between them (and their fans) is fierce, and fans are as partial to their football teams as they are to their baseball teams.

The San Francisco 49ers ("The Niners") are the home team; ticket office tel: (415) 656-4900; www.49ers.com/. The team's home stadium is not actually in San Francisco, but in Santa Clara, just south of the City. For information on Levi's Stadium, access www.levisstadium.com/.

And in Oakland, the team is The Oakland Raiders, but not for long; tel: (510) 864-5000; www.raiders.com. The team is scheduled to move to Las Vegas and begin to play there in 2020—if not before—disappointing their ardent fans. But a new, adequate stadium was needed, and satisfactory offers and plans were not forthcoming.

Ice Hockey
The Bay Area professional ice hockey team, The San Jose Sharks, plays at the 17,500-seat SAP Center in San Jose, tickets: www.sjsharks.com. Some locals call the SAP Center the "Shark Tank".

Basketball
The Bay Area basketball team, the Golden State Warriors, generally plays in the Oracle Arena in Oakland; www.nba.com/warriors. The season runs from November through April. At this writing, a new 18,000-seat arena and community are being built just south of the AT&T baseball complex. Upon completion the Chase Center will maintain parking for almost 1,000 vehicles, a large public plaza and retail units. The T-Third light rail system will service the facility, and by 2021 a new subway line will link this southern area all the way north through downtown toward Chinatown.

Horse Racing

Golden Gate Fields is in Berkeley, at 1100 Eastshore Highway, off Interstate 80, tel: (510) 559-7300; www.goldengatefields. com. Check the website for the live racing and simulcast day schedules.

Outdoors and free

First, everyone walks. There is little to say about walking in San Francisco except that everyone does it. Walking is a favorite exercise, and here in this moderate climate, many people walk 365 days a year. People walk to work whenever they can, wearing business suits and walking shoes (with women changing to dress shoes at work). For exercise, people walk up and down the hills, slowly or quickly, singly or in groups, along the Embarcadero, in the parks, at Crissy Field, along the 3½-mile Golden Gate Promenade, and across the Golden Gate Bridge. The best walking is where the views are breathtaking: the trails in the Presidio and just about anywhere in Golden Gate Park. And if you are hardy, Ocean Beach certainly qualifies, even when the fog and wind are fierce.

The same holds true for running, just about any day of the year. People run anywhere they can, whenever they can. If you are a serious runner—or even a not-so-serious runner—check the calendar of events on pages 226–231, and enter one of the numerous races San Francisco puts on during the year. Also check www.runguides.com/san-francisco/runs for all the current races.

Dog Walking

Brisk dog-walking is good exercise and an excellent way to meet neighbors. While dogs are not allowed in most parks (signs are generally posted at entrances), some parks have areas designated "off leash" where dogs may run freely, and some neighborhood parks have dog runs. Golden Gate Park has several off-leash areas, as do Crissy Field and Ocean

Beach. There are many more neighbourhood dog-friendly parks: A current informational website is Bring Fido: www. bringfido.com/attraction/parks/city/san_francisco_ca_us/

San Franciscans celebrate their dogs as they do anything else. See if the "Barkathon" continues or the World Dog Surfing Championships (which may be nearby in Pacifica). The Dog Fest is an annual pleasure. And participate in the Best Dog Costume event. If these events have disappeared, surely some other event for the pooches will be on the dog-lovers' calendar.

And note that some restaurants—especially those with patios—are dog-friendly.

Hiking

You can appreciate the beautiful natural resources of the area in dozens of locations within the city, but the entire Bay Area is a wealth of opportunities that can take many pleasant years to explore. In the city itself, though, and in addition to the two major parks described below, McLaren Park (the city's second largest), Glen Canyon Park, Bernal Park, Lincoln Park, and others have hiking trails. Consider especially Crissy Field, Ocean Beach, or the Ridge Trail, which stretches from Lake Merced to Golden Gate Park, and which will eventually circle the bay.

Sierra Club, a nationwide environmental and outdoors association, puts on a year-round schedule of hikes, backpacking trips, and other activities, plus social events. Bay Chapter: 2530 San Pablo Avenue, Berkeley, tel: (510) 848-0800; www. sierraclub.org/san-francisco-bay.

Golden Gate Park

Golden Gate Park, dating from about 1865, is one of the country's major urban parks, comprising some 1,017 diverse acres (411.6 ha) and welcoming hundreds of thousands of people each year. With rolling hills and meadows, fragrant forests, stunning museums, and seemingly endless variety, the park starts in the city and ends by the sandy beaches at the edge of the continent. For an up-to-date calendar of attractions and events, access its website: https://goldengatepark.com/.

Within its confines there is an arboretum and botanical garden, a conservatory of flowers, a lake where you can rent a boat and another where you can sail a model. The Japanese Tea Garden is next to the world class De Young Museum—as spectacular outside as well as within https://deyoung.famsf.org/. And another crowning glory, the California Academy of Sciences is an amazing, world-class natural history museum: www.calacademy.org. And in the park itself, almost every weekend there is an event, a concert, or a happening.

The park begins at the Panhandle, between Oak and Fell Streets, which is lined by some of the oldest trees in the city. East of the 19th Avenue bisect, the park is the most civilized. Here are the museums, tennis courts, playgrounds, the exquisite Strybing Arboretum and Botanical Gardens, as well as Stow Lake, the largest in the park. The lovely Sharon Meadow has been renamed Robin Williams Meadow, honouring the actor and comedian who got his start in San Francisco and lived long here.

West of 19th Avenue, where the fog may hover for days, are the activities that take more space: golf, doggie runs, horseback riding, soccer, polo, fly-casting, and model boat sailing. Especially beloved are the bison in the large paddock on John F. Kennedy Drive, at about 39th Avenue. Throughout the park there are the hiking trails and bicycle paths, forested groves, and lawns and meadows for picnics or games of Frisbee.

If you are around in February and March, look for the exquisitely blooming Queen Wilhelmina Tulip Garden, adjacent to the Dutch Windmill at the western end of the park (and then go for a beer at the Beach Chalet and enjoy the ocean view). And, at the eastern beginning of the park is the National AIDS Memorial Grove, with thousands of plantings to memorialize those who lost their struggle against AIDS.

On weekends and holidays and for some special events, major roads are closed to traffic. These are good days to rent a boat or bike at the Stow Lake Boathouse, or to take an official Segway tour of the park, the tours initiating at Tea Garden Drive behind the Temple of Music. In general, people bike or rollerblade, stroll or jog, visit the museums, listen to a concert, or just hang out with family and friends. There is not one foggy or rainy day of the year that the park is not appreciated and enjoyed. This is Golden Gate Park.

GGNRA

The Golden Gate National Recreation Area (GGNRA) spans more than 75,000 acres (30,352 ha) and 115 miles (185.1 km) over a three-county area and is the largest urban national park in the world. It protects 1000 historic structures, 27 rare and endangered species, and islands whose habitats are threatened. Some 20 million people visit the GGNRA each year. It includes parts of San Francisco itself as well as the wilder reaches outside the city. In the city it includes The Presidio and

The Embarcadero

The Embarcadero has stretched its arc along the Bay for 150 years, but for decades in the 20th century no one could enjoy it, with a double-decker freeway obscuring the view. In 1989, however, the Loma Prieta Earthquake damaged the highway, and San Franciscans demanded it be torn down. Now, after refurbishment, the Embarcadero promenades are glorious and the dining and marketing opportunities bring San Franciscans day and night.

Start by exploring the Ferry Building, a landmark that survived the 1906 earthquake and fire, and—after a US$ 100 million renovation—is a vibrant community resource, with a dozens of upscale shops and eateries, and an outdoor market. The north promenade then takes you to Pier 15 and the city's beloved Exploratorium, the hands-on science museum, and on to Pier 39 and Fisherman's Wharf. To the south of the Ferry Building—with its even-numbered piers—you will see sculptures along the waterside and restaurants of all levels, and eventually you will come to the AT&T Baseball Park, where you might take in a game. And, adding to the "only in San Francisco" charm, in either direction as you walk on, you will be passed by the colorful vintage streetcars as they glide along the tracks between rows of stately palms. San Franciscans can love their waterfront once again.

Crissy Field, and the beaches mentioned below, Fort Mason, and even sites that might surprise you: The Cliff House, and Alcatraz Island. Among the most popular attractions outside the city are the Marin Headlands directly across the Golden Gate Bridge, and Muir Woods.

Larger than Golden Gate Park (almost twice as large as New York's Central Park), the Presidio's 1,410 acres (570.6 ha), sometimes called "the jewel of the Pacific," are part of the GGNRA, an urban national park. The fragrant forests, unspoiled beaches, and coastal bluffs are open to the public, including many miles of paved roads and hiking trails, plus a golf course, bowling alley, and tennis courts for more structured recreation. For a fuller description, see page 44.

Closed to vehicles, Crissy Field is one of the gems of San Francisco. Transformed from 100 acres (40.5 ha) of asphalt to an exquisite shoreline national park, it now encompasses a promenade for jogging or strolling (part of the 400-mile (643.7-km) Bay Trail), paths for bicycling, grassy fields and picnic areas, tidal marshes welcoming to native wildlife, and access to the bay for boardsailing.

Water, Water, Everywhere …

Open Water Swimming

Yes, San Francisco is on the ocean, but swimming in the cold waters off the city's beaches can not only be chilling, it can definitely be risky; some of the most inviting-looking beaches have dangerous undertows and rip tides, so swimming, and wading—even in waters that appear calm—may be unsafe. You will see some surfers in their wetsuits, but it's best to sun yourself, jog, or walk along the beaches to enjoy the view, and to consider the city's pools for relaxing and a steady swim.

One good beach in the city is the GGNRA's China Beach, off the Sea Cliff neighbourhood at Camino del Mar. Down a steep trail, the beach is fairly protected from the tides, but still pay attention, for there are no lifeguards on duty. Nearby Baker Beach has great views and is popular.

Bay swimming is more attractive, but it's not as simple as just jumping in the water in your bathing suit. The water is cold, and for most of the year, it's best to have a wetsuit. Your cap should be brightly colored, and you should have a swim mask (or goggles). Crissy Field has a swimming beach, and the rowing clubs listed below are also swim clubs and have popular swim events. For good swimming possibilities in the Bay Area, check http://rhorii.com/BABP/bestswim.htm.

- SwimArt puts on private, small-group open water swims: to Alcatraz, Bay Bridge to Aquatic Park, Bridge to Bridge, and more; http://swim-art.com/index.htm. Their FAQ page offers helpful information about open water swimming: http://swim-art.com/openwaterinfo.html.

Surfing

San Francisco itself may not be the best place for surfing for beginners, but, experienced surfers do try at Ocean Beach and at Fort Point in the city, and at others close by. Beginners often surf at Pacifica's Linda Mar Beach, and experts also go down to Half Moon Bay. Windsurfers tend to use Lake Merced and the more challenging area at Crissy Field. Check the various websites for information on best locations around the Bay Area for beginners to advanced: www.nerverush.com/top-5-places-surf-san-francisco/; or https://matadornetwork.com/destinations/north-america/united-states/san-francisco/guide-surfing-san-francisco-bay-area-beginners-experts/

Pool Swimming

The multi-sport fitness clubs listed below all have swimming pools, and "Park and Rec"maintains nine municipal public pools. Prices are reasonable, especially if you buy a series. Swim lessons are also available: http://sfrecpark.org/recreation-community-services/aquatics-pools/.

Water Sports

- Sailing: Opening Day on the bay in Spring can be an awesome sight with hundreds of vessels taking over the water, displaying their sails. They come out in force again during special events such as fireworks or the aerial displays of the Blue Angels. For people without boats, it is sometimes possible to sign on as crew. Try the Saint Francis Yacht Club; tel: (415) 563-6363; www.stfyc.com/, or the Golden Gate Yacht Club; tel: (415) 346-2628; www.ggyc.com/, both membership clubs located in The Marina.

- Rowing— Dolphin Swimming and Boating Club: 502 Jefferson Street, at the foot of Hyde Street; tel: (415) 441-9329; www.dolphinclub.org/. A group of hardy folk who swim in the Bay year round and row on the Bay and on Lake Merced. Try also the South End Rowing Club, next door: 500 Jefferson; tel: (415) 776-7372 http://serc.com/. In Golden Gate Park, as mentioned above, you can rent a boat at the Stow Lake Boathouse, and the same goes for Lake Merced Boathouse: Harding Road and Skyline Boulevard http://sfrecpark.org/permits-and-reservations/indoor-facilities/lake-merced-boathouse/.

- Kayaking—City Kayak, Pier 40; tel: (888) 966-0953; www.citykayak.com. Visit the scenic city destinations from your rental kayak. See the skyline around the bay, Alcatraz, the Golden Gate Bridge, etc. Get recommendations and advice from the company—especially as to the weather and conditions.

- Fishing—The city's municipal piers—at Fisherman's Wharf, Pier 7, or the Municipal Pier near FortMason, west of the Wharf—allow fishing in the heart of the city (as does Crissy Field) and people occasionally reel in flounder, rockfish, cod, bass, perch, or crabs. www.wildlife.ca.gov/licensing. Which fish are safe to eat, in this age of pollution and overfishing? Access the County of San Mateo Health System: www.smchealth.org/fishsmart. For Lake Merced,

https://oehha.ca.gov/fish/press-release/press-release-fish/
fish-advisory-san-franciscos-lake-merced-north-lake-
offers. And see page 157 for sustainable fish information.

Bicycling

For sports cycling, the entire Bay Area has excellent trails on
an extremely varied terrain, from mountainous to flat, and often
with outstanding views. Rec and Parks maintains the McLaren
Bike Park (in McLaren Park), for people of all ages and levels.
In the city, bikers also head for Golden Gate Park, along the
Great Highway, the Golden Gate Promenade, and around Lake
Merced. And people pedal along the sidewalk on the Golden
Gate Bridge, leading to some of Marin's most outstanding trails.

Participate with Critical Mass, the gathering of cyclists on
the last Friday evening of each month, when up to 2000 riders
pedal happily (and loudly) around the city, somewhat like the
rollerblade evening described below. www.sfcriticalmass.org/
For information about this and just about everything about
cycling in the city and Bay Area, check out the San Francisco
Bicycle Coalition (www.sfbike.org).

In addition to the Ford GoBike bike share program described
on page 132, you can rent bikes, especially for biking around
Golden Gate Park and other areas. https://parkwide.com/. For
Golden Gate Park, you can also rent your bikes (and in-line
blades) at Golden Gate Park Bike & Skate: 3038 Fulton Street;
tel: (415) 668-1117; http://goldengateparkbikeandskate.com/.
Within the park is the Stow Lake Boathouse with rowboats and
bikes for rent.

Inline Skating

For inline skating, many people take their gear to Golden
Gate Park, where a rollerblade hockey game can sometimes
be found near the tennis courts. The Marina Green or the
Embarcadero are also popular, but basically people skate just
about any place they want.

On Friday evenings, join the Midnight Rollers, and with hundreds of other skaters follow a serpentine course through the north part of the city and back to the starting point at the Ferry Building. Starts about 9:00pm; tel: (415) 752-1967; www.cora.org/friday.phtml.

Multi-sport Fitness Clubs

Urban San Francisco offers dozens of neighbourhood fitness and crossfit clubs, and storefront gyms—many with spas and other amenities. Yoga, pilates, and martial arts studios also are popular in the neighborhoods. In addition to their standard facilities, some offer scheduled athletic events, tournaments, and social gatherings.

- City-wide—The YMCAs offer aerobics, yoga, and dance classes, swimming pools, and racquetball courts.Four addresses in the city: www.ymcasf.org .
- City-wide—UCSF Campus Life Services: http://campuslifeservices.ucsf.edu/fitnessrecreation/services/fitness_centers/fitness_centers. The University of California San Francisco has several fitness and recreation centers. The Bakar Fitness & Recreation Center at Mission Bay—a major part of the ultra-modern biotech center—has three floors of activities and a rooftop pool: 1675 Owens Street, tel: (415) 514-4545.
- Embarcadero—Bay Club at the Gateway: 370 Drumm Street, tel: (415) 616-8800; www.bayclubs.com/gateway/. The Gateway club has the only outdoor swimming pools downtown, nine tennis courts, and a fitness center. For other Bay Clubs in San Francisco and the Bay Area, access www.bayclubs.com/.
- Masonic—Koret Health & Recreation Center, 2130 Fulton Street, tel: (415) 422-6811; www.usfca.edu/koret. Part of the University of San Francisco, Koret emphasises the "health" part of recreation. The facility has classes,

cardiovascular equipment, an interactive biking zone, a large indoor pool, sports clubs and an outdoor adventure program.

Asian Disciplines

As to martial arts and yoga, there are so many small dojos and teaching academies for so many different disciplines, it's best just to plug "martial arts San Francisco" into your browser and choose what's best for you. The same holds true for yoga, which has its own varied and specialized studios, but also classes in the health clubs and spas.

- Martial Arts: www.expertise.com/ca/san-francisco/ karate-taekwondo-martial-arts
- Yoga: https://fitt.co/san-francisco/ find-flow-17-yoga-studios-san-francisco/

Tennis

In addition to private clubs, more than 150 free public tennis courts dot the city's parks; they are "first-come first-served, except those in Golden Gate Park, which takes reservations. http://sfrecpark.org/recprogram/tennis-program. For listing of the city's courts—both public courts and private clubs—access www.tennissf.com/SF-Tennis-Courts.

For general group activities, events and classes with other tennis enthusiasts, consider joining the San Francisco Tennis Meetup: www.meetup.com/San-Francisco-Tennis-Meetup/?_cookie-check=I9W2b92nFn6j8m8L

Golf

Golf is a year-round sport, despite the winter rains and the summer fog, but San Franciscans are hardy, and swathed in sweaters and jackets, they wait patiently for their tee. There are a few private membership clubs in the city, and many clubs around the Bay Area are open to the public.

It may be surprising that there are six public golf courses in this small city; some are nine holes only, but full of twists and turns—and often breathtaking views. Access the Rec & Parks website for information on the courses and also how to register for the Resident Golf Card. http://sfrecpark.org/parks-open-spaces/golf-courses/.

Skiing

Some of the best skiing in the country takes place on the ski slopes of the Sierra Nevada, only a four-hour drive from San Francisco. In the winter, daily weather updates report the snow level and depth of snow pack of areas such as: Lake Tahoe, Incline, Alpine Meadows, Yosemite, and Bear Valley. Be prepared to carry tire chains in your car and from time to time to be stuck in the mountains until the roads are cleared of snow. Sunday night traffic off the mountains can be slow. CalTrans maintains a website for current highway conditions: www.dot.ca.gov/cgi-bin/roads.cgi.

Other Sports

- Basketball—You can probably pick up a basketball game in the Golden Gate panhandle, Dolores Park, at some of the city's playgrounds, the Moscone Recreation Center in the Marina, or the Potrero Hill Recreation Center; www.sfstation.com/guides/hoops-guide-16-best-basketball-courts-in-san-francisco/.
- Bowling—There are several bowling alleys in the city. It seems, though, that locals rave about Presidio Bowl: 93 Moraga Avenue, tel: (415) 561-2695; https://presidiobowl.com/contact/. Twelve lanes, a bar and grill, leagues and events, plus "glow in the dark" bowling on weekends. Downtown in SoMa, the Yerba Buena Ice Skating and Bowling Center at 750 Folsom Street also offers a "dance-club atmosphere", Sunday night family specials, and SoMa-style food and drink; tel: (415) 820-3532; www.

skatebowl.com/bowling. And there's ice skating there year-round. Check it out.

"SHOP TILL YOU DROP"

All Day, Every Day

As small and compact as it is, San Francisco's stores sell everything you need for your lifestyle. Nothing is hard to find; San Francisco being a totally-wired city—you'll find .everything you want on your browser. Whereas the large malls and chain stores are open all day on Sunday, neighborhood shops may close on Sundays or open for shorter hours

Getting to know your neighbourhood will help you get the personal, neighborly service that makes people feel at home. San Franciscans support their local businesses when they can. The city actively encourages people to buy locally, supporting the neighbourhood businesses. For information, check www. shopdine49.com.

Where to Shop

A description of the city's shopping districts must begin directly on Union Square, where department stores rule the scene. At this writing, Macy's is still the major department store—but reports indicate are that it may close in the next few years. Saks Fifth Avenue and Neiman Marcus are the most fashionable of the clothing chains. But the streets that surround Union Square house smaller, upmarket shops, both local boutiques and branches of national chains. Gump's, the most elegant and prestigious of old San Francisco shops, has entrances on both Post and Maiden Lane. Just across Market Street—now an extension of the Union Square area—is the huge vertical Westfield Centre shopping mall.

Some areas are known for a particular focus: art galleries downtown and around the Civic Center, antique shops on lower Jackson and on Sacramento near Presidio, modern furniture below Potrero Hill, appliances South of Market or in the Mission. South of Market also sees some outlets of the huge nationwide superstore chains. Some neighborhoods have fought to exclude the megastores, trying to preserve both the character of their areas and the small independent merchants. So, some of the large stores are just outside the city limits, but easy to get to. In any case, with both large chain stores and local businesses to choose among, you should have no trouble finding what you want.

Clothing

Clothing shops near Union Square may sport the most-recognized designer labels and the highest prices, but even the outlying districts sell interesting clothes at prices that match the quality and design. Shopping is almost a game for many San Franciscans who, however, tend to brag about how little they paid for an item of clothing or an accessory. It is not likely that you would find any damaged or inferior merchandise, but of course the quality reflects each manufacturer's approach.

Sales assistance in the smaller shops may be more personal than in the larger stores, but customer service is generally good no matter where you go. And, although many shops have been in their locations for years, stores do come and go. Check a particular shop's website make sure it's still there and to ascertain its hours.

Department stores and small shops carry children's clothing, shoes, and equipment and Target also has a large children's clothes department. Small shops tend to be clustered in family neighborhoods. For information on children's shops and services (as well as articles of interest and schedules of child-oriented events), pick up Bay Area Parent or access its website, www.bayareaparent.com/. Also check out the "best" shopping for kids in your browser.

Paying the Bill

Except for some small shops, stores accept the major credit cards. A few might still take a personal check on a California bank when you produce photo identification, although fewer do so now that almost everyone has a credit or debit card. People do not bargain on prices, as a rule, but if the merchandise is damaged and you still want to buy it, you may be given a discount.

Ask about the store's refund policy. The large stores and chains generally make refunds with no questions asked if you bring back the merchandise and the receipt within a reasonable length of time; they will also exchange ill-fitting goods for a larger or smaller size, or even a different color. Some stores will exchange for other merchandise only. Stores are not required to make refunds, and each store sets its own policy. An "all sales final," is often displayed, especially during a sale. If you have doubts, ask in advance.

Shopping Centers

Small shopping malls that cater to locals—with markets, repair shops, pharmacies—cluster in the different neighborhoods in San Francisco. The larger malls are generally anchored by a large department store, surrounded by dozens of smaller specialty stores. Stonestown Galleria and Westfield Center are the largest and most varied shopping malls in the city, rivaling those that sprawl just outside the city;

In addition to the malls listed below, these tourist destinations—the Cannery, Pier 39, The Anchorage, and Ghirardelli Square—hold some interesting and offbeat shops, and the massive Canton Bazaar in Chinatown stocks imported goods. Also, keep in mind the Ferry Building Marketplace for your markets and other shops.

- Market Street—
  Westfield San Francisco
  Centre: 865 Market at
  5th Street. An enormous
  vertical shopping mall,
  anchored by the upscale Nordstrom
  and Bloomingdales, plus dozens of stores, a large day
  spa, a food court, and a cinema.
- FiDi—Crocker Galleria: 50 Post Street, near Montgomery. A multi-story glass-domed mall of boutiques and eateries; its cafe-style tables and chairs under the skylight give the feeling of eating outdoors in any season.
- Embarcadero—Embarcadero Center: Battery and Sacramento Streets. A three-level shopping, dining, and cinema complex, spread across four buildings connected by walkways, and with a parking garage.
- Potrero Hill—Potrero Center: Neighborhood shops, anchored by a Safeway,
- Pacific/Presidio Heights—Laurel Village: 3500 California Street, past Presidio. An excellent varied local mall.
- SoMa—Metreon: 4th and Mission Streets. Part of the Moscone Center and Yuerba Buena Gardens complex, Metreon hosts dozens of shops, eateries, and a multiplex cinema.
- Sunset—Stonestown Galleria: 19th Avenue at Winston Drive. The enormous Stonestown Galleria contains shops, a multiplex cinema, and restaurants.

Best Prices

The superstores listed here offer extremely good prices and an extensive selection for your household and electronic needs or repair; there are also some clothing warehouse shops that are well-stocked and reasonably priced. But look at your neighborhood merchants as well, who may offer more personal service both during the purchase and afterwards.

- Clothing: Burlington Store #114, 899 Howard Street, tel: (415) 495-7234; www.burlingtoncoatfactory. com/store-details-Store-114--899-Howard-Street--San-Francisco--CA--94103-3037. aspx?id=806c9f7f-7cd6-4320-890b-41dcc8cc43d9.
- Computing: Apple Union Square: 300 Post Street, tel: (415) 486-4800; www.apple.com/retail/unionsquare.
- Computing & Electronics: Best Buy: 1717 Harrison Street, tel: (415) 626-9682; www.bestbuy.com
- SF Flower Mart: 640 Brannan Street, tel, (415) 392-7944 www.sanfranciscoflowermart.com/ .
- Furniture: Ikea, 4400 Shellmound Street, Emeryville, tel: (510) 420-4532; www.ikea.com/us/en/store/emeryville

- General/Food: Costco: 450 10th Street; tel, (415) 626-4388; https://m.costco.com/warehouse-locations/san-francisco-ca-144.html.
- General: Target: Stonestown Mall, tel, (415) 680-2914; https://www.target.com/sl/san-francisco-stonestown/3264 Other locations around the Bay Area.
- Hardware: Discount Builders Supply: 1695 Mission at 13th Street, tel: (415) 621-8511; www.discountbuilderssupplysf.com/#.
- Home Supply and Decoration: Bed Bath & Beyond: 555 Ninth Street, tel: (415) 252-0490); https://stores.bedbathandbeyond.com/San%20Francisco-CA-94103-38
- Home Supplies: Home Depot, 2 Colma Boulevard, Colma, tel: (650) 755-9600; Building Trade: at 91 Colma Boulevard is Home Depot Pro, tel: (650) 758-3410. Also at 303 East Lake Merced Boulevard, Daly City; tel: (650) 755-0178.
- www.homedepot.com/l/Daly-City/CA/Daly-City/94015/1092
- Shoes: DSW (Designer Show Warehouse): 400 Post Street, (415) 956-3453; http://stores.dsw.com/usa/ca/sanfrancisco/dsw-designer-shoe-warehouse-union-square.html.

BOOKS

Independent bookshops shine in San Francisco, despite being outdone by Amazon and ebooks. But San Franciscans are determined to support their independent bookshops. San Francisco Travel recommends ten independent bookstores: www.sftravel.com/article/10-independent-bookstores-where-you-can-find-perfect-gift. The independent bookseller Books, Inc has three shops in San Francisco and operates Compass Books at the airport: www.booksinc.net. And some bookshops also have sections on foreign languages:

- Chinatown—Eastwind Books & Arts: 1435 Stockton Street, tel: (415) 772-5888; www.eastwindbooks.com.

- Cow Hollow—Juicy News, 2181 Union Street, tel: (415) 441-3051.
- Financial District—Fog City News: 455 Market Street, tel: (415) 543-7400; www.fogcitynews.com/home.html
- Haight—Booksmith, 1644 Haight Street, tel: (415) 863-8688; www.booksmith.com/
- Japan Center—Kinokuniya Bookstore, 1581 Webster Street, in the Japan Center, tel: (415) 567-7625; www.kinokuniya.com/us/index.php/fho003

And … Not far from the City

Depending on where you live, these excellent and varied shopping malls around the Bay Area offer a wide variety sometimes different selections:

- Corte Madera: Town Center; The Village
- Daly City: Serramonte Center and Westlake Shopping Center
- Palo Alto: Stanford Shopping Center
- Pleasanton: Stoneridge Shopping Center
- San Bruno: Shops at Tanforan
- San Mateo: Hillsdale Shopping Center
- Walnut Creek: Broadway Plaza

Factory outlet malls offer good prices because the stores are run by the companies themselves, bypassing the wholesaler and retailer. Several outlet malls are located within an hour's drive of the city and all are open on Sunday with ample parking. Premium Outlets: www.premiumoutlets.com/outlet/san-francisco/stores.

NATIONAL HOLIDAYS AND LOCAL EVENTS

Holiday and festival dates may vary from year to year, often depending on the day of the week on which the event falls, and many national holidays are celebrated on Monday, no matter the actual date they commemorate, giving workers a long weekend break. On national holidays, all government offices are closed, including the Post Office; except for Christmas and Easter, the largest stores and supermarkets may be open for at least part of the day. Banks are closed on national holidays and by law may not be closed more than three days in a row, but on any day cash can be had from the ubiquitous ATM machines. Federal holidays in the calendar appear in boldface.

As for the purely local events, do not forget that San Franciscans love to party. When there is nothing official to celebrate and no occurrence to remember, the city creates its own. You can find a parade, street fair, race, or walk in honor of a charitable cause almost every weekend of the year. Note how San Francisco shows its appreciation of its multi-culturalism through the annual festivals of many other countries. San Franciscans may work hard, which they do, but for the rest of the time they want just to enjoy themselves—whatever is the most fun on that day.

January
- **1: New Year's Day**
- All month: Dine-About-Town: More than 100 fine restaurants offer lunches and dinners at special prices in this week-long celebration.

LOOKING FOR EVENTS

The website of the city's tourist Office, San Francisco Travel, is the most wide-ranging in its coverage of events around the city, with daily updates: www.sftravel.com/article/event-calendar#/94112-san-francisco/all/today. Check these links as well:
- www.sfgate.com/
- www.sfbg.com
- www.sfstation.com
- www.sanfranmag.com
- www.bay-insider.com
- www.sftourismtips.com/san-francisco-events.html

- **Third Monday: Martin King Jr. Day.** In honor of the civil rights leader slain in 1968.

February
- **Third Monday: President's Day**
- Dates vary: Chinese New Year. Weeks of activities, culminating in the Golden Dragon Parade, with marching bands, dragons, lots of firecrackers, and lots of fun.

March
- Sunday closest to March 17: Saint Patrick's Day Parade. All the Irish bars celebrate well into the wee hours.

April
- 1: Saint Stupid's Day Parade on April Fool's Day: Costume parade starts at Justin Herman Plaza and goes up Market Street.
- Mid-month: Cherry Blossom Festival at the Japan Center. A Grand Parade, arts and crafts, tea ceremonies, performances, all held on two successive weekends.
- Mid-April: Baseball season begins: Opening games for San Francisco Giants and Oakland A's.
- End of April: Opening day on the Bay. Sailing season starts with a boat parade and a blessing of the fleet.

May
- 5: Cinco de Mayo: Latin American festival produced by the Mission Neighborhood Centers, showing Latin American cultures, with music, dance food, and more; around Valencia Street between21st and 24th Streets.
- Third Sunday: Bay to Breakers Race. 7.5 mile (12.07 km) race, from the Bay to the ocean. A San Francisco "happening", drawing 100,000 runners, would-be runners, and some people in outrageously fun costumes.

- Black and White Ball. The whole city comes to this charity benefit held in various venues. Wear only black or white, dance, and listen to the music.
- **Last Monday: Memorial Day**
- Memorial Day Weekend: Carnaval. Large and lively multi-cultural festival and parade in the Mission district.

June

- All Summer: Stern Grove Midsummer Music Festival, 19th Avenue and Sloat Boulevard at the Stern Grove Amphitheater; tel: (415) 252-6252; www.sterngrove.org/. Free outdoor concerts every Sunday in the Concert Meadow of a lovely park.
- Early month: Escape from Alcatraz. Triathlon contest: 1.5 mile (2.4 km) swim to Alcatraz, 18-mile (29-km) bike ride and 8-mile run, finishing at the Marina Green.
- Mid-month: Fiesta Pistahan: Celebrating Filipino arts and culture: two days of music, arts & crafts, traditional food.
- Mid-month: San Francisco Jazz Festival: Two weeks of jazz, in venues around the city. Dates vary.
- Fourth Sunday: SF LGBT Pride Celebration. Week-long festivities and an enormous parade attracting a million people from around the world. This includes the annual Dyke March, as well. Second largest event in the State (after the Rose Bowl Parade), with 200 floats, people strolling alone or as couples, celebrating on until all hours.

July

- **4: Independence Day** (Known as the Fourth of July). Celebrate with thousands of San Franciscans at the Waterfront Festival, near Pier 39. Live concerts, activities for the whole family, culminating in exciting fireworks to end the night.
- Early July: Fillmore Jazz Festival: Fillmore Street: Thousands of jazz enthusiasts flock to various stages for

this long-established jazz festival. Along Fillmore, blocks stalls of arts and crafts, and gourmet food and drink keep the folks coming.

- Mid-month: San Francisco Marathon. Twenty-six mile (41.8 km) course from Golden Gate Park to the Civic Center.
- Late in month: Two-day event of a Ginza Bazaar and O-bon Dance. The Bazaar features food booths, an auction, homemade crafts, and more. The O-Bon dance features outdoor colourfully-dressed Japanese folk dancers.
- Dates vary: San Francisco Ethnic Dance Festival. Dozens of international ethnic dances, performed at the Opera House by local troupes and soloists.

August

- Date varies: Football season begins. San Francisco 49ers pre-opening game.
- Early month: Jerry Day. Concert and fun, celebrating the birthday of Jerry Garcia, the late leader of the Grateful Dead.
- Outside Lands: An annual music and arts festival in Golden Gate Park (near the Polo Field) that definitely highlights gourmet food from creative San Francisco chefs.
- Eat Drink SF; A large food festival held primarily at Fort Mason, offering sampling of San Francisco's amazing culinary creations.

September

- **First Monday: Labor Day**.
- Ghirardelli Chocolate Festival: on Beach Street, southern side of Ghirardelli Square. A two-day celebration of chocolate.
- Mid-September: Annual Comedy Day celebration at Robin Williams Meadow in Golden Gate Park. A day for comedians and a million laughs.

October

- Around October 1st: Blessing of the Animals at Grace Cathedral. On the Feast Day of Saint Francis of Assisi, the patron saint of animals.
- Early month: Litquake. Literary festival showcasing Bay Area writers. Readings, films, discussions at various venues.
- **Second Monday: Columbus Day**. Columbus Day parade celebrates the Italian heritage in San Francisco. Festivities, in North Beach and at Fisherman's Wharf, including a blessing of the fishing fleet.
- Around Columbus Day, Fleet Week: The U.S. Navy comes to town, and the Blue Angels, precision Navy flyers, take to the skies over San Francisco.
- Closest to full moon: Chinatown Autumn Moon Festival, annual harvest event in Chinatown. Dragon Parades, events and activities—on Grant Avenue/
- Mid-month: Open Studios. Artists all over town open their studios to the public.
- Mid-month: Hardly Strictly Bluegrass festival in the Hellman Hollow of Golden Gate Park. Join the crowds for three days of free bluegrass in gorgeous outdoor settings.
- Late Fall: San Francisco Opera and Symphony season officially begins;
- 31: Halloween. Celebrated around the Civic Center that puts on a Ghost Walk, and also in the Castro, with wonderfully outrageous costumes. One of the major events of the year.

November

- 2: Dìa de los Muertos. Mexican honoring of the dead in the Mission, with a fiesta, exhibits, and parade, lighting of candles at a specially-constructed altar.

- **11: Veterans Day**. Parade along Market Street to the Ferry Building.
- **Fourth Thursday: Thanksgiving Day**.

December
- Dates vary: Christmas Tree and Chanukah menorah lighting in various venues around the city: Union Square, Ghirardelli Square, Fisherman's Wharf.
- All month: Nutcracker Suite performed by San Francisco Ballet. Plus the Dance-Along Nutcracker.
- San Francisco Ballet full season begins.
- **25: Christmas Day**.
- 31: New Year's Eve: Fireworks along the Embarcadero, parties and events all around town.

CHAPTER 8

THE BAY AND BEYOND

> ❝East is east, and West is San Francisco.❞

> **— O. Henry**

OVER LAND AND ON THE SEA

A Wealth of Choice!

Northern California is so varied and beautiful—with wild bluffs, forests, mountains and ridges, fertile valleys, charming towns, and even a 14,000-foot (4,267.2-m) volcano (Mount Shasta) a bit farther north—that it is hard to suggest just a few outings for those who are here only a short time. There is also so much to relish within just a few hours of the City by the Bay in any of the four directions—yes, even to the west on the ocean itself—that there will certainly be something to appeal to your imagination, time, and budget. It should be no surprise that many of the attractions have to do with the appreciation of the natural beauty of the area; after all, it is California that you are here to see. You can't see it all right away, but you can get an idea of what the areas have to offer and immediately start thinking about coming back.

The Islands

Right in the middle of San Francisco Bay are several important Islands. Most people have heard of Alcatraz, the former notorious prison, and hardy tourists like Angel Island, with its nature trails. Fewer people explore the man-made Treasure Island, a former naval station and site of a World's Fair, but now with many attractions of its own.

Alcatraz, the former maximum security prison isolated on a wind-swept rock in the middle of the bay, is now a landmark, part of the Golden Gate National Recreation Area (GGNRA) and administered by the National Park Service (https://www.nps.gov/alca/index.htm). Over its 250-year history, it has

Alcatraz Island commands a 360-degree view of San Francisco Bay.

served as a military post and a rather inconvenient prison, as all supplies including fresh water had to be brought in by boat. Having closed in 1960, by 1969 it was occupied for about two years by a group of Native Americans, who claimed it as their right.

For a trip just to Alcatraz, expect to spend about three hours, including the ferry and the audio-guided tour. And, since the ferry leaves from Pier 41, it is easy to start first with a morning visit to the tourist shops at Pier 39, to have a coffee while admiring the view, and then get on the ferry at the time you reserved and head out onto the Bay.

Take the guided tour of the prison and then walk around the island and see the nesting birds and the life in the tide pools. Or, think perhaps of taking the evening tour that displays the entire Bay Area sparkling with lights. It is spectacular.

Angel Island is a state park and wildlife refuge (https://angel-lisland.com/). It is the largest of the islands in the Bay, and it is popular for picnics, hiking, and biking. The views are splendid. The trails are well kept, but for non-hikers there is also a guided tram tour that gives an overview of the island and its long and varied history. The native Miwoks were here for centuries before the Spaniards displaced them. The American government used Angel Island as a military base and then for 100 years as an infamous quarantine station for immigrants. Some of the buildings from that era still stand. Now, it is preserved for recreation and for wildlife, and is popular with tourists and locals alike.

Treasure Island, a man-made island created for a 1939 International Exposition, is tied to its neighbour, Yerba Buena, both reached by the Oakland Bay Bridge. Primarily, Yerba Buena holds a major Coast Guard installation, but there are three parks, all with views. Treasure Island, though, is more interesting. Previously a naval base, now it is actually a San Francisco neighbourhood, for several thousand people live there. Development of new homes, commerce, and hotel rooms are forecast, but for now it's just fun to go kayaking in a sheltered cove or relax at one of the beach bars. Go for beer or wine tasting (even in an old navy submarine!), eat well or picnic, and always enjoy the great views. And all of this just under the Bay Bridge, not far at all.

Another island is mainly the small residential town of Alameda, and most of the island has been developed. Originally a peninsula attached to Oakland, the dredging of a canal on the north created the island. On the south, there is a stretch of beaches. (https://alameda.gov.)

A Day on the Pacific Ocean

West of the Bay, there's the ocean. For a wonderful and educational experience, bring your warm jacket, hat and take a boat trip out onto the Pacific Ocean. Some 27 miles (43.45 km) off the shore of San Francisco is the Greater Farallones National Marine Sanctuary, craggy islands that are a federally-protected marine ecosystem encouraging to whales, dolphins, seals and seabirds as they feed and breed (https://farallones.noaa.gov/). The Farrallon Islands National Wildlife Refuge itself is one of the country's largest seabird rookeries (nesting season is from March through August), and its beaches welcome sea turtles, seals, and even the large Stellar's sea lions that are on the Endangered Species List (www.fws.gov/refuge/farallon_islands/).

Only researchers are allowed onto the wild, foggy, windswept islands, but boat tours circle the area to view whatever wildlife happens to be there at the time. Naturalist guides also help you spot whichever whales are on their seasonal migrations, and some summer cruises even take you farther out to the edge of the Continental Shelf itself. Although cruises usually go ahead as scheduled, rain or shine, occasionally they are canceled, depending on the state of the sea. And it is no joke: make sure you have protection from the weather. You are almost 30 miles (48.28 km) out into the Pacific Ocean, after all.

Migration seasons:
- Blue whales (June through October)
- Humpback whales (June through November)
- Pacific White Sided Dolphin (June through November)
- Great White Shark (August through November)
- Grey Whales: (December through May)
- Sperm Whales (November through April, although rarely seen)

Several companies offer whale-watching tours. Check the Internet sites for current schedules and prices.
- The Oceanic Society: Fort Mason Center; tel (800) 326-7491; weather information: (415) 256-9524; www.oceanic-society.org.
- San Francisco Bay Whale Tours: Pier 39; tel: (415) 706-7364; https://sanfranciscowhaletours.com/.

Ah, Sausalito!
Just across the bridge, more distant adventures start. Here are some adjectives to describe Sausalito: quaint, picturesque,

romantic, heavenly, Mediterranean, eclectic, adorable. On your way to experiencing them all, start by heading to the historic Ferry Building and wander around until it's time for the ferry to take you across the bay. Sausalito awaits! Here you will step off the boat into yet another beautiful Bay Area world. Bridgeway is the bayfront promenade, where as you browse the shops you might see San Francisco gleaming in the sun or, as is quite likely, socked in by a blanket of beautifully-white fog. The next street in is Caledonia, also with shops and restaurants to explore. That is all there is here: exquisite beauty, sunshine, and fun. So enjoy your afternoon. Some people call Sausalito paradise. See if you agree: www.oursausalito.com/visiting-sausalito.html

If you decide to drive, crossing the Golden Gate Bridge—with the bay to your right and the ocean on your left—stay in the right lane and turn off at the first opportunity, into the scenic overlook point. As you gaze at the panorama (if the weather cooperates), think of the Native Americans who lived here for a thousand years, think of the Spaniards who "discovered" the bay, after Sir Francis Drake passed it by (probably on one of those foggy days when he could not see a thing!) and marvel in the beauty as they must also have done. Then get back on the road for the next turnoff winding down into dreamy Sausalito, which actually is quite Northern-California real.

If you are driving (or even if you're taking the ferry), this might be the opportunity to continue up Highway 101 another fifteen minutes, to take in Tiburon, another lovely waterside town with stunning views (www.destinationtiburon.org/).

Muir Woods and Mount Tamalpais

Some tour companies offer combined excursions to Sausalito and Muir Woods, near Mill Valley, but no matter how you plan your time, Muir Woods alone is an opportunity to walk among some of the tallest and oldest trees in the world (www.nps.gov/muwo).

Only 12 miles (19.3 km) north of the Golden Gate Bridge at Mill Valley, up and down steep roads and finally down into an isolated valley, you will find an ancient coastal redwood forest, Muir Woods National Monument. Here in this primeval forest, you can walk among awe-inspiring 1,000-year old giant trees reaching 260 feet (79.25 m) up into the sky. You can see tall Douglas fir, big-leaf maples, tanbark oak, and bay laurels nestling under their even taller, majestic neighbors. This is the way Northern California might still look if it had not been for loggers, and these beauties too might have been cut in the 1800s if the valley had been more accessible. And thanks to a declaration in 1908 by President Theodore Roosevelt, the sequoia sempervirens—that grow only along the Pacific coast and reach no farther than 20 miles (32.2 km) inland—have been protected and preserved. Except for Big Basin State Park (see below), an even larger stand of redwoods, and which is about 55 miles (88.5 km) south of San Francisco, this is the only close-by place you will see these original growth lovelies. (Note that the famous, massive sequoia sequoiadendron giganteum grows only in California's Sierra Nevada Mountains, not close enough by.)

Above Muir Woods is Mount Tamalpais, the highest mountain the region, reaching up 2571 feet (www.parks.ca.gov/?page_id=471). On sunny days it has great views, it has nice trails for hiking and a restaurant and is a favorite with the locals for a day's escape from city life.

FARTHER AFIELD: THE WINE COUNTRY

Paradise Awaits!

The Wine Country deserves a book of its own (and several have been written), but even this necessarily brief overview can say the one important thing: go! No matter how short your time, no matter if you are someone who prefers a martini to the fruit of the vine, the Wine Country is not to be missed. There is wine tasting in hundreds of wineries to be sure, but there are also dazzling views, splendid parks, spas that offer hot volcanic mud baths, a petrified forest and a geyser, hot-air balloon rides, charming towns to stroll, golf courses galore, and numerous restaurants that serve the local bounty and the counties' own wines. So, it is best to spend a few days, if you can. Since these two spectacular valleys are so close to San Francisco, even if you can spare only one day from your exploration of The City, you can still get an idea of what the Wine Country has to offer. Then, without doubt you will begin your planning to come back for more. Nine million visitors come to these valleys each year, and many of them are locals who come back time and time again.

The Vines and the Wines

California grows grapes and produces wine in large portions of the state, starting in the south near Santa Barbara, stretching north to Mendocino, and thriving through the central San Joaquin Valley and as far to the east as the Sierra foothills up into the Gold Country. However, the two best-known and revered valleys—which are known as the Wine Country—are Napa and Sonoma. Fortunately, these are within an hour's drive of San Francisco, by car or on a tour. If you have had enough of fog and cool winds for a day or so, there is nothing like the Wine Country to warm your soul.

Make no mistake: some of the wineries you visit may be charming and small, homey and folksy, but wine is big business here and nothing less. Eighty five per cent of all American wine is made in California, selling almost 300 million cases of wine in the United States. Employing more than half a million people in more than four thousand wineries, and hosting some 23 million visitors, the wineries in Calfiornia add some $57 billion just to California's economy.

Resources

For detailed information about the Wine Country (more than you could possibly use on a short visit), before you go, access as much information as you can online:

- Napa Valley: www.napavalley.com.
- Napa Valley Wineries: www.napavalley.com/wineries/.
- Sonoma County: www.sonomacounty.com.
- Sonoma Valley: www.sonomavalley.com.
- Sonoma Valley Wineries; www.sonomavalleywine.com/.
- Sonoma Valley Wine Trolley: www.sonomavalleywinetrolley.com/.
- The Wine Country: www.winecountry.com.
- Napa Valley Vintners; https://napavintners.com/index.asp.
- Touring the Wine Country: www.thespruce.com/tour-napa-valley-and-sonoma-county-3510916.
- Wine train: www.winetrain.com.

The Wineries

In the Napa and Sonoma valleys, there are hundreds of wineries; some were damaged in the devastating fires of 2017, but just about all have recovered and are open for business. Check the websites listed above.

Napa alone has some 400 wineries. Almost all have tasting rooms, with opportunities not just to taste the wines, but to learn about the grapes, the winemaking process, and the differences that give the wines their own particular essence. Some of the wineries also have picnic tables and gift shops, and some offer full meals to show off the range of their wines.

Although the wineries produce several different kinds of wine, many are known for particular types of wine. If you are a true wine aficionado and intend to taste the wines of just one or two types of grapes, do your research in advance to maximize your time. And do not forget to try the various Zinfandels in the wineries of both valleys. "Zin" is a California experience not to be missed.

The Climate

So, now you are in the Wine Country sun and the air is probably gloriously clear. In fact, it is the climate and the soil that make these valleys produce the exquisite wines they do. Both valleys have the moderate climates one associates with Mediterranean countries; warm dry summers and fairly mild, wet winters. Yet both areas experience several microclimates: areas closer to the coast are affected by the Pacific fog and winds and have cooler days, while inland valleys, protected by the surrounding hills, are warmer. When the winter damp season ends and the hills turn from lush green to golden yellow, when the days are warm and the nights cool, the grapes ripen slowly and evenly. Wine aficionados pay attention to the weather and if there is any drop of rain, for these affect whether the harvest will be good, fine, or—as one always hopes—exceptional.

The Grapes

Although there are many different grapes grown in the valley, those linked below command the most acreage in the valleys. If a wine highlights the grape on the label, it is a "varietal", meaning that 75 per cent of the wine is made from that grape alone. Others used for blending make up 25 per cent or less.

- Napa: https://napavintners.com/napa_valley/grape_varieties.asp.
- Sonoma: www.sonomacounty.com/articles/sonoma-wine-facts.

Sparkling Wines

Sparkling wines seem to be a world unto themselves. There are many wineries that specialize in sparkling wines, and some have elegant grounds and gourmet meals in beautiful settings. These wines are called "sparkling" because the name Champagne may be applied only to sparkling wines that are produced in the Champagne region of France. Thus, even though the wonderful bubblies of the Wine Country employ the traditional French methode champenoise, they still are designated as "sparkling wines." (It's true that some old-time producers may use the name California Champagne according to a 2005 international agreement on wines, assigning the name solely to Champagne in France.)

- www.sonoma.com/blog/sparkling-wines-of-sonoma-county/.
- www.napavalley.com/guides/napa-valley-sparkling-wine/.
- www.californiachampagnes.com/sonoma-and-marin-counties/.
- http://winecountrygetaways.com/wine-regions/napa-valley/champagne-sparkling-wine-trail/.
- www.bookerandbutler.com/sparkling-wineries-napa-sonoma/.

In Between Tastings …

There's much more than wine in the valleys, enough to keep you here another few days, or to come back again and again.

Balloon Rides

Colorful hot-air balloons soar high above the Wine Country, giving their passengers a sublime overview of the valleys and little towns below.

Balloon rides start shortly after sunrise, when the breezes are mild and the air is fairly stable. They do not take off if the winds are too strong. The rides last up to about two hours. The balloons float between 500–2,000 feet (152.4–609.6 m) above the valley floor, and the baskets hold 2–4 people, some up to 8–10. Prices generally are toward $200 per person. Pilots are FAA-certified, and although the flights are safe, most companies require passengers to read the safety rules and affirm in writing that they have read them. Note that meeting places vary.

- Napa—Balloons Above the Valley: 603 California Boulevard, Napa 94559; tels: (800) 464-6824; (707) 253-2222; https://balloonrides.com.

- Napa—Napa Valley Aloft: 6525 Washington Street, Yountville; tel: (707) 944-4400; www.nvaloft.com.
- Napa—Napa Valley Balloons: 4086 Byway E, Napa, tel: (707) 944-0228; tels: (800) 253-2224; www.napavalleyballoons.com.
- Sonoma—Wine Country Balloons: 397 Aviation Boulevard Santa Rosa, tel: (707) 538-7359; (800) 759-5638; www.balloontours.com.
- Sonoma—Up & Away Ballooning: 1458 Lincoln Ave, Calistoga, tel: (707) 836-0171; www.up-away.com.

Petrified Forest

The Petrified Forest at 4100 Petrified Forest Road, Calistoga (between Santa Rosa and Calistoga) is what remains of an ancient redwood forest that was buried millions of years ago during a massive and long-lasting volcanic eruption (tel: (707) 942-6667; www.petrifiedforest.org). Hot ash mixed with rains over thousands of years buried the toppled trees. Then, organic matter, silicon, and oxygen, piled high during millions of years, slowly petrified and turned to stone. Hidden until erosion and the upward movement of the earth finally exposed some of the tips of this Pliocene forest, excavations about 150 years ago found an astounding forest of massive redwoods, completely made of stone. The forest is open daily.

Jack London State Historic Park

Jack London State Historic Park is in Glen Ellen, off Arnold Drive at London Ranch Road (tel: (707) 938-5216; www.jack-londonpark.com). Named after Jack London (1876–1916), a famous and prolific San Francisco-born writer, whose most celebrated book was *Call of the Wild*, the park was originally London's 1400-acre (566.6-ha) ranch. Now visitors can see the buildings that remain, including the ruins of Wolf House, which London designed and built, but which burned down in 1913, just weeks before he and his wife were to move in. The furniture that he designed is also on view. After London's death in 1916, his widow built The House of Happy Walls, which is now the park's museum and visitor center. A memorial to London, there are photographs and exhibits about his life, and a gift shop that sells his books.

There is, however, much more to the park. Evidence of previous occupants—from early natives to miners and their old homesteads—can be seen as you walk along the hiking and nature trails. (Do stay on trails, avoiding the poison oak and occasional rattlesnakes.) Not far away—about 0.5 mile—is a lake with a dam and bathhouse built by London, and there are wonderful views of the Valley of the Moon. You can walk up to the summit of Sonoma Mountain, or you can ride a bike or horseback along the several ridges (reservations tel: (707) 933-1600). In addition to self-guided tours, there are some that are docent-led. In Spring, there are interesting Wildflower Walks.

Picnic Provisions

If you have spent the morning wandering in the parks, or if you are heading to one of the wineries that has outdoor tables, you are going to want a delicious picnic. You have come to the right place.

- Sonoma—Sonoma Cheese Factory: 2 Spain Street, tel: (707) 966-1931; www.sonomacheesefactory.com/. This cheese factory is the home of all the varieties of Sonoma Jack. The deli offers local breads and meats, all the "fixin's" for a picnic, including local wines and beers. Look around, for there is a lot to choose from.
- Napa—Oakville Grocery: 7856 Saint Helena Highway, Oakville, tel: (707) 944-8802; www.oakvillegrocery.com. An oldtime country store—"picnic-friendly"—with the most modern of artisan cheeses, meats, smoked fish, local produce, and California wines. The bakery offers fresh, homemade pastries and good coffee.

Mud Baths

Since the late 1800s, when the railroad made the area easily accessible, visitors have flocked by the thousands to "take the waters" at Calistoga's many spas. Deep in the earth, an underground river flows over magma—molten rock—and it is this naturally hot mineral water that provides the waters for the town's spas, as well as the Calistoga Water that is served in so many restaurants. Today, there are spas with lodgings, day spas, and even spas for couples. Make sure to reserve in advance.

Yes, mud baths. Most of the spas feature a relaxing bath—covered up to your neck—in hot volcanic ash, mixed with peat and hot mineral water. It is not nearly as weird as it sounds. As you stay almost supine in the tub of hot mud, the minerals and heat draw out the toxins from your body, and you emerge—after having been scraped off, of course—relaxed and ready for the next healthful rounds: often a shower in hot mineral water, a steam, and then a massage. By the time you're done, you do not remember that you ever had a care in the world.

- Dr. Wilkinson's Hot Springs Resort, 1507 Lincoln Avenue, tel: (707) 942-4102; www.drwilkinson.com.
- Golden Haven Hot Springs Spa and Resort, 1713 Lake Street, tel: (707) 942-8000; www.goldenhaven.com.
- Baths at Roman Spa: 1300 Washington Street, (707) 942-2122; www.bathsromanspa.com.

Old Faithful Geyser

It is no accident that with those underground waters heated by the deep pockets of magma, there is a geyser right in the middle of Calistoga. Take the time to visit Old Faithful Geyser, at 1299 Tubbs Lane; tel: (707) 942-6463; www.oldfaithfulgeyser.com. There are three "Old Faithful" geysers in the world: the most famous for Americans is in Yellowstone National Park, another is in New Zealand, and the third is here in Calistoga, California.

"Old Faithful" is less a name than a category, referring to a geyser that erupts on a regular, periodic basis. As the water boils deep underground, it expands and moves into empty spaces, shooting upwards in a cloud of steam and scalding water. Calistoga's Old Faithful erupts every 45 minutes or so, its boiling water and steam shooting 60 feet up into the sky. It is truly amazing. The exhibit on geysers and earthquakes explains how these phenomena occur and that there may well be a correlation between deviations in the eruptions of the geyser and the appearance of earthquakes. Fortunately, the area was spared during the fire of 2017, and the exhibits are open to the public.

To the North: Reyes National Seashore

To the west of the Wine Country is where you'll find pure nature at its best. Some 30 miles (48.3 km) north of San Francisco on California Highway 1, there is a spectacularly wild peninsula that juts 10 miles out into the ocean, its bluffs overlooking the not-so pacific crashing waves. This is Point Reyes National Seashore, and there is nothing else like it (www.nps.gov/pore).

Here are vantage points to view the migration routes of the grey whales (seen especially from Chimney Rock and the Point Reyes Lighthouse), as well as sea lions, harbor seals, and even the seemingly indolent elephant seals on the beaches below. Shore- and seabirds abound. Tide pools teem with life. Off the 147 miles (236.6 km) of trails that traverse the area of 85,000 acres (34,398.9 ha), you might also get a glimpse of the rare Tule elk (at the north end), or some of the 30 other species of land mammals that have found a welcoming—and since 1962 federally protected—habitat. About 20 per cent of all California's flowering plant species are represented here so something is no doubt blooming at any time of the year. And, this is definitely earthquake territory, for the peninsula sits atop the northern end of the San Andreas Fault. Along the trails, you will see evidence of the earth having moved violently, but you will not notice that it is always moving slightly north, even as you stand admiring the view.

Start at the Bear Valley Visitor Center, which has information about the park, current exhibits and the flora and fauna to be seen, plus historical artifacts. And go on from there.

When you can finally bear to tear yourself away from the park, stop for a while at one of the charming coastal towns— Inverness, Point Reyes Station, and Olema—that have refused the encroachment of development. And do not miss Drake's Estero, a protected National Seashore, home to thousands of species of wildlife, in a true marine wilderness.

East to the Sun: Oakland and Berkeley

Back from the north, why not spend a day in the East Bay sunshine, when tourists back in San Francisco are braving the fog and wind? Both Oakland, with its population of about 420,000, and the university town of Berkeley, have attractions not to miss. If you are going to do both in one day, rent a car and drive over the Oakland-San Francisco Bay Bridge—one of the country's longest spans—completed in 1936 (and completely modernized in 2013), just before its more famous neighbor, the Golden Gate Bridge. Stop off at Treasure Island and visit its wineries, browse the antique dealers and admire the lovely views. Otherwise you can take BART, which is simple and cheap, but which may require more time getting from site to site than you may want.

Oakland is humming these days, having well recovered and moved on from its decades of decline (www.oaklandnet.com/). See the amazingly expanded zoo from its overhead tram (www.oaklandzoo.org) and stroll around or take a gondola cruise on Lake Merritt, the tidal lagoon and wildlife refuge that is so popular with locals.

Do plan to spend some fun time at Jack London Square, a waterfront destination in itself. There is always something going on there: the liveliest farmer's market in the East Bay, restaurants, shops, recreation, and even hotels. And then there is Yoshi's, a jazz club that sees international performers and large Oakland crowds. In fact, if you want just to visit Jack London Square, add to the fun by taking the Alameda-Oakland ferry across the bay directly from the Ferry Building to the Square (tel: (510) 749-5972; www.eastbayferry.com). The views are wonderful, of course, as they would be.

Uptown (which actually is downtown) has become a fun entertainment and arts destination, its restored historic buildings holding galleries, restaurants, nightspots, a symphony hall, movie theaters and more. And Rockridge, a village in itself, is a charming neighbourhood along College Avenue, with its bungalows and little shops and cafés.

- The Oakland Museum of California (OMCA) at 1000 Oak Street, tel: 98880 625-6873; www.museumca. org. The only museum to focus on California: its art, history, geography, and natural sciences. Do not miss the permanent exhibit of photographs by Ansel Adams.
- The African American Museum and Library: 659 14th Street, tel: (510) 637-0200; www.oaklandlibrary.org/ AAMLO. The history of African Americans in California.
- The Chabot Space & Science Center: 10000 Skyline Boulevard, tel: (510) 336-7300; www.chabotspace.org. Chabot is a wonder, starting more than a century ago as an observatory but is now a modern interactive museum and planetarium.

Berkeley may be known as a "university town," but, as you will see, it's much more (www.cityofberkeley.info/visitors/). Perhaps best remembered as being one of the radical, hippy branches of the University of California, Berkeley actually offers some of the best education in the country. More than 20 Nobel Prize winners have done their research here, and the school is famed for its academic excellence.

Start by strolling the major street near the university: Telegraph Avenue teems with coffee houses, bookshops, and artisan stalls that sell interesting handmade "this and thats". And then move on to see more.

- Lawrence Hall of Science: One Centennial Drive, tel: (510) 642-5132; www.lawrencehallofscience.org. An interactive science museum.
- Berkeley Art Museum and Pacific Film Archive (BAMPFA): on the university campus, tel: (510) 642-0808; www.bampfa.berkeley.edu.
- Berkeley Repertory Theater ("Berkeley Rep") 2025 Addison Street, tel: (510) 647-2949; www.berkeleyrep.org/index.asp. A year-round selection of innovative theatre.
- Tilden Park: In the Berkeley hills just north of Highway 24, Fish Ranch Road exit, turn right at Grizzly Peak Blvd. www.ebparks.org/parks/tilden. The lovely 2077 acre (840.53 ha) park has a botanical garden of California plants, with picnic areas and camping facilities; Lake Anza is good for fishing and swimming (in season), and there's a popular 18-hole golf course.
- Berkeley Rose Garden: 1200 Euclid Avenue, tel: (510) 981-6660; www.cityofberkeley.info/contentdisplay.aspx?id=12048. Some 1500 rose bushes and 250 varieties.
- University of California Botanical Garden: 290 Centennial Lane, tel: (510) 643-2755; http://botanicalgarden.berkeley.edu/. Succulents, redwoods, and greenery of all sorts.

To the South

The best attractions to the south of San Francisco cannot really be said to be in the Bay Area, but if you are ready for longer ride or a two-day excursion, it's well worth considering a trip south toward the beautiful and interesting Monterey Peninsula. To begin with, think of taking the slower scenic and curvy ocean road (California Highway 1) rather than the multi-lane inland highways that get you where you are going faster, but without the charm. Highway 1 will take you eventually to Monterey (and its spectacular aquarium and famous Cannery Row), the craggy cliffs of wild Big Sur, or the charming town of Carmel-by-the-Sea, and you will have a lovely ride. You will pass small beachside towns—often socked in by fog or buffeted by wind, but which sometimes sparkle gloriously in the sun. And the vast ocean on your right and the mountains on your left, as you curve around the coastal road, will take your breath away.

- Monterey: www.monterey.org/
- Monterey Bay Aquarium: www.montereybayaquarium.org/
- Monterey Cannery Row: www.canneryrow.com
- Carmel-by-the-Sea; www.carmelcalifornia.com
- Big Sur; www.bigsurcalifornia.org/
- Santa Cruz: http://www.santacruz.org

Note that there are some impressive places to visit on the way. If you are going to go as even as far as Santa Cruz, about 75 miles south of San Francisco, take time for two important parks, and stop off for an afternoon in Palo Alto (www.cityof-paloalto.org/visiting/default.asp).

Año Nuevo State Reserve is about 55 miles (88.5 km) south of San Francisco, and it is amazing (www.parks.ca.gov/?page_id=523). Here on the windy beaches the enormous elephant seals come to breed; they rest, they mate, and then they give birth in the sandy dunes. First the males battle to see who is going to get the best gals, and then the females just lie around until it is time to give birth in the dunes. Breeding season is December-March, and guided walks allow people to come fairly close to these huge animals (who are usually doing nothing to the human eye), but not too close, for these are wild animals, despite how peaceful they look; not only is it dangerous to get too close, it is a federal offense to bother them.

Big Basin State Park, 65 miles south of San Francisco at Boulder Creek, is home to some 18,000 acres of old growth—and recovering—coastal redwoods (www.parks. ca.gov/?page_id=540). Big Basin is the state's oldest State Park (established 1902). There are some 80 miles (128.8 km) of trails, numerous waterfalls, and abundant wildlife, including egrets, herons, and California woodpeckers. Sometimes you can see deer, raccoons, bobcats, and once in a rare while, even a mountain lion or two.

The Peninsula is also home to that unmapped area designated as "Silicon Valley", which refers to where so many of the innovations of the Information Age have been taking place. The major towns are Sunnyvale, Santa Clara, Cupertino, Palo Alto, and Saratoga. Perhaps the most interesting for visitors is San Jose; this bustling city has an excellent Children's Discovery Museum (www.cdm.org), and the San Jose Museum of Art (http://sjmusart.org), plus an enormous 930-square foot Monopoly outdoor game in a park (www.monopolyinthepark. com).

Between San Francisco and San Jose, though, is Palo Alto, the ineffable center of Silicon Valley, home to the lovely Stanford University campus and its Art Museum, the Hoover Institution, and the Stanford Linear Accelerator Center (www. cityofpaloalto.org/). If you just want a pleasant lunch and an afternoon of shopping, visit the upscale Stanford Shopping Center, where everything is there for you to find: www.simon. com/mall/stanford-shopping-center.

CHAPTER 9

BUSINESS AND EMPLOYMENT

> ❲The extreme geniality of San Francisco's economic, intellectual and political climate makes it the most varied and challenging city in the United States.❳

> — **James Michener**

BUSINESS ON THE PACIFIC RIM

From its earliest days, San Francisco has been a city of opportunities seen and grasped. Even today, whether you are coming to start your own business or for a job, you will find that San Francisco opens its doors to those who are qualified—and who understand how the city works. But be wise. In these changing economic and regulatory conditions, it is also especially important to understand what is happening nationally and in all of California as you start your research just for the Bay Area.

California's economy ranks about the 6th in the world and the Bay Area among the top 25 economies. San Francisco plays a crucial part in the economy and trade of the vast Pacific Rim, and with some of the world's major international corporations based here, it is sometimes called the "Wall Street of the West." With the city's well-established ties to Asia, finance and commerce along the Rim long dominated the most important parts of the economy of the city and the Bay Area region. Currently, exports have reached about $25 billion, having grown 30% in the last decade. China is the largest foreign market, but Asia in general accounts for more than half the activity, with Canada and Europe next. The GDP of the entire Bay Area is currently about $430 billion. In fact, if you are immigrating to the United States to participate in these industries, note that San Francisco is particularly welcome of newcomers. Immigrants make up about a third of the city's population, and reports are that some 12,500 are entrepreneurs. The city's

Immigrant Rights Commission stresses that immigration helps power the local economy.

Just in finance are the headquarters for Wells Fargo (the city's largest employer), Bank of the West, and Bank of the Orient; the Pacific Stock Exchange, Charles Schwab & Co, a U.S. Mint, the Federal Home Loan Bank, and the Federal Reserve Bank of San Francisco. The Bay Area also has among the highest concentration of venture capital investment in the country—particularly in the booming tech and artificial intelligence industries—further enhancing the region's importance as one of the most concentrated financial hubs in the United States.

However, the focus of the city has changed, and technology is now paramount, employing some 80,000 people. Headquarters of international corporations include—to name just a few—Salesforce (which will soon have more staff than Wells Fargo), Twitter, Airbnb, Dropbox, Dolby, Yelp, Uber and Lyft, and dozens of multi-national technology services. Also, Facebook/Instagram (with 23,000 employees) with its primary campus in Menlo Park, now is housing a large employee contingent in a tower in San Francisco.

But—as with just about everything in the Bay Area—categories overlap, even locations. Just south of the city—in "Silicon Valley"—are some of the most important international technological corporations: Apple, for instance (with some 12,000 employees in Cupertino), plus Cisco, Facebook, Google, Hewlett-Packard, Intel, Netflix Oracle, and Tesla. Some of their staffs prefer to live in San Francisco than on the Peninsula, so companies shuttle them to and from work each day.

For the city itself, tourism is still one of its largest revenue-generating industries, sustaining more than 66,000 of the city's jobs. Often rated by travel magazines as the nation's most popular vacation spot, San Francisco is currently visited by some 25 million visitors who spend more than $9 billion in the city each year. Other than vacationers, the city is also a draw for some 200 trade shows, conventions, and business meetings. International visitors account for just under half of all hotel guests, and these explore the city every day, spending their money at tourist attractions, in the downtown and outer shopping districts, and especially at the city's restaurants.

Don't be discouraged by the power of the large corporations. San Francisco encourages start-ups, and small, locally-owned businesses and restaurants. In fact, despite the invasion of nationwide chain stores and franchises, community-grounded businesses continue to characterize the city, from tourist-oriented kiosks and eateries of all quality and prices, to services the citizens need, to the funkiest or most elegant fashion boutiques. Many businesses succeed, yet some fail, certainly owing to economic variables, but also often owing to an incomplete understanding of how the city works. Much will depend on the amount of knowledge you have at the outset—including that all-important aspect of location—and how organized and funded you are in your approach. Although it seems that business and financial information change day-by-day, here are some general websites that should be helpful in thinking about business.

- www.eventbrite.com/o/san-francisco-sba-entrepreneur-center-7819349965
- www.sfsmallbusinessweek.com/about-us/
- www.census.gov/quickfacts/fact/table
- http://sfced.org/why-san-francisco/facts-figures/

THE START-UP

Make sure you understand the legal and financial intricacies of opening a business and the risks involved. Start with the U.S. Small Business Administration (SBA), located on the sixth floor of 455 Market Street. SBA, an agency of the federal government, helps anyone who wants to open a small business; tel: (415) 744-6820; www.sba.gov/offices/district/ca/san-francisco. It is also the largest source of long-term small business financing in the nation. Loans are made to qualified applicants by private lending institutions that participate in the SBA program.

- The San Francisco African American Chamber of Commerce: 1485 Bayshore Boulevard; tel: (415) 749-6400; website www.sfaacc.org. Helps to connect African American business owners to the global market.

- Asian Business League of San Francisco: PO Box 191345, tel: (415) 670-9022; www.ablsf.org. This is a membership organization for Asians in business, providing seminars, workshops, networking events.

- The Better Business Bureau that services San Francisco is at 1000 Broadway in Oakland; tel: (510) 844-2000 or (866) 411- 2221; www.oakland.bbb.org. The BBB provides information on companies, including lists of those with good records.

- The Renaissance Entrepreneurship Center: 275 Fifth Street, tel: (415) 541-8580; www.rencenter.org; Non-profit entrepreneurial training organization that works in conjunction with SBA and some private businesses, offering training and help for people wanting to create their own businesses. Also in Bayview at India Basin Plaza, 1325-B Evans Avenue; tel: (415) 647-3728.

- Mission Economic Development Association (MEDA): 2301 Mission tel: (415) 282-3334; fax: (415) 415-282-3334; www.medasf.org This bilingual (Spanish and English) association in the heart of the Mission provides counseling, technical assistance, and loan packaging services (through the SBA and small lenders) to people (especially Latinos) wishing to set up a new business or improve an existing business.

- San Francisco Chamber of Commerce: 235 Montgomery Street, tel: (415) 392-4520; fax: (415) 392-0485; www. sfchamber.com. A non-profit membership association of more than 2,000 local businesses of all sizes.
- San Francisco Small Business Network: PO Box 225336; tel: (415) 731-2859; www.sfsbn.org. This group promotes and lobbies for small business and education programs, aiming to strengthen and unify the voices of small business owners.
- San Francisco Business Times: 275 Battery Street, Suite 940; tel: (415) 989-2522; fax: (415) 398-2494; www. bizjournals.com/sanfrancisco; An excellent newspaper and online resource for current business information and business-related reports.

Networking

San Franciscans are friendly and open both professionally and socially, so you should have little trouble meeting people and becoming an active member of the professional communities. For networking, consider joining the following groups:

- The City Club of San Francisco: 155 Sansome Street, 10th Floor; tel: (415) 362-2480; www.cityclubsf.com. A multi-purpose professional and social club that accommodates breakfast speakers, conducts networking forums, and organizes special events.
- The Commonwealth Club of California: 110 The Embarcadero tel: (415) 597-6705; www. commonwealthclub.org. This prestigious public affairs group invites well-known and interesting people to speak at meal-centered meetings (breakfast, lunch, dinner, receptions). Also organized are special and social events geared to current issues; outings to cultural and sports events.

An aerial view of San Francisco's Financial District at night and the Bay Bridge in the background.

- Golden Gate Business Association, 584 Castro Street, tel: (415) 862-4422; www.ggba.com. San Francisco's oldest GLBT business organization, GGBA includes professionals, business owners, and artists, and it conducts networking events and a variety of business-related programs.
- National Association of Women Business Owners, San Francisco: 237 Kearny Street, tel: (415)333-2130; www.

nawbo.org/san-francisco-bay-area. NAWBO provides networking, business, and social contacts. It also has links with women's business groups worldwide.

- Professional women's Network (PWN): 25 Holly Park Circle: http://pwnetwork.com/contact-pwn/. Social and professional networking at lunches on the first Friday of each month.

- Rotary Club of San Francisco: 588 Sutter Street, tel: 300 Montgomery Street, tel: (415) 335-9717; www.sfrotary. com. Rotary's local businesses members take on and fund civic projects to help communities worldwide. The usual meeting location is at the Sir Francis Drake Hotel at 450 Powell Street, most Tuesdays at noon. Check the website for specifics.

- World Affairs Council of Northern California: World Affairs Center, 312 Sutter Street, Suite 200; tel: (415) 293-4600; www.worldaffairs.org/. The Council holds programs on foreign policy issues, organizes events with international guests, and has forums on current issues, plus special and social events.

THE JOB SEARCH

San Francisco has long been home to plentiful jobs, traditionally in finance, international trade and especially in tourism. Now with upwards of 80,000 people employed in technology-related industries and with even more coming to the skyscrapers that have been built to hold them, obviously the focus has changed. Technology brings jobs, and the plentiful workforce brings more tech firms. Employment also focuses on the leisure and hospitality fields, in locations around the extensive University of California medical complex and bioscience companies in Mission Bay. Multimedia companies tend to thrive, and Lucasfilms has its headquarter in the Presidio.

Yet if there are jobs, they are easily filled, and the unemployment rate in San Francisco hovers around 3.5%, below the national average. Make sure your résumé and cover letter are well organized and presented. Networking—check the opportunities above—is always helpful.

Average wages in San Francisco are currently about $85,000 annually, but think carefully about your lifestyle, for the cost of living in the city is well above the national average, and although salaries are high, they may not stretch as far as you think, especially when the cost of housing is the highest in the country.

• www.glassdoor.com/Salaries/san-francisco-salary-SRCH_ IL.0,13_IM759.htm
• www.payscale.com/research/US/ Location=San-Francisco-CA/Salary

In order to apply for a job, you might be asked to prove that you are legally permitted to work in the United States; foreigners may be asked to take an English-language test. In addition, some companies will test you on the skills you claim to have, in addition to checking samples of your work and references.

If you are coming to the city without a job, start your search before arrival by looking at the websites of employment agencies and the San Francisco Chronicle (www.sfgate.com). The Sunday issue has an extensive career section containing articles, advertisements for career development, and a major section of classified ads for job openings.

In addition to listing yourself with the employment agencies, try to take advantage of the organizations that help people to develop their capabilities, to present themselves well, and to understand and access the San Francisco job market:

• California Employment Development Department: www. edd.ca.gov/Find_a_Job.htm. EDD works with state and local agencies in employment and training.
• Jewish Vocational Service and Career Counseling (JVS): 225 Bush Street, Suite 400; tel: (415) 391-3600; www. jvs.org. JVS, a non-sectarian. non-profit job counseling

and employment agency, organizes workshops, provides opportunities for networking, and conducts skills training programs,

- Media Alliance at the Pacific Felt Factory, 2830 20th Street, Suite 102, tel: (415) 746-9475; https://media-alliance.org/. A non-profit association for communications and general media professionals. The Jobfile lists available positions.

Employment Agencies

The dozens of employment agencies in the city offer temporary and permanent jobs. Basically, just check your browser for jobs available in your field. Or look, as usual, at those grouped as "the best": www.expertise.com/ca/san-francisco/employment-staffing-agencies#provider17. Some agencies are nationwide, and their listings might be broader for the area than those just in the city:

- Kelly Services Inc; www.kellyservices.com; Nationwide, matches jobseekers to temporary positions in several fields, including clerical and accounting.
- Manpower; www.manpower.com; Nationwide, specializes in recruitment, training, selection of job candidates, and listings of jobs.

Also, some agencies specialize their categories, such as:

- ABA Staff: www.abastaff.com. Legal and technology jobs and professional services.
- ProGayJobs: www.progayjobs.com; Specializing in jobs for the GLBT community, with a wide range of full-time and temporary positions.
- The Job Shop: www.jobshopsf.com; temporary and permanent positions in architecture and accounting, sales, marketing, advertising, financial services, and more.
- Mayor's Youth Jobs+: http://sfyouthjobs.org/. Works with various non-profit and governmental entities to find jobs for young adults.

CHAPTER 10

SAN FRANCISCO AT A GLANCE

> *It is an odd thing, but every one who disappears
> is said to be seen at San Francisco.*

— Oscar Wilde

Official Name
City and County of San Francisco

Flag
A gold border on a white background with the crest of a phoenix rising from the fire in the center of the flag. The crest sits on top of the motto, *Oro en Paz*, *Fierro en Guerra* (Gold in Peace, Iron in War).

Time
Greenwich Mean Time minus eight hours (GMT -0800) during Standard Time and minus seven hours (GMT -0700) during Daylight Savings Time. San Francisco is on Pacific Standard/ Daylight Savings Time. Three hours behind Eastern Time Zone (New York).

Area
Land area: 46.9 square miles (121 sq km); tip of peninsula between Pacific Ocean and San Francisco Bay.
Including ocean and bay portions within city/county limits: 128 square miles (332 sq km).

The Hills
Although there are 42 hills of varying heights throughout San Francisco, the seven major, well-known hills are: Nob Hill, Telegraph Hill, Russian Hill, Rincon Hill, Twin Peaks (two together), Mount Davidson (the highest in the city) and Mount Sutro.

Main Districts

Union Square, Financial District, SoMa (with Mission Bay, Dogpatch, Bayview and Hunter's Point) and Nob Hill; Chinatown, North Beach, Telegraph Hill, and Russian Hill; Pacific Heights, the Marina, Cow Hollow, and the Presidio; Japantown, Western Addition, and the Haight; The Mission, The Castro, Noe Valley, Glen Park, and Bernal Heights; The Sunset, The Richmond, and OMI.

Climate

Predominantly cool weather owing to ocean currents and winds sweeping through the Golden Gate. Winters tend to be rainy and cool. Summers can be foggy and windy, especially in the mornings. Warmest temperatures are generally in Spring and Fall. Average yearly rainfall: 20 inches (51 cm).

San Francisco Climate			
Month	Average High Temperature	Average Low Temperature	Average Rainfall
January	55°F	41°F	4.4 inches
February	58°F	45°F	3.2 inches
March	60°F	45°F	3.1 inches
April	64°F	47°F	1.4 inches
May	66°F	48°F	0.2 inches
June	70°F	52°F	0.1 inches
July	71°F	54°F	0 inches
August	72°F	55°F	0.1 inches
September	74°F	55°F	0.2 inches
October	70°F	51°F	1.2 inches
November	62°F	47°F	2.9 inches
December	56°F	42°F	3.1 inches

Population
San Francisco: 875,000 (2018)
Metropolitan Area: 4.6 million

Ethnic Groups
Caucasian (53.6%), Asian (35.3%), Chinese (21.4%), Latino of any race (15.3%), African-Americans (6.1 percent). Largest Asian population in America outside of Hawaii. One-third of the residents were born outside of the country.

Government Structure
The City and County of San Francisco is a metropolitan municipality with a consolidated government: a mayor and board of supervisors, elected by the populace.

Official Language
English is the "common and unifying language" of the United States. It is the official language of California. In San Francisco, much city information and election ballots are in English, Spanish, and Chinese.

Voltage Rating

The standard electric current in the United States is 110–115 volts (60 Hz). Wall outlets take plugs with two flat prongs and a round ground pin above. Cell phones and foreign electronics should convert voltage automatically; if so, the appliance will need only an adapter.

Currency

U.S. dollar (USD or US$)

Industries

Banking and Finance, technology, biosciences, tourism, manufacturing, electronics.

Famous Earthquakes:

April 18,1906: magnitude 8.25 on the Richter scale; 28,000 buildings were destroyed; more than 3,000 people died.
October 17th, 1989: magnitude 6.9 on the Richter scale. The Embarcadero Freeway was damaged and then demolished.

The Transbay Transit Center was damaged and has been completely rebuilt and expanded, linking it with the adjacent skyscraper, and now named the Salesforce Transit Center.

Airports

One international airport: San Francisco International Airport (SFO); 14 miles (22 km) south of San Francisco; website: http://www.san-francisco-sfo.com

City Attractions

- Highest Point: Mount Davidson (282 m / 925.2 ft)
- Lowest Point: Sea level
- Shoreline: 29 miles (46.7 km)
- Steepest Streets, with 31.5 per cent of grade: Filbert Street, between Leavenworth and Hyde; 22nd Street between Church and Vicksburg
- Longest Street: Mission Street (7.29 miles / 11.7 km)
- Oldest Street: Grant Avenue (Originally Dupont)
- Oldest Square: Portsmouth Square
- Oldest Building: Mission Dolores, completed in 1791
- Tallest Building: Salesforce Tower
- Victorian Houses: 14,000
- Golden Gate Park: Established 1870, city's largest park at 1,013 acres (410 ha).

SOME WELL-KNOWN AMERICANS

George Washington (1732–1799)

"The Father of Our Country." General who led the American armies to victory over the British in the Revolutionary War, and beloved first President of the United States. Official celebration of his birthday: Presidents' Day, the third Monday in February.

Meriwether Lewis (1774–1809)

Asked by President Thomas Jefferson (1743–1826) to lead an expedition to the unexplored Western frontier. Lewis and his friend Will Clark set out in 1804. Over one and a half years, they navigated the Missouri River, crossed the Rockies and followed the Columbia River to the Pacific Ocean.

Abraham Lincoln (1809–1865)

One of America's greatest presidents. Lincoln preserved the Union during the Civil War and abolished slavery, but was assassinated for his efforts. Official celebration of his birthday: Presidents' Day, the third Monday in February.

Susan B. Anthony (1820–1906)

Civil rights leader, working for abolition of slavery and then for women's suffrage. Called "the Napoleon of the Women's Rights Movement."

Geronimo (1829–1909)

An Apache born Chiricahua Goyaałé and later nicknamed Geronimo. Fought against the United States to preserve the independence of Native Americans and their tribal lands. Brave and determined as he was, he could not succeed.

Louisa May Alcott (1832–1888)

Prominent woman writer, whose most enduring novels are *Little Women* (1868–1869) and *Little Men* (1871).

Mark Twain (1835–1910)

Revered humorist and writer of adventure stories, including *Life on the Mississippi*, *The Adventures of Tom Sawyer*, and *The Adventures of Huckleberry Finn*. Credited with saying, "The coldest winter I ever spent was summer in San Francisco."

Alexander Graham Bell (1847–1922)

Inventor of the telephone and the "photophone," which transmitted sound over a beam of light, the forerunner of the wireless, laser, and fiber optics technology of today.

Jack London (1876–1916)

San Francisco-born writer, whose most famous book is *Call of the Wild*. Some of his vigorous stories of surviving hardships and travail were based on his own life.

Franklin Delano Roosevelt (1882-1945) and Eleanor Roosevelt (1884-1962)

Thirty-second president of the United States, Franklin Roosevelt, brought social programs and justice into modernity, and saw the country through most of World War II. His widow, Eleanor, remained an activist on social issues and women's rights, wrote a newspaper column, and was appointed by President John Kennedy as the United States' ambassador to the United Nations. She was admired by people around the world.

John Steinbeck (1902–1968)

California-born novelist, whose writings emphasized the hard lives of poor workers during the Great Depression. His most lasting works are *Of Mice and Men* and *The Grapes of Wrath*. Much of his work takes place in the Salinas Valley-Monterey area of California. Steinbeck won the Nobel Prize for Literature in 1962.

Francis Albert Sinatra (1915–1998)

One of America's first "teenage heartthrobs," Frank Sinatra's singing career as a pop vocalist kept his name always at the top of the charts. Among his 250 million records, his recordings of *My Way*, *Strangers in the Night*, *New York, New York*, and *It Was a Very Good Year*, remain perennial favorites. As an actor, his movie credits included *From Here to Eternity*, for which he won an Academy Award, and *Guys and Dolls*.

John F. Kennedy (1917–1963)

America's 35th President. Young, charming, and energetic, Kennedy's presidency brought a refreshed idealism and energy to the United States. Assassinated in 1963, he did not live to see his programs for justice and civil rights put into effect.

Lawrence Ferlinghetti (1919–)

A proponent of the movement called "The Beat Generation", which rejected the traditional values of the 1950s. An influential poet, Ferlinghetti has for 50 years been a powerful challenge to entrenched artistic and literary interests. His City Lights Bookstore in San Francisco is a well-known center for intellectuals and poets. Named first San Francisco Poet Laureate in 1998.

César Chávez (1927–1993)

Founder of the United Farm Workers, he organized a 5-year strike of California grape pickers. Remembered as a powerful force for the rights of migrant workers. His birthday, March 31, is a California state holiday, the only one honoring a Mexican-American in the United States.

Martin Luther King (1929–1968)
Pivotal and inspirational figure in the American Civil Rights movement, Martin Luther King was awarded the 1964 Nobel Peace Prize. Official celebration of his birthday: Martin Luther King Day, January 15th.

Muhammad Ali (1942–2016)
Born Cassius Clay, but in embracing Islam (as a Sunni Muslim) refused to retain his "slave name". A boxer and heavyweight Champion of the World, Ali was named Sportsman of the Century in 1999. Ali was respected both for his athleticism and for being outspoken for his beliefs. He received the Presidential Medal of Freedom in 2005.

Dianne Feinstein (1933–) and Kamala Harris (1964–)
Senators from the State of California, both are Democrats and outspoken leaders for justice and equality.

Jerry Garcia (1942–1995)
San Francisco-born, lead guitarist of the psychedlic rock group The Grateful Dead. Epitomized the freedom-loving attitude of the times, Garcia was seen as a guru by legions of devoted fans, called "deadheads".

Arnold Schwarzenegger (1947–)
Bodybuilder and star of *The Terminator* movies, former Governor of California.

Robin Williams (1951-2014)
Stand-up comedian and famous movie actor (*Mrs. Doubtfire*, *Good Morning, Vietnam*, *Awakenings*). Lived in San Francisco

until his death in 2014. The Sharon Meadow in Golden Gate Park has been renamed for him.

Barack Obama (1961–)
Forty-fourth president of the United States, and the first African-American to be elected president. He served two terms, from 2009–2017.

ABBREVIATIONS, ACRONYMS ... AND SLANG

San Franciscans often personalize names when speaking, making them shorter or cuter, or just more efficient. Although sometimes you will see the slang in writing, generally it is used only in conversation. Acronyms are pronounced as though they were words.

- American Conservatory Theater: A-C-T
- As soon as possible: A-S-A-P
- Bay Area Rapid Transit: Bart
- Bay Guardian: The Guardian
- California Department of Transportation: Caltrans
- Disk Jockey: D-J
- El Camino Real (Road leading to the South Bay): The Camino
- Financial District: Fi-Di (acronym)
- Fisherman's Wharf: The Wharf
- Freeway 101: One Oh One
- Freeway 280: Two Eighty
- Freeway 5: The 5
- Golden Gate Bridge: The Bridge
- Golden Gate Park: The Park
- Golden Gate Recreation Area: G-G-N-R-A
- Haight Ashbury district: The Haight
- Lesbian, Gay, Bisexual, Transgender: L-G-B-T

- Mark Hopkins Hotel bar: Top of the Mark
- Museum of Modern Art: MoMa (acronym)
- Oakland Athletics: The A's
- Pacific Bell: Pac Bell
- Pacific Gas and Electric (PG&E): P-G-'n-E
- Sacramento: Sacto (The state capital)
- *San Francisco Chronicle*: *The Chronicle*
- San Francisco: The City
- San Francisco Forty Niners (football team): The Niners
- San Francisco Giants (baseball team): The Giants
- San Francisco Municipal Transportation Agency: The Muni
- San Francisco International Airport: The Airport, or S-F-O
- San Francisco-Oakland Bay Bridge: The Bay Bridge
- San Mateo County Transit: SamTrans
- South of Market: SoMa (acronym)
- Streets west of Arguello: The Avenues
- Thank God it's Friday: T-G-I-F

CULTURE QUIZ

SITUATION 1

Your new colleagues have set up a Saturday night dinner at a trendy restaurant in the Mission. It's a going-away party for the department head. On Saturday, when you're thinking about what to wear, you realize you have no idea how dressy you should look. And you don't have the home telephone numbers of anyone who will be there. What do you wear?

Ⓐ You don't want to take a chance on dressing too casually for this important occasion, and you want to impress your new colleagues. So you wear what you would wear to the office—a sports jacket and tie for a man, a suit and silk blouse for a woman.

Ⓑ This is San Francisco and the dinner is in the trendy, young Mission District, so you don't think you have to get dressed up at all. You put on some casual clothes—decently pressed slacks and a sweater—and know you look "put together," but not overly dressed.

Ⓒ It's the weekend and you've previously noticed people wearing jeans, even in the trendiest of restaurants. You put on your clean jeans and a good shirt and make sure you look put together and trendy, yourself. You want to fit in with your new friends, and this is probably what they will wear.

Comments

The answer is B. Unless you're sure it's a dressy occasion in an upscale (expensive) restaurant, you don't need to wear business clothes for an evening out. So, wear something casual and comfortable, but make sure you look good or presentable. San Franciscans—even those who would have chosen answer C and wear jeans—make sure that no matter how casual their dress, they show they care about their appearance. In a city where people spend a lot of time keeping fit, it's not surprising that they would want to flaunt the results of their efforts.

SITUATION 2

You are an older person who has decided to retire to San Francisco. When you are settling into your new home, you call PG&E to have your electricity hooked up. The telephone representative asks your name and then immediately calls you by your first name. You are surprised by such familiarity from someone you've never met; you come from a culture that respects both age and formality, and where strangers are addressed by their last name, prefaced by Mr. or Ms. You don't like it that someone you don't even know, and who hasn't even told you her own name, seems to show you no respect. How do you handle this?

Ⓐ You just say politely, "Excuse me, but I'd prefer you to call me by my last name."

Ⓑ You try to be friendly and respond, "If you're going to call me by my first name, at least tell me yours."

Ⓒ You don't bother to say anything. This could just be a person who is not well-bred, so let it go. You probably won't be put in the same situation again.

Comments

If it's important to you to be called by your last name, then say so. In that case, the answer is A. The telephone representative on the phone shouldn't be insulted and the situation will have resolved itself. Answer B is somewhat acceptable, but since this is a business telephone call, there's no point in adding a second artificial and insincere friendliness to that of the first. Answer C is the best option, but understand that the person isn't being rude. Americans generally call people by their first names, often upon first meeting. This has now extended itself to business calls, and although you might take such behavior as undue familiarity (even some Americans do), here it's often seen as friendliness, trying to put the customer at ease. So, you might as well get used to it, or on days when you decide more formality is required, resort to answer A.

SITUATION 3

You have finally moved into the new apartment you've purchased in Pacific Heights. It's just the apartment you've been looking for, in the district you wanted, and with all the amenities you hoped for. You're excited, and you tell the good news to a colleague at work. You say what street the apartment is on and all the things you like about the place. You are surprised when your friend asks you how much the apartment cost. You are not used to talking about money and think the price of the apartment is no one's business but your own. What do you say?

Ⓐ You just laugh and say, "Wow, much more than I thought it would," and then change the subject to a general one of how expensive housing in San Francisco is.

Ⓑ You say how much it cost you.

Ⓒ You explain that in your culture people don't talk openly about money the way people do in the United States, and that it isn't something that you can do.

Comments

People in the United States are often more open about discussing the specifics of money than in other countries. Sometimes they crow about how little they've spent on something and other times they remark (with pride) on how expensive something was. The answer here is A. You never have to say what something cost you, so B is wrong. As for C, comparing your country's cultural ethos with those of the United States would be a fun conversation over a drink sometime, but not in this conversation, where it would seem that you're reproving your colleague, who is, after all, only following American norms.

SITUATION 4

You're patiently standing in line at the cinema to buy your ticket to a popular new film, when a guy sneaks past you and the others and inserts himself toward the front of the line. He clearly hasn't come to join friends who are waiting for him. No, he's just a line jumper. You don't like this, because you've been patient, and the others in line have been, too. What do you do?

Ⓐ Nothing. You're new here and you shouldn't be the one to make a fuss. Let the San Franciscans handle it. Besides, if it's so important for him to get in sooner, let him. It's a big theater with a lot of seats, and the film will start at the same time for everyone.

Ⓑ Be polite. Say kindly, "Excuse me, but the line is back there." Hope he takes the hint and goes back where he belongs. If he doesn't, just shrug and let other people take the next step.

Ⓒ React firmly, and make sure he hears you. Yell loudly, "Hey, buddy, the line's back there!" and gesture behind you to the end of the line where people are waiting.

Comments

Actually, any of the above answers are acceptable, although B might be most effective, if making him do what's fair is important to you. It just depends on your mood of the moment. San Franciscans are tolerant of aberrant behavior—on most days and in most situations—but if they feel like saying that something bothers them, they do. So, gauge the situation and see what suits you. If you choose C, however, be prepared for a response in the same tone and manner you've used.

SITUATION 5

You've just moved here from abroad and are settling in. One day, you're sitting on the bus with your eight-year-old daughter. Two young men board and take seats close by. After a few minutes, one leans over and kisses the other on the mouth. Your daughter asks, "Why are those men kissing?" What do you say?

A You don't know what to say, so you just say, "Beats me, I haven't the slightest idea," and then try to distract her by pointing to something out the window.

B You laugh and say, "We always knew San Francisco was different, didn't we?"

C You say, "They're just showing affection toward each other. Usually it's between a man and a woman, but occasionally a man will love another man, or a woman will love another woman. That's their choice."

D You tell her your opinion of homosexuality (or of public displays of affection) and that it is against your principles. She's old enough to understand.

Comments

Public affection may not be common in your culture, but it is common in San Francisco, no matter the sexual orientation. So, it's best to tell your daughter the truth, one way or the other. The best answer is C, for San Francisco teaches tolerance and expects it in return. But if you're adamant in your opposition either to openly-expressed affection or homosexuality, you'll no doubt already have begun at home to explain clearly your carefully-considered views on life. But, even if your answer is D, don't be loudly judgmental in front of the affectionate couple. And think it over. This is San Francisco; if you don't approve of any of the various lifestyles here, perhaps you're in the wrong place.

SITUATION 6

You are driving home late at night, after a business dinner during which you've shared a couple of bottles of wine. You're not drunk, just tired. Just as you get to the traffic light you see it is about to turn red. Nobody is coming in either direction so you speed up and get through the instant it becomes red. But a police car parked to the side turns on his flashing lights and directs you to pull over to the side. He asks you to step out of the car. You know that you've been drinking and driving. You also know you shouldn't have dashed through the traffic light as it was turning red. How do you handle the situation?

Ⓐ You have an early meeting in the morning. You act friendly with the police officer and explain that you had a late business dinner and are concerned about your important meeting in the morning. Take out your wallet and ask the police officer how much the fine will be, so you can pay him directly and go home.

ⓑ You're tired and just want to go home and go to bed. You're not drunk, and lots of people dash through the light at the last minute. You take out your wallet and fold a US$ 50 bill around it, and smile as you hand it to the police officer.

ⓒ You know this will be a stain on your record and that you will have to go to the police station and perhaps have your license suspended. Admit to the officer that you were wrong, accept the penalties as they unfold according to the particular situation, and vow to yourself that you will never do either again. And don't.

Comments

Clearly, the answer here is C. Never (never!) attempt to bribe or even pay a fine to a police officer, for that too could be seen as bribery. If you have no defense to your actions, apologize and follow the instructions of the officer; the penalties will be severe—even more so if this is not your first offense. They could involve license suspension or restriction, a course in safe driving, a fine, or even real jail time. If you are taken to the police station by the officer, call your lawyer, or ask for one if you don't know one. You might also contact your embassy or consulate for a lawyer, although it is not the embassy's responsibility to get you out of jail. The answer C is obvious, but the question was put in to remind you never to drink and drive, never to offer money to a police officer, and never to run a red light, which is not only illegal but also dangerous. San Francisco is tolerant of unusual behavior, but not of breaking laws or endangering others.

SITUATION 7

Coming to San Francisco alone, with no family in tow, you have taken a good job as a manager in a major bank. After you've been there a few weeks, your boss suggests you go out for drinks after work. You assume he wants to talk about business and your new job. When you get to the bar, however, it is clear he is interested in you personally, and after two cocktails he puts his hand on your leg and suggests you go back to his apartment for a "nightcap." What do you do?

Ⓐ You are extremely attracted to the man, he seems very nice, and being new in town, you don't have a relationship at present. So you decide to go back to his apartment with him. He's also important in the bank, so a relationship with him might help you get ahead.

Ⓑ This bothers you, and you tell him his behavior is inappropriate. You push his hand off your leg, and tell him if he does this again, you'll report him for sexual harassment.

Ⓒ You thank him for the offer, but say firmly that it's not a good idea to have a personal relationship with a colleague. Then, after finishing your drink, you thank him again, say you'll see him at work tomorrow, and leave.

Comments

The answer is C. It isn't a good idea to have a personal relationship with a colleague, and in fact, they rarely help someone get ahead in a company. And there's no point getting angry, if you want to stay happily in this new job. Instead of accepting a drink with him after work, which may well have had personal overtones that you didn't catch, you might have suggested a lunch instead. Yet sexual harassment is a tricky issue in the United States, and personal relationships in the office—including even the occasional friendly pat on the back—must be paid attention to. If you come from a culture where men and women friends are physically affectionate (kisses on cheeks, pats on backs, friendly hugs), you'll have to gauge each situation carefully in the United States. Shaking hands is always an accepted thing to do.

SITUATION 8

Your family is visiting you. It's their first time in the United States and you want them to have a good time. You make a reservation at a typically-San Francisco restaurant near Union Square. As your family is still tired from a long flight, you book early, imagining a nice leisurely dinner and lingering over a cup of coffee, hearing all the news and gossip from home. But at the end of the meal, just as you're finishing your coffee, the waiter comes over and asks, "Would you like anything else?" When you say, "No, thank you," he comes back immediately with the bill. It's clear that he intends for you to pay and leave, even though you're not ready. What do you do?

Ⓐ You pay and leave. You're not happy with the situation and make a mental note not to come back to this restaurant again. You also leave a slightly smaller tip than you would have, had you not felt rushed.

Ⓑ You say, "Thanks, but we're not quite ready to leave. We want to stay another fifteen minutes, or so." If the waiter responds nicely, you make a mental note to give him a large tip.

Ⓒ You pay and ask whether there's a table at the bar where you can continue your conversation. If there isn't, you leave and find another place—perhaps a cocktail lounge or nice bar—where you can linger awhile.

Comments

In the United States, many restaurants generally open early and expect to reseat the table several times in the evening, allocating a certain amount of time for each party to eat and then leave. This is called "turning" the tables. Waiters make most of their income on tips, so it is also to their advantage to have as many different parties of diners at a table as possible. Here the best answer is B, and your waiter should be accommodating, since the time when the table will be free can be gauged, but if the server isn't happy with the idea, try answer C. There may be a free table at the bar, but on a weekend night, don't count on it. Otherwise, just pay your bill and find somewhere else. But realize that the waiter is probably just following the policy of that restaurant, the same as in many others.

DOS AND DON'TS

So, now you're in San Francisco, perhaps here to stay. Your belongings have arrived, your children are in school, you've most likely started to work at a job with new colleagues, and even your dog has made friends in the park. What comes next? That's clear: building your life in a city that may have civil laws, but seems to have few rules—or even guidelines—for individual behavior. But certainly, it must. Actually, there are very few, and San Franciscans, being an outspoken lot, will let you know when you've broken some—no doubt arcane—taboo. Pay attention to those around you, and ask if you have a question. Herewith are just a few reminders of what San Franciscans know.

DOS

- Do remember that the climate in San Francisco is ever-changing. Unless there is a definite heatwave, think about taking a jacket when you go out. And, because summer is a cool and foggy season, women don't usually wear white shoes and white clothing as though they were in the tropics. Do wear light-colored suits and shoes, if you like, but not necessarily white. The same holds true for men.

- Do understand that San Francisco accepts people for who and what they are. Thus, people's lifestyle choices— whether you approve of them or not—are their business and not yours. Don't show disapproval or in any way try to impede behavior that you think is inappropriate, unless it is obviously criminal, illegal, or endangering others.

- Do be careful when you are out late at night; petty crime, pick-pocketing, and purse snatchings do exist, especially in some peripheral areas South of Market or the Tenderloin. Do take the usual precautions that you would in any large city; stay on well-lighted, well-populated streets, and if you must go into a neighborhood that is "iffy," go in a group.

- Do carry only the particular credit card you're going to use at that time. And if you're not driving, leave your license at home, or in your hotel safe (unless it's your identification). There's no point losing everything all at once.

- Do realize that Americans may be casual, even in first encounters. Don't be offended if you are called by your given name immediately upon meeting someone. This holds true even when you make a business call: expect to be called by your first name and don't insist on formality in response.

- Do remember that San Francisco has had a high rate of HIV and Aids. If you meet someone and are considering an intimate relationship, do practice "safe sex," no matter how "safe" you think your new partner may be. Or you and your partner might decide together to have AIDs tests; several clinics offer free and confidential testing. (See page 125.)

- Do be a generous tipper in a restaurant. Servers earn low salaries and depend on their tips. Generally, the tip is not included in the bill, so if the service is good, add somewhere about 20 per cent. If the service is not good, leave less or inform the management that you were not treated well. In some restaurants, a tip is included in the bill if the party has six people or more.

- Do be on time for a social engagement. San Francisco is an "early town," and even on weekends, you may well be invited to someone home for dinner at 7:00 or 7:30 pm. Both at someone's home or at a restaurant, arrive within ten minutes of the specified time. Call if you're going to be late. And, if you change your plans and can't eat where you've reserved, call to cancel the reservation. Don't just not show up: in some of the better restaurants, if you've guaranteed the reservation with your credit card, you could be charged the entire amount of the dinner.

- Do offer the person you're with a taste of your dinner when you're in a restaurant. That's what people do. And don't be offended if someone asks—or, heaven forbid!—even reaches over and spears a little bite off your place. Do feel free to accept a taste of your friend's dinner when offered, but don't feel obliged, if you don't want to.

- Do remember that San Franciscans dress casually. It depends on your social group and where you're going, but it's often okay to wear jeans in the evening—if they're clean or adorned, and you don't look sloppy.

- Do remember that smoking is illegal in all restaurants and bars and public spaces. This is one instance when you can admonish someone else, if they are smoking in a prohibited area and it is offending you. Do be polite but firm.

DON'TS

- Don't call the city Frisco. Do call the city San Francisco, or The City. If a local asks whether you live in Marin, for example, you might answer, "No, I live in The City."

- Don't call the towns or the rest of the Bay Area "suburbs". Do refer to the areas as "The East Bay" (east); "Marin" (north); "The South Bay" or "The Peninsula" (south).

- Don't be upset if a new acquaintance who has expressed warm interest in knowing you doesn't call you to get together. This happens; people are busy in their lives and with their friends and colleagues. If this happens, wait a short while and then do take the initiative: call and suggest a definite day for a movie or a dinner or a hike—or whatever you have in common. You might say, "Would you like to see the film at the Roxie next Saturday?" Then you can negotiate a time. Or if the person doesn't seem interested, drop it and don't pursue it further.

RESOURCE GUIDE

IMPORTANT NUMBERS

- **Dire emergencies: Medical/Fire/Criminal** 911
- **Alternate number for emergencies**   (415) 553-8090
- **Police, non-emergencies**   (415) 553-0123
- **Poison Control**   (800) 222-1222
- **Poison Control: SF General Hospital**   (800) 876-4766
- **City Services: 24-Hour Hotline**   311
- **Telephone operator Dial**   0
- **All transportation information**   511
- **Pacific Gas & Electric power outages**   (800) 743-5000
  Pet emergencies: SPCA Vet Hospital   (415) 554-3030
- **Animals in distress**   (415)554-9400
- **Phone Directory Assistance**   411
- **AIDS/HIV Nightline**   (415) 434-2437
- **Alcoholics Anonymous**   (415) 674-1821
- **San Francisco Unified School District**   (415) 241-6000

HEALTH EMERGENCIES

Emergency Services

First see if you can stabilize the patient and if CPR is necessary. Have someone call the 911 or poison control numbers
above. Response to a 911 call will be by a Fire Department
ambulance. Paramedics will stabilize the patient during the trip
to the hospital. In the case of a sudden trauma, transport will
likely be to San Francisco General. For burns, transport may
be to Saint Francis Memorial. In other cases, the ambulance
will probably be directed to the nearest hospital that has an
available Intensive Care Unit (ICU).

One Medical provides primary and specialized care in locations around the city (tel: (415) 523-6317; www.onemedical.
com). Same day appointments.

AMBULANCES

- **King American Ambulance**   (415) 931-1400
- **American Medical Response** (415) 922-9400
- **Saint Joseph's Ambulance**   (415) 921-0707

24-HOUR HOSPITAL EMERGENCY ROOMS (BY AREA)

- **Castro/Hayes Valley / Mission**
  California Pacific Medical Center
  (Davies Campus)
  Castro Street at Duboce
  Tel: (415) 600-6000
- **Tenderloin, Van Ness, Civic Center**
  Saint Francis Memorial Hospital
  900 Hyde Street
  Tel: (415) 353-6000
- **Haight/Sunset**
  Saint Mary's Medical Center (DignityHealth)
  450 Stanyan Street
  Tel: (415) 668-1000
- **Mission/Potrero Hill**
  San Francisco General Hospital
  1001 Potrero Avenue
  Tel: (415) 206-8000
- **Sunset/Avenues**
  UCSF Medical Center
  505 Parnassus Avenue
  Tel: (415) 353-1238
- **Western Addition**
  Kaiser Permanente (For members)
  2425 Geary Boulevard
  Tel: (415) 833-2200

WALGREENS 24-HOUR PRESCRIPTION PHARMACY

- **Castro/NoeValley**
  498 Castro Street
  Tel: (415) 861-3136

TRAVEL INFORMATION

- **San Francisco International Airport**
  www.flysfo.com
- **Oakland International Airport**
  www.flyoakland.com
- **Amtrak** (trains)
  www.amtrak.com; www.actransit.org
- **Greyhound** (bus)
  200 Folsom Street
  http://locations.greyhound.com/us/california/san-francisco
- **SF Travel Association**
  www.sftravel.com

VISITOR INFORMATION

- **San Francisco Visitor Information Center**: Corner of Market and Powell; lower level of Hallidie Plaza, tel: (415) 391-2000, www.sftravel.com.
- **CityPass**: www.citypass.com. Packaged one-pass admissions to some of the top city attractions, including public transport.
- **City Government**: http://sfgov.org/visitors. The city's website offers visitor opportunities by category.
- **Go San Francisco Card**: www.gosanfranciscocard. com. Admission to more than 25 attractions for one price, including the Big Bus Hop-on Hop-off bus.
- **National Park Service Visitor Information**: 102 Montgomery Street, in the Presidio, tel: (415) 561-4323, www.nps.gov.
- **California**: www.ca.gov

FEDERAL INFORMATION

- **National Federal Information**
  www.usa.gov
- **Department of Homeland Security: Citizenship and Immigration**
  www.dhs.gov
- **Customs and Border Protection**
  www.cbp.gov
- **Internal Revenue Service**
  www.irs.gov
- **Social Security Administration**
  www.ssa.gov

LOST CREDIT CARDS

- **American Express**
  Tel: (800) 327-1267
- **MasterCard**
  Tel: (800) 627-8372
- **Visa**
  Tel: (800) 847-2911

TELEPHONE: COUNTRY AND AREA CODES

Country Code for USA: 1

Area Code for San Francisco and most of Marin: 415

Area Code for Napa/Sonoma 707

Area Code for Berkeley, Oakland, and much of East Bay: 510

Area Code for South Bay: 650

International calls: prefix 011 and then the country code: cell phones, press + before the country code

Operator: 0

Toll-free numbers: 800, 888, 866, 877

Non-toll free numbers: any that start with 700 or 900.

CONVERSION TABLES

One U.S. gallon = 3.8 liters; 0.85 Imperial gallons

One kilo = 2.2 pounds

100 grams = 3.5 ounces

One liter = 1 quart, 2 ounces; about 4 cups

One teaspoon dry measure = about 5 grams

One tablespoon = 14.3 grams

One stone = 14 pounds

One centimeter =.39 inches

One meter =39.3 inches; 3.3 feet; 1.1 yard

One kilometer = 0.62 miles; one mile =1.6km

212° Fahrenheit = 100° Centigrade

32° Fahrenheit = 0° Centigrade

98.6° Fahrenheit = 37° Centigrade

VOTER INFORMATION

- **Democratic Party**
  100 Broadway Street
  Tel: (415) 626-1161
  www.sfdemocrats.org
- **Republican Party**
  150 Sutter Street
  Tel: (415) 379-0595
  www.sfgop.org

LGBTQ RESOURCES

- **SF LGBT Center**: 1800 Market Street, tel: (415) 865-5555; www.sfcenter.org. Full program to support the LGBT communities: career counselling, computer lab, social activities, and much more.
- **James C. Hormel Gay and Lesbian Center**: San Francisco Public Library: 100 Larkin Street, tel: (415) 557-4400; https://sfpl.org/?pg=0200002401. Broad collections documenting history and culture in the Bay Area.

- **San Francisco Gay Men's Chorus**: 526 Castro Street, tel: (415) 865-3650; www.sfgmc.org. The chorus presents major concerts each year, plus outreach concerts for community groups. Audition for the chorus, or even if you can't sing, volunteers are always needed to keep track of wardrobe, ticket sales, production, etc.
- **Women's Building**: 3543, 18th Street, tel: (415) 431-1180; www.womensbuilding.org. Multi-cultural center for women and girls, providing a wide range of tools for full participation in society. Multilingual.
- **Eureka Valley-Harvey Milk Library**: 1 José Sarria Court (at 16th, near Market), tel: (415) 355-5616; https://sfpl.org/index.php?pg=0100002301. Memorial branch of the Public Library, has well-organized materials of interest to the LGBT communities.
- **Pacific Center**: 2712 Telegraph Avenue, Berkeley, tel: (510) 548-8283; www.pacificcenter.org. LGBT resource and support for the entire Bay Area.

MEETING PEOPLE BY VOLUNTEERING

You will meet people at work, at your gym, walking your dog in the parks, and through other means, especially by volunteering for community or non-profit organizations, often in the arts. Many of the cultural performance sites and museums described in Chapter 7 have opportunities for volunteering. For professional and business networking, see page 257.

- **The San Francisco Volunteer Center**: 1675 California Street, tel: (415) 928-8999; www.thevolunteercenter.net. Coordinates volunteers in community-wide projects. Volunteer Match: www.volunteermatch.org/search/. Lists possibilities for volunteering, from mentoring with your professional skills, tutoring students, driving people to medical appointments, and more.

- **Project Homeless Connect**: 25 Van Ness Avenue, Suite 340, tel: (855-588-7968); www.projecthomelessconnect. org. A city-sponsored set of projects to help the San Francisco homeless.
- **Hands On Bay Area**: 1504 Bryant Street, Suite 100, tel: (415) 541-9616; www.handsonbayarea.org. Connects people with projects in schools, parks and non-profits.
- **SFCASA** (San Francisco Court Appointed Special Advocate Program): 2535 Mission Street, tel: (415) 398-8001; www.sfcasa.org. Supporting foster children in need of help, in different ways and guiding them through the court system, as necessary.
- **Friends of the San Francisco Public Library**: 391 Grove Street, tel: (415) 626-7500; www.friendssfpl.org. Friends raise money for the library, help operate the several bookshops, and support the library in other ways.

FURTHER READING

FICTION

- Chabon, Michael. *Telegraph Avenue* (2012)
  The book may actually be set mostly in the East Bay—Berkeley and Oakland—but the city's surrounds, while quite different, are also part of why the Bay Area is so amazing.

- Hammett, Dashiell. *The Maltese Falcon* (1930)
  Classic "hard boiled" detective novel set in San Francisco in the 1920s. Novel was made into a classic film starring Humphrey Bogart.

- Kerouac, Jack. *On the Road* (1957)
  The "bible of the Beat Generation", so entrenched in San Francisco, Kerouac and his friends take to the road—with their poetry and drugs—to find themselves.

- London, Jack. *San Francisco Stories* (2010)
  A collection of London's stories of San Francisco, edited by Nattgew Asprey. London is most famous for his book, *Call of the Wild* (1903), about the sheepdog Buck, adapting to survive in the Klondike.

- Maupin, Armistead. *Tales of the City* (1978–2014)
  A cult favorite, bestselling nine-volume series of witty novels (soap operas, actually) that recreate the atmosphere of San Francisco in the 1970s and 1980s, published over several decades.

- Norris, Frank. *McTeague: A Story of San Francisco* (1899)
  Writing at the same time as London, Norris' gritty tale of avarice and violence takes place in turn-of-the-century San Francisco.

- Seth, Vikram. *The Golden Gate* (1986)
  A novel in verse form, depicting the lives of a group of San Francisco yuppies in the 1980s.

- Stadler. *Landscape Memory* (1995)
  An unusual and captivating story taking place after the 1906 earthquake: a love story of two men as they and the city rebuild themselves, shown through dozens of versions of a painting.

- Steinbeck, John. *The Grapes of Wrath* (1939)
  Grim, Pulitzer Prize-winning novel of sharecroppers during the Great Depression, driven from their home by drought, joining migrant workers of California.

- Tan, Amy. *The Joy Luck Club* (1989)
  Charming novel, relating the interconnected woes and joys of four Chinese women who have immigrated to San Francisco, and their American-Chinese daughters.

- Twain, Mark. *Roughing It* (1872)
  Tales of frontier California and San Francisco in the 1860s. Descriptions of the Comstock Lode, the famous silver mines.

NON-FICTION

- Bonné, Jon. *The New California Wines* (2013)
  Wines and producers of California and the changes to viniculture and the innovations of the "new generation" of winemakers.

- Kamiya, Gary. *Cool Gray City of Love: 49 Views of San Francisco* (2013)
  This reflective and varied book portrays both landmarks and byways that show why walking is the best way to see San Francisco.

- Madonna, Paul. *All Over Coffee* (2007)
  Just a fun look at San Francisco, through poetry and a comic strip-looking depiction of San Franciscans and their world.

- Rich, Nathaniel. *San Francisco Noir (The City in Film Noir from 1940 to the Present)* (2005)
  Details and trivia about the film industry's focus on the city, especially in "film noir."

- Richards, Rand. *Historic San Francisco*: A Concise History and Guide (2011)
  A compact history of the city from its beginnings, descriptions of sites, and tours that show the city's highlights.

- Shilts, Randy. *The Mayor of Castro Street: The Life and Times of Harvey Milk* (1982)
  The story of the San Francisco gay activist and first gay man elected to public office. Assassinated in 1978, he remains the symbol of cohesive gay politics that is making a difference.

- Solnit, Rebecca. *Infinite City*: A San Francisco Atlas (2010)
  An atlas of San Francisco that shows the city's possibilities and spirit through maps and essays.

ABOUT THE AUTHOR

Frances Gendlin has held leadership positions in magazine and book publishing; she was Editor and Publisher of *Sierra*, the magazine of the Sierra Club, a worldwide environmental organization, and was the association's Director of Public Affairs. As Executive Director of the Association of American University Presses, she represented the 100-member publishing houses to the public and fostered scholarly publishing interests. In 1997, she wrote *Rome At Your Door*, a widely-read guide to living in that city. In 1998, using the same format, she wrote *Paris At Your Door (Living & Working Abroad: Paris)*. This is the third edition of the San Francisco guide, now titled *Culture Shock! San Francisco: A Survival Guide to Customs and Etiquette*.

While she was growing up, her family moved several times to different areas of the United States, each with its own characteristics and culture, climate, and cuisine. This has led her to appreciate new cultures, to wonder about their differences and similarities, and to try and understand them. All her life she has enjoyed travel and new adventures, meeting interesting people and making new friends.

After living in San Francisco for 20 years, Frances Gendlin then moved to Paris, fortunate at that time to know intimately two of the most charming cities in the world. Still spending time in both cities and now the winter months in Puerto Vallarta, Mexico, she has added that third city to the list. Her fictional memoir, *Paris, Moi, and the Gang: A Memoir ... of Sorts* was published in 2010.

INDEX

Titles in the **CultureShock!** series:

Argentina	France	Philippines
Australia	Germany	Portugal
Austria	Great Britain	Russia
Bahrain	Greece	San Francisco
Bali	Hawaii	Saudi Arabia
Beijing	Hong Kong	Scotland
Belgium	Hungary	Sri Lanka
Berlin	India	Shanghai
Bolivia	Ireland	Singapore
Borneo	Italy	South Africa
Bulgaria	Jakarta	Spain
Brazil	Japan	Sri Lanka
Cambodia	Korea	Sweden
Canada	Laos	Switzerland
Chicago	London	Syria
Chile	Malaysia	Taiwan
China	Mauritius	Thailand
Costa Rica	Morocco	Tokyo
Cuba	Munich	Travel Safe
Czech Republic	Myanmar	Turkey
Denmark	Netherlands	United Arab Emirates
Dubai	New Zealand	USA
Ecuador	Norway	Vancouver
Egypt	Pakistan	Venezuela
Finland	Paris	Vietnam

For more information about any of these titles, please contact the Publisher via email at: genref@sg.marshallcavendish.com or visit our website at:

www.marshallcavendish.com/genref